D0710393

Negotiating Justice

Negotiating Justice

Progressive Lawyering,
Low-Income Clients, and
the Quest for Social Change

Corey S. Shdaimah

NEW YORK UNIVERSITY PRESS
New York and London

NEW YORK UNIVERSITY PRESS
New York and London
www.nyupress.org

Library of Congress Cataloging-in-Publication Data
Shdaimah, Corey S.
Negotiating justice : progressive lawyering, low-income clients, and
the quest for social change / Corey S. Shdaimah.
p.   cm.
Includes bibliographical references and index.
ISBN-13: 978–0–8147–4054–5 (cl : alk. paper)
ISBN-10: 0–8147–4054–5 (cl : alk. paper)
1. Attorney and client—United States. 2. Practice of law—United
States. 3. Legal ethics—United States.   I. Title.
KF311.S522 2009
347.73'17—dc22   2008041185

New York University Press books are printed on acid-free paper, and
their binding materials are chosen for strength and durability. We
strive to use environmentally responsible suppliers and materials to
the greatest extent possible in publishing our books.

Manufactured in the United States of America
10 9 8 7 6 5 4 3 2 1

Contents

Acknowledgments

My first thanks are to the clients and lawyers who participated in the study that is the subject of this book. They allowed me into their offices and homes to generously share their time, their thoughts, and their experiences. They willingly explored with me actions, values, and beliefs, even when these were not flattering to themselves or others. The impressive combination of indignation, strength, and humor with which they met what seemed to be crushing difficulties was both inspirational and humbling. I often find myself thinking of the people who participated in this study, wondering how their lives have continued to unfold.

Northeast Legal Service's executive director agreed to let me conduct this research at NELS and believed in its importance. She provided a number of opportunities (formal and informal) to discuss my work in progress and offered feedback on various portions of the analysis. She and NELS staff members also supplied me with information and documentation about NELS whenever I pestered them with queries, and provided a place to meet when necessary.

A number of scholars graciously shared feedback and suggestions during various stages of the research and writing. Jim Baumohl read several iterations of the manuscript, and I am grateful for his input. Most valuable and fun were our discussions, which sharpened my analysis. Sandy Schram challenged my thinking and offered encouragement, particularly in my preliminary analysis and in the social change chapter. Thanks to Carolyn Needleman for guidance on study methods and to Raymond Albert for providing opportunities to share my work. Folks at the Law and Society Association and the Cause Lawyering Project were nurturing from the beginning. I especially appreciate the generosity of Austin Sarat, Stu Scheingold, and Frank Munger and talks with co-conspirator Steve Meili. Peter Margulies provided suggestions for chapter 6. There are too many other people who sat with me for an hour (or three) or read bits and pieces of articles to name here. All of their feedback made a difference.

I am also grateful for the comments and enthusiasm of law students, lawyers, legal services programs, and clinical and public interest law professors. The opportunity to engage with current and future practitioners shored up my commitment to scholarship that is relevant to the problems and practices of real people and convinced me of the resonance of my work.

I am lucky to have Debbie Gershenowitz as my editor. Her guidance and input were respectful of my voice while challenging me to clarify the framework, audience, and purpose for my work. She helped to make this a better manuscript and I have enjoyed every one of our conversations.

Brooke McEntyre and Ingrid Löfgren provided excellent research assistance and lively discussion, which were much appreciated. Thanks to Jamnian Thinchuai, Sam Dalke, Anna Jakubas, Carina Ozaki, and Jaqueline Souza. They are the young adults who helped to take care of my children and enriched all of our lives in so many ways. Without their help this would not have been possible.

There are so many reasons to thank Judie McCoyd. She is candid critic, peer reviewer, intellectual companion and, most important, my friend. My wonderful family: Amichai, Cliel, Elad, and Sagi, have been encouraging fans. Their patience, humor, and love remind me of what is most important.

Some of the ideas developed in chapter 3 were adapted from "Intersecting Identities," published in *Cause Lawyers and Social Movements*, edited by Austin Sarat and Stuart Scheingold, © 2006 by the Board of Trustees of the Leland Stanford Jr. University, by permission of the publisher.

Initial framework for chapters 4, 5, and 6, relying on a preliminary analysis of the first 30 interviews, was sketched out in "Dilemmas of Progressive Lawyering," published in *The Worlds Cause Lawyers Make*, edited by Austin Sarat and Stuart Scheingold, © 2005 by the Board of Trustees of the Leland Stanford Jr. University, by permission of the publisher.

Preface

The Master's Tools

The master's tools will never dismantle the master's house.
—Audre Lorde[1]

Ellis is an elderly African American man who lives in a declining neighborhood in Northeast City.[2] We met in his house in the summer of 2002. The curtains were drawn and the house was dark. When we began our interview he opened the curtains to let in some light. Ellis recalled his neighborhood's finer days:

> When we were coming up where we would go to school and enjoy ourselves and work and try to help the family and help others–I—I mean, the way it is now you can't do that. It's getting terrible now. Now when I got on this street—oh man, it was so nice. You could walk on this street, you wouldn't have to uh, you couldn't even find a piece of paper on this block. The way it is now, they don't do nothing; they don't even want to clean up the blood.

Now a widower, Ellis lives alone. The living room where we sat was full of pictures of his late wife and their children.

Ellis told me that he and his wife had trouble with their mortgage company. Despite their timely payments, it seemed to them that the bills were getting higher and higher. No matter when they sent the payments, the mortgage company told them that they were late. And it appeared that the payment due dates were getting earlier and earlier. At first, Ellis tried to deal with the mortgage company directly:

> I kept calling them, they said you have to speak to the manager and then they put me on hold and next thing you know—"beep beep beep beep

beep." And then I call them back again and they said he's on the other line and I never did get a chance to speak to him. I would call about two or three days out of a week to call them and tell them about the bills and all.

Ellis learned about Northeast Legal Services (NELS) from a friend. "One of my best friends had told me about it and I was in trouble about mortgage and stuff like that. He told me to go down there and that's when I went. And I found out that they were the best and that's why I went." Ellis and his wife, who has since died, came to NELS in 1999 one day during intake hours. There, "each one of us had to get a number and then tell them who we wanted to talk to or what we wanted to talk about and they said, 'We'll let you speak to Marjorie.'" Marjorie came down to the intake area where Ellis and his wife were waiting and called them in. In my interview with her, she explained that she usually meets with elderly clients downstairs so that they don't have to climb the one flight to her office. Ellis said he found Marjorie kind and reassuring. His wife was relieved after their first meeting and was sure that everything would be fine. "Because the way she talks, she don't talk like the other lawyers. The other lawyers say, 'I see about this,' or 'I see about that' and different things like that." Of Marjorie, he said, "The way I felt, just like my wife said, God sent us an angel. And that was Marjorie MacDonald."

Marjorie devoted time and effort to Ellis's case. Eventually she was able to reduce their mortgage: "She said they done dropped it all the way from 44,000 all the way to 20." She told Ellis, "If they ever start over again doing the same thing to let her know." Ellis has had to call Marjorie repeatedly, as the mortgage company continues to plague him. She has made herself available over the course of their three-year relationship. Ellis met with Marjorie periodically, first with his wife and then, after she died, on his own. They supplied whatever documentation she required. In each case, Marjorie goes over the letters and payment schedules with Ellis, reviews his payment records and, if necessary, responds on his behalf. Based on his experience, he thinks that people who do not have lawyers "have a hard time. They will have a hard time. Because they'll never make it without one."

Ellis's wife experienced a great deal of stress from the mortgage problems. He and Marjorie both feel as though her death may be attributable to this stress. "Even the hospital was saying she was under too much stress. That's what they were saying 'cause her pressure kept going up." He is concerned for himself.

Every time I would go and look at that letter, when they send me the bill saying that I owe this and owe that, when I go to my doctor they said, "You still under a lot of stress." My—they would take my pressure they says, "You still taking your pressure pills?" I says yes. They said, "It ain't doing no good."

Ellis is eager to discuss his legal problems and offer his opinions about lawyers, Northeast City, mortgage companies, and justice. He appears lonely—during our interview he shares pictures and stories, mostly of his recently deceased wife of nearly 49 years and his children. One picture that he carries in his pocket shows his wife and him when they were just married, with Ellis in a uniform from the armed forces. His youngest son has drug problems and is involved in illegal activities. He unsuccessfully tried to help him and he felt the need to sever contact with him to protect his home and property (and his wife).

While Ellis seems lonely and eager to talk, he is far from isolated or pathetic. He is outraged by changes in his neighborhood and works hard to protect it. He told me that he had provided information about suspected arson and calls the police when necessary. Himself a senior citizen, Ellis is active on his block, helping others and encouraging them to seek legal help.

Now I be sending a lot of different ones down [to NELS] when I, you know, see that they really need help and I'm trying to get my neighbor over there [points] two doors from me to go down—have me take her down there. See she's 89. Each one on this block has a senior citizen to take care of. And I take care of her. And then another up the street. And I always take them different places, take them to get their checks cashed and all of that. So I'm going to get them down there. Because I told them this is the best.

Ellis is one of 31 clients whom I interviewed. While each story is unique, Ellis's story illustrates a number of themes that I explore in this book, including trauma, oppression, and multiple impacts of poverty, from the mundane to the severe. So are the stories of resilience and persistence. Like the majority of NELS's clients, Ellis lives in a poor section of Northeast City. His life contains a number of stressors: health problems, the recent death of his wife, and a son who has drug problems. When he first became entangled with legal problems, he tried to resolve them on his own. The agency, in this case a private lender, proved evasive and unresponsive to his efforts. Ellis was treated so badly that he suspects that they were trying to defraud him.

Ellis learned about NELS by word of mouth and came seeking assistance, not quite sure what they could do but with no other options. He was surprised to find a lawyer who listened to him, who appeared to care about him and his wife, and who acted on their behalf. He is not really sure what Marjorie did, but he feels that his legal problems were resolved, at least temporarily. After his initial respite, however, he faced renewed problems with his mortgage company. Marjorie continues to assist him. Although she is pressed for time, she is sensitive to his recent loss and recognizes that his ongoing difficulties with the mortgage company would be difficult for him to resolve on his own. After his experience with Marjorie, Ellis advocated for others in similar situations by encouraging them to seek legal assistance from NELS. He is also clear that he thinks it is not fair that the mortgage company treats him the way they do.

In this book, I explore the meanings that legal services lawyers and clients like Ellis and Marjorie give to their work within systems that they perceive as fundamentally inequitable and hostile to the claims of poor people. Law has long been seen as a problematic but necessary tool for working for social justice (however defined). Much has been written about the potential for disempowerment in lawyer-client relationships, which is said to privilege expert knowledge and channel energy into practices that preserve the status quo. This particularly troubles lawyers who dedicate careers to representing poor clients. However, few studies have explored the perspective of lawyers and clients who choose to use what Lorde has called the "master's tools."

Audre Lorde contended that "the master's tools will never dismantle the master's house." With them, "only the most narrow perimeters of change are possible and allowable." While she cautioned that the master's tools are imperfect and even dangerous in their potential to preserve the prevailing social order, she nevertheless advocated using them. This was because the master's tools and discourses were available to her, and she believed that oppression should be fought wherever, whenever, and however possible. Lorde also used the master's tools because they formed a bridge between power and lack of power and between those who are powerful and those who are deprived of power. Like Lorde, lawyers and clients in this study have taken up the master's tools to chip away at the master's house from within. Lawyers and clients with pressing needs do not reject legal tools that, in their very use, acknowledge the authority of legal systems and of lawyers. For the lawyers and clients in this study, as for Audre Lorde, the challenge is to take up the legal tools at their disposal for radical purposes and with a critical perspective.

This book is an account of "situated" practice. By this, I refer to the way lawyers and clients practice within the context of their daily routines, personal and professional opportunities and constraints, and existing social and political arrangements. From the situated practice of lawyers and clients, it is clear that rigid theoretical prescriptions for practice are bound to fail. In the messy world of legal services, lawyers and clients alike learn to be flexible. If lawyers are truly open to their clients and clients truly open to their lawyers, even foundational ideals they bring to their work become open to revision and to competing values, like compassion or the importance of face-to-face practice with clients. Scholars who ignore the rich and problematic understanding that arises from situated practice risk providing incomplete and irrelevant critiques and interpretations. Failure to attend to those engaged "on the ground" is one reason for the mismatch between theory and practice. Lawyers and clients see their work together as a type of realistic radicalism rather than capitulation or system conservation. Their practices do not amount merely to a strategic or haphazard muddling through, but form an internally consistent and morally informed ethic of risk.[3]

Lawyers and clients find ways to navigate systems of which they are highly critical. By listening to them discuss how they accomplish this, we better understand their views on the nature of justice and the workings of the legal system. This book asks how the lawyer-client relationship hinders and facilitates the achievement of social justice goals. Relying on over 50 interviews with urban legal service lawyers and their clients during 2002 and 2003, I consider the themes of autonomy, collaboration, transformation, and social change. These are themes central to "progressive" lawyering literatures, those critiques of legal practice that value equality, social justice, and the dignity of all clients, which I review in greater detail in chapter 2. Based on the data, I offer a revised understanding of these themes that reflects how lawyers adapt their ideals to the exigencies of practice, and perhaps more important, to the circumstances and understandings of clients. I analyze the experiences

and aspirations of lawyers and clients and the trade-offs and negotiations they make together in working for short-term material assistance
as well as more abstract notions of justice, fairness, and dignity in a system that both groups find oppressive. To begin, I introduce the lawyers
and clients interviewed and the legal services organization that brought
them together.

1

Clients and Lawyers

I mean, am I changing the world? No. But the revolution still isn't happening and at some basic level this office, legal aid programs and myself personally make a difference in people's lives . . . on basic bread and butter issues. . . . [T]here are people in this office . . . who have a lot of trouble . . . that we're playing at the margins, that we are not fermenting the revolution. And we're not. We're not. We really are not. And that's fine. I mean I can live with it. But no, I love this job, this is a great job. And we do make a difference, both individually and on issues that affect our client population. And *but for* the work we did, things would be considerably worse for our clients.   —Steve, a Northeast Legal Services lawyer

I just think that when you got certain stuff that you're not clear about, you get a professional to handle it, so that is what I did. . . . It's a process that's not a familiar process for most people. And it's something that a professional should handle. There's no way in this world I would go and file legal proceedings and not know what I'm doing.   —Dara, a NELS client

A one-page flyer, written in both English and Spanish, distributed by Northeast Legal Services (NELS), opens with a heading in large print: "Do you have a LEGAL problem or question? *We want to help you!*" NELS is a nonprofit legal services organization with a centrally located main office and one neighborhood branch office serving a large urban center. Its flyer offers assistance for questions as well as problems. It does, however, require that clients understand their problem to be a legal one, and might deter those who are unsure if their case meets this criterion (see chapter 4). This flyer, as well as NELS's website that contains a similar message (but does not emphasize the legal aspects), both note that assistance is available in other languages but explain that this might not be immediately available:

> Note to people who do not speak English: We are committed to serving you, but have few regular staff members who speak languages other than English or Spanish. If possible, please have a friend or family member come with you for your first visit, or call in advance so that we can make sure an interpreter is available.

NELS is committed to assisting non-English-speaking Northeast City residents through a language access project. NELS reports serving clients who speak Arabic, Cambodian, Cantonese, Creole, English, French, German, Italian, Korean, Laotian, Mandarin, Polish, Portuguese, Russian, Sign Language, Spanish, and Vietnamese.

Flyers are distributed when NELS does community outreach and, in some cases, NELS contact information is provided by local government agencies. For example, Northeast City's child protective services inform legal guardians that they can seek representation from NELS, as do appeal forms for Social Security Disability Insurance. In some cases, clients are referred through the court system, including many of the family advocacy clients. Most clients, however, must go through a screening process.

Each unit has its own intake process. Some units (such as the housing unit) have telephone intake, and others (such as the elderly law unit) go to centers where potential clients congregate. NELS's intake generally requires a potential client to come to their offices. At one time NELS had up to six neighborhood offices, but these were reduced due to funding cuts. The lack of neighborhood presence is a burden for clients who often have to travel far on public transportation, or who may have disabilities or may be caring for other family members. Martin, a NELS lawyer, remarks that when NELS reduced its number of neighborhood offices, it tried to minimize this concern by increasing telephone intake:

> When I started working here we had five offices, so there were four neighborhood offices and then the midtown office. So it was easier for people to get in to see NELS, just physically easier. Now we only have two offices. And when we did, I think we tended to allow more phone intake

program-wide. The preferred method I still think, for most units, is for
walk-in intake.

Walk-in intake is conducted during limited hours; particular units do intake on particular days. Janet, a client, said that NELS did not help her
over the phone: "No, they just said you have to go down there, they didn't
really help me on the telephone. They said you just have to go down between such and such days, such and such hours." Clients who inquire
over the phone are given the office's hours of operation. Clients who arrive at undesignated times are turned away and told to return during intake hours. There is also a general walk-in intake every day from 9 a.m. to
12 noon at the main office, and only on Monday, Wednesday, and Friday
from 9 to 12 at the neighborhood office. Clients who arrive at the correct
time and day wait to be called. As Janet explains:

> Yeah. You just walk in, you fill out the forms. You go back and you talk to
> another lady doing intake and then she's the one referred me to Steve. . . .
> I was there most of the day. . . I waited quite a while before I got, before I
> was seen. In fact I remember I was falling asleep [laughs]! But then when
> I had an appointment, I didn't wait. But just the first initial time, I waited
> a long time.

Waiting time varies, although clients at the neighborhood office were more
likely to complain of lengthy wait times. Elizabeth, who sought services at
both offices, made the comparison: "No. I didn't have to wait a long time
[at the main office]. That was good. Now [at the branch office]! I had to
wait about a hour, 2 hours. I waited a long time. They don't see people
after 12 o'clock. Lot of people in there." As Janet indicates, once a person
goes through the intake process and becomes a client, she then schedules
appointments with the individual paralegal or attorney handling the case
and does not have to wait.

Lawyers and paralegals in most units participate in the intake process.
They determine which cases are eligible based on a variety of criteria
that include client's income and the area of law involved. Clients come to
NELS in a variety of ways, and each unit has its own guidelines for interviewing clients and determining whether or not they will take on cases
beyond NELS's universal income eligibility requirements. Some call lawyers directly. Other clients are referred by social service agencies, other
public interest law organizations, or, in the case of the family division, by

the courts. My client sample includes people who enlisted the assistance of NELS via each of these routes.

NELS does not accept all clients who apply for assistance. According to e-mail correspondence with its director:

> The truth about eligibility decisions is that they vary depending on the unit's situation . . . how many other cases came in recently and how swamped we are, along with an evaluation of the merits and likelihood of success, our expertise, time it will take, impact for the greater client community of handling this, etc. Some places are much better than we at putting those variables into writing . . . but they do change so often, that we do it on an ongoing basis, usually at unit meetings. But then there is the hard rule on certain cases . . . no one over the income limit, no Social Security insurance cases, because the private bar will do them, no divorces . . . because they're not seen as urgent and they can be done by private attorneys very cheaply, no employment discrimination (which we used to do) because they are so immense for one person's benefit, etc. Of course, tho I say those are "hard" rules, even they could be broken if there is an exceptional situation.

Selection criteria have been discussed in the literature and came up regularly in my conversations with clients and lawyers. I will discuss them further in chapter 6.

Legal services programs are not all of a piece.[1] With approximately 100 employees that include administrators, lawyers, paralegals, and social workers, NELS is one of the largest public interest organizations in a city with quite a few. It is well integrated in a collaborative and diverse public interest law community. From its inception, it kept close ties with local law schools and a wide variety of community organizations. NELS is a highly regarded, sought-after public interest law practice. Pete, a lawyer in the benefits unit, was attracted not only by the prestige and reputation, but by the caliber of the legal work that came out of NELS and the opportunity to work with highly qualified professionals:

> When I made the move over to NELS, uh, we have, you know, without being like a braggart, you know, one of the top welfare practices in the country in terms of the collection of critical mass of people who have been doing this for a long time that have, you know, experience and perspective and who are really hard-working and thoughtful and, um, it's a

very unique organization. It serves both this kind of like a traditional, you know, neighborhood law center in the sense that we do individual cases but we also are for all intents and purposes a state and in some ways a national back-up center.[2]

While NELS engages in both individual and impact work, most lawyers have large caseloads and constant client interaction, in keeping with its legal services mission "[t]o help low-income residents obtain justice by providing them advice and representation in civil legal matters, advocating for their legal rights and conducting community education about legal services." NELS has a number of operational divisions. These address either substantive legal issues such as Social Security benefits, employment or housing; or serve particular populations such as those in need of language assistance or the elderly. Participants in this study represented lawyers and clients from most of NELS's units.

All clients must meet NELS's means test of having an income of no more than 125 percent of the federal poverty line.[3] With management approval, NELS also accepts clients "with exceptional expenses or circumstances" whose incomes go up to 187.5 percent of the federal poverty line. An example of such a case provided by a NELS intake supervisor was a client who recently found employment, making him ineligible for services, but who had previously been unemployed and still had a high level of debt. In short, all clients experience some level of financial and social distress. In 2006, NELS handled nearly 17,000 cases. The number of people assisted in some way exceeds this, however, as a NELS administrator explained: "This number excludes many brief encounters where legal advice was dispensed, such as brief phone calls from individuals, other practitioners, or social service providers seeking our assistance."

The Research Site: Northeast Legal Services

The Founding of Northeast Legal Services

The city that I call Northeast City[4] is a de-industrialized urban center. Like many similar cities, it suffered a loss of well-paid blue-collar jobs and outward migration to the suburbs of the more affluent citizens over the last few decades. Today, Northeast City contains a core of struggling older communities, where a significant portion of the residents endure high rates of unemployment, violent crime, inadequate housing, under-resourced public schools, and areas with high concentrations of extreme poverty. These communities have disproportionate numbers of minority residents, female-headed households, and immigrants. The central business district of the city is vibrant, and a number of poor neighborhoods are undergoing a process of gentrification that is encouraged by Northeast City's government. Community groups and housing advocates claim that this has made housing even less affordable for Northeast City's poorest residents and has had a deleterious effect on communities.

NELS was formed in the mid-1960s, a time when legal services programs were started around the country and legal services careers enjoyed a surge of popularity. Lawyers influenced by social and intellectual changes sought to create a different kind of legal assistance to the poor. At that time, critiques of traditional legal aid bureaus and offices abounded, and a new kind of lawyering for the poor was championed. The critiques decried the conventional stance of legal aid as disempowering. They also criticized the narrow provision of particular (and very limited) types of legal services and the limited pool of clients that, according to the critics, was based on inaccurate and self-serving determinations of deservedness. These programs did not mount any kinds of systemic or policy-related claims, and did not challenge the state or its administrative apparatus in any way. The evolution of legal services programs as we currently think of them was the product of social and intellectual ferment within the profession and outside of it. This was pioneered by organizations such as the National Association for the Advancement of Colored People that developed a social change–focused litigation strategy. It was also the product of a new generation of lawyers such as Edgar and Jean Cahn and Charles Reich, who wrote for and advocated to an (albeit limited) audience impatient with the glacial pace of social change.[5]

There was much contention within this group about how legal work could optimize social change, and the extent to which clients could and should be involved in the process.[6] There was consensus that many of the existing government systems were fundamentally inimical to the interests of poor people and minorities; that the law could and should be used for social change; and that in order to mount these challenges lawyers needed to create a new form of practice to use the legal system against itself, challenging legal institutions to live up to the promise of equal justice.[7]

To some extent, these new legal services programs gained the support of the organized bar and institutional interests on the federal and local levels. However, this support often came from different motivations and was drawn from a more conservative conception of legal services. For example, while some wanted to use legal services for radical social change, others saw it as a way to channel societal grievances into relatively tame legal frameworks. It also meant that, in practice, legal services lawyers were often criticized by their national and local professional counterparts.[8]

NELS was one of the first of this new breed of legal services programs. It was founded at the initiation of members of the Northeast City Bar Association, although it was not supported by all private attorneys or members of the organized bar. Lawyers who had been with NELS from the early days reported that NELS encountered hostility from local attorneys and judges and that it took some years for NELS to be accepted and respected by the broader legal community.

Founders of NELS in Northeast City sought to create a legal services program on the new model. In some cities, existing legal aid programs sought new federal funding without changing their mission or model of practice. According to Joe, a former NELS director, in Northeast City "the decision was made to close down the [existing] legal services organization although we acquired some of those employees."

NELS followed the new model of storefront offices that served communities in their own neighborhoods. Ben, a longtime consumer lawyer with NELS, described how NELS had provided a variety of services in locations throughout Northeast City:

> We had offices all over the city so . . . we'd have like five different consumer units and you'd have to have meetings of all the consumer lawyers in all the different offices, same thing with welfare and employment and social security and all the other things we do.

Like other longtime NELS lawyers, Joe describes with a tinge of nostalgia his first experience in a NELS neighborhood law office:

> You had to travel through the community on a daily basis and I think that had a healthy effect. And literally, I mean I would, you know, drive to the office, park my car and as I walked from wherever I parked to the office literally you would talk to people on their porches . . . and they would interact with you about their legal problems before and after work . . . You were this outside professional coming in and although you thought of yourself differently as a professional than perhaps other lawyers downtown, reality was that you were a stranger in that community.

And a stranger in a lot of ways . . . and so I had a lot to learn. But I think people were eager to teach you and to interact with you and were appreciative. But I think that was helped by the fact there were informal opportunities to interact as well as formal opportunities.

Joe and other lawyers practicing in these years associate lawyering in the community setting with the generalist practice model. Lawyers did not "screen out" cases and often had very little experience practicing law, but they were open to serving the needs of the clients as they came:

When I started we were all generalists in the law. There was no specialization. And people would drop in with a problem; you wouldn't know what that problem would be. And we'd be expected to respond to that problem and I think that was a great challenge for lawyers. We were all young lawyers at the time in the program. There really were no senior lawyers so the level of experience was much, much lower than it is today in legal services. And that generalist approach in some ways, I think, made the institution closer to the communities that they served.

Although Joe's tone is somewhat nostalgic, he does not romanticize the early years. The generalist neighborhood practice often lacked professional experience; it was also hectic and confusing. As another attorney, Barry, observed: "We probably didn't have all the tools we needed to practice law the way we would have liked, so there are trade-offs."

Nor does Joe romanticize all aspects of being in a neighborhood. He noted that over time, drug problems in poor neighborhoods grew worse and with drug use came concerns for safety. Leslie, a client of the benefits unit, echoed worries about safety at the remaining neighborhood office: "I was a little skeptical because I really didn't like being [in the neighborhood office], 'cause it can be a little ah [laughs]! It's not like it used to be." In addition to concerns for safety, Joe observed that as the lawyers matured along with legal services, their own lives and obligations grew more complicated as they started families of their own and desired more regular schedules.[9] Most lawyers did not live in client neighborhoods, so when connections to poor communities became more attenuated through the closing of neighborhood offices, no one picked up the slack outside of the formal work context.

Over time, due to a combination of cuts in state funding and restrictions placed on federal funding, NELS closed most of its neighborhood offices. This was a painful decision, and most lawyers saw it as a survival mechanism with unfortunate consequences. Today, only two offices remain. One is a storefront neighborhood operation and the other is NELS's main branch, located in the heart of Northeast City in proximity to the seat of city government, the city bar association, and private and other public interest law practices. Although there is some overlap in the services provided and the type of clients served in the neighborhood and branch offices, some units only provide legal services to clients in one location.

The "feel" of the neighborhood office and the main office are very different from one another, as noted by clients and lawyers alike. The main office is newer. Erica, a client, summed it up: "Nice and clean. Professional." The offices are quieter, and the flow of incoming clients is regulated at the entrance. Clients come in at the street level and approach an intake window, where there is someone to receive and direct them. Clients directed further are sent to NELS offices, which take up several floors of the building. The main reception area, on the fourth floor, has parquet floors. Elizabeth notes: "The office is different!" She finds the main office "much cleaner and much better, moderized (sic). It's nice." By contrast, the remaining neighborhood office is "really run down."

The NELS neighborhood office is in a converted shoe store, located at a busy intersection in a low-income neighborhood. The basement contains offices, conference tables, and law books. The first floor has a reception area that is separated by a sliding window from an office area for paralegals and office staff. The reception area also serves as an intake space. Marcia, a lawyer who represents children on issues of Social Security Disability Insurance, worked in the neighborhood office before moving to the main office for personal reasons. She described the neighborhood office as drastically different:

> I mean, you know, I was in the basement of a shoe store for eight years! I mean, we revamped and kept my feet—pulled out the drawer, the bottom drawer of the desk to keep my feet up because the mice—you know? I mean, you know, it's just so different.

Although clients familiar with both offices noted the differences, they did not attribute other differences to the physical surroundings. Elizabeth explained that she felt comfortable in both offices. Lilly, another client, saw advantages to the neighborhood office in view of the clients who used it:

I felt they were comfortable in the area. First of all, it's not overly manicured. It's a comfortable place, a neighborhood place. And if you can
walk in to a neighborhood place, I think it helps. And that was important
there. It might not be the cup of tea for other people, but I think the level
of comfort is important for the client coming in so they're not intimidated. Because they could be easily intimidated. It's the law, it's something
they're not sure of. Many of them are not American born and so they
could be intimidated and that's not fair.

Lilly had not visited the main office, but it made sense to her that the offices looked and felt different: "It's Midtown. . . . They are right for that
neighborhood, the other would be wrong for this neighborhood . . . I
would expect Midtown to be more manicured."

Although clients did not remark on differences beyond the physical,
lawyers who had worked at both offices or had worked at other neighborhood offices before coming to work in the main office thought that the
differences also pervaded the work atmosphere. Again, Marcia:

It's just a totally—and people dress differently. You know what I mean?
The whole atmosphere at the neighborhood office is different. I was up at
[Main] and [Cross] in our neighborhood office and I lived up there. . . .
And that's a great place to work. It's much more like legal services.

In trying to explain the differences, Marcia noted several factors. One difference that resonates with Ben and Joe's accounts is that the neighborhood office is physically present in the neighborhoods they served: "It
made a difference that we were physically where the clients were. In their
neighborhood." This facilitated personal connections that fostered a feeling of investment in the neighborhoods and helped lawyers stay attuned
to the legal needs and emerging concerns of residents. These offices hired
local staff.

We were very invested. And a lot of paralegals that work up there came to
NELS out of high school and they are very invested in making a go of it.
I mean making this neighborhood office work. And it does [work]. They
produce some of the most nationally recognized work. Like they've done,
they were the leaders on a piece that came out recently . . . about what
happens to people after they've been in prison. In terms of welfare, employment, you know, once they come out. What the re-entry legal issues

are. And so given that neighborhood they really saw—and likewise with the predatory lending. They—that was happening right there and so you miss some of that down here [at the main office].

NELS's proximity to the neighborhoods where people live also indicates the kind of service NELS provides. NELS lawyers focus on the legal issues that arise within the daily lives of the people in the neighborhoods. Steve, a NELS lawyer, referred to these as "bread-and-butter" services.

Bread-and-Butter Legal Services

"Bread-and-butter" legal services practice for the poor might be viewed as outdated, a throwback to the '60s or '70s, as suggested by some advocates for "new" kinds of legal services practice.[10] While in theory legal services is not a zero-sum game, there is competition for scarce legal services jobs and for even more scarce legal services.[11] This suggests that legal services providers must allocate resources and that the provision of certain types of legal services mean that others will likely go unheeded. Despite the criticism of bread-and-butter legal services (discussed in greater detail in chapter 3), a significant portion of legal services lawyers continue to provide direct representation to clients for mundane and arguably classical services that are of vital importance. Clients still request assistance with housing, access to public benefits, help with landlord-tenant conflicts, relief from predatory loans, and assistance fighting charges of child neglect and abuse. Assistance with the quotidian aspects of life is necessary in the face of the violence of routine, systematic oppression, more harmful for being so very ordinary.[12]

Attention to situated practice allows us to see why clients still need and want legal assistance, why and how lawyers respond to them, and how both lawyers and clients make sense of their needs and how they strive to meet them. The extant literature is short on such discussion. Almost without exception, studies of legal services have failed to solicit the views of clients. A more careful look at clients' and lawyers' perspectives reveals that routine work for the poor is significant for individuals as well as the broader society. It permits us to transcend the falsely polarizing dichotomy between individual representation and so-called impact practices, dedicated to changing the world by changing the law. Moving beyond the classic version of that argument, lawyers and clients in this study do not debate the relative merits or glamour or importance of these polarities of practice. In fact, they engage in systemic as well as individual change personally and institutionally and take for granted the importance of both. They make strategic choices arising from their hard-won understanding of the possible, which is often different from their own (and others') utopian visions. While lawyers and clients in this study have a vision of justice that calls for systemic change, they are at the same time engaged in what might be disparaged as tinkering.

In this study, I examine a group of legal services lawyers' and clients' understandings of the work they do together. All of them worked together on issues of individual importance to clients. Some of the cases were also tied to broader notions of social justice. Even in discussing the more mundane cases, without exception clients and lawyers articulated some alternative vision of social justice and decried the workings of a system they viewed as unjust. These discussions helped me to understand some ways in which power and resistance are manifest in relationships between lawyers and clients and in their approaches to the outside institutions they challenged together.

Lawyers and clients engage in forms of social critique. However, this kind of social change work often falls below the "radar" of progressive lawyering theories. This is partly a result of theorists' failures to seek input from lawyers who are engaged in such practices on a daily basis. More important, it reflects a failure to seek the perceptions of clients who can best provide us with insight on how they view the work they do with legal services lawyers.

The following chapter briefly reviews the theoretical framework and methods employed in this study. The subsequent four chapters are organized around recurring themes that emerged in interviews with lawyers and clients. I have grouped these themes using concepts central to the progressive lawyering literature: notions of social change, autonomy, collaboration, and transformation. These chapters discuss lawyer and client perspectives and values as shaped by and through the constraints and possibilities of their day-to-day realities. In each chapter, I discuss how the concepts can and should be altered to encompass the experiences and aspirations of lawyers and clients.

Chapter 3 focuses on lawyers' and clients' understanding of the role of law in social change. Working for justice within a system perceived as oppressive and hostile presents challenges to lawyers hoping for social change. However, most consider it an obligation to assist clients rather than ask that they "wait for the revolution." Lawyers find that working with clients on a daily basis helps to reinforce the importance of their work. Clients also view the systems they encounter as oppressive and unfair, not as a place to seek justice. Even so, they believe that with the help of a lawyer it *might* be possible to navigate the legal system and other government bureaucracies successfully. Clients and lawyers often work together to create narratives of an unjust system. This means that for both, working within the system is a necessity and should not be confused with an acceptance of the legal system and/or the government. Neither should it indicate acceptance of the values embodied in encounters with such bureaucracies. This distinction might seem trivial or merely semantic to scholars and critics, but this chapter traces why and how it is very important to both lawyers and clients. It examines how lawyers and clients weigh the risks and benefits of any particular strategy in the short and longterm. I also examine how lawyers and clients see themselves and their struggles as resisting and oppositional, despite the fact that they take place in conventional legal forums using the "master's tools" (often with considerable relish!). I suggest that future scholarship must attend to practice and should be concerned with how visions of social justice and tactics of social change are played out in the contingent realities of everyday lives. To ignore this is to risk further injustice, even if intentions are "good."

Chapter 4 focuses on the concept of autonomy, which is central to most theories of progressive lawyering. Such theories assume clients to be competent and entitled to make informed decisions. According to the literature, progressive lawyers should be on guard to facilitate rather than impede client autonomy. Clients and lawyers are equals and therefore lawyers should resist dominant conceptions of practice in which the lawyer knows best and should make decisions for the client, even if lawyers do so in the client's purported best interest.

Many lawyers champion autonomy, but are unsure what it means in practice. Do we let clients make decisions that we believe are detrimental? Do we force clients to be autonomous (as we see it) by forcing them to follow certain procedures or take certain actions even if they would rather delegate these to their lawyers? Or does autonomy include allowing clients to abdicate their autonomy? Many of the lawyers struggle with such questions and have trouble balancing autonomy with other values that inform their practice, such as care and compassion.

Chapter 4 also discusses the narrow, prevailing view of autonomy, and how client perspectives suggest the need to revise it. It juxtaposes autonomy against the service-oriented retainer model that poor clients believe wealthy clients enjoy. This reveals how the autonomy debate plays into discourses of dependence pervasive in current social welfare policy and the double standard we hold when we ascribe meanings to behaviors and attitudes. The chapter asks that we redefine autonomy more broadly, to include not only the legal issue at hand and the lawyer-client relationship, but the context of the clients' lives. Most clients view "handing over" a particular problem as responsible behavior: they believe people should entrust specialized problems to people with specialized knowledge. In fact, clients castigate friends and relatives who fail to do so as not taking charge of their affairs responsibly. Relying on lawyers ultimately makes clients more autonomous both by allowing them to make decisions informed by professional expertise and by "freeing up" their time to take care of other, sometimes more pressing, issues.

Collaborative lawyering models, the focus of chapter 5, portray lawyers and clients as what Gerald López has called "co-eminent problem solvers."[13] This term is rooted in a belief that both lawyers and clients can and should contribute knowledge and skills to the relationship. While most lawyers espouse this notion in theory, many find it inefficient in practice. Asking or allowing clients to collaborate is not feasible because clients may not be reliable and also because doing so involves a greater time investment. Lawyers and clients find ways to collaborate that do not so much involve clients taking on "lawyer roles" as allocating tasks according to the specialty of each. Lawyers may ask clients to gather information or seek extra-legal resources. Also, many clients will go as far as they can on their own to solve problems before turning to lawyers, a form of what I call serial collaboration.

This chapter also explores a number of ways in which lawyers and clients collaborate that have gone largely unnoticed in the literature. Lawyers and clients work to "name, blame, and claim": that is, they recognize problems as legal issues, attribute responsibility for these problems, and use the legal system as a means to hold others accountable.[14] Lawyers and clients talk about how they need *each other* for this—it is not merely the lawyers who magically take a problem and make it "legal." This work often has political implications, for lawyers and clients together create a narrative of responsibility that allows both to understand individual problems within a broader social, political, and economic context. Such work is important to clients, who are often subject to ongoing messages that hold them solely responsible for their plight. Often mistreated by the bureaucracies ostensibly designed to assist them, most are "taught" that they are politically inefficacious.[15] Lawyers who respect and listen to clients counteract these messages and foster incipient understandings of political self-efficacy and, in some cases, advocacy on behalf of others. Collaboration of this type is also important to lawyers because it shores up their understanding of their role. It reinforces the larger importance of their work at a time when most legal and professional forums are hostile to notions of systemic responsibility or widespread reforms.

The most important facet of legal services lawyering examined in chapter 6 of this book is that it takes place through ongoing interaction between lawyers and clients. Legal services lawyers and clients spoke of a practice centered on the individual client that was often transformative for both client and lawyer. Clients sought material assistance from NELS. They also experienced empathy, respect, and a feeling of connection that was highly valued by clients who are often ignored, judged, or even abused by a host of legal and other government bureaucracies. Lawyers also found relationships with clients personally and professionally significant as a source of inspiration, challenge, and feedback for the work that they do in systems that seem impervious to change.

Most lawyers and clients had trouble characterizing their relationships, not finding words that fit their understanding. Some said it was like friendship in that there was openness, caring, and affinity. Both lawyers and clients who used this term also recognized that their relationship was unlike friendship in that it was bounded and that there was an inequality of disclosure. Others used the term professional to indicate that lawyers were not judgmental, that they were competent and willing to put their skills in service of the clients, and that lawyers acted respectfully and were not overly familiar or patronizing. Clients and lawyers using this characterization also qualified it. They distinguished their lawyers who were caring and had a down-to-earth approach from those who distance themselves by using legal jargon and mystification.

Lawyers and clients alike noted the difficulties that such a complex relationship had, how hard it was to give and receive bad news, and how hard it was to be honest about, and open to, the suffering and harsh conditions that people experience. Empathy, humor, and the importance of legal representation to clients and lawyers help them to weather these difficulties. This chapter ends by reflecting on how openness and empathy toward clients lead lawyers to temper their abstract ideals of progressive practice.

In the final chapter, I show that the practices of lawyers and clients are something more than a collection of haphazard adaptations to political contingencies. While many of the practices reviewed in this book might look to some like a muddling through that comes from a practice that eschews reflection, this is not the case. Lawyers and clients work together within an internally consistent and morally informed ethic of risk. Drawing on Sharon Welch's feminist ethic of risk, I examine the way in which the practice of public interest law is informed by a dual commitment to social justice and the necessity of getting one's hands dirty. Lawyers who believe they should help and clients who need and desire assistance in a climate that both perceive as hostile to their claims are faced with a need to consider strategy: they do not have the luxury of armchair philosophers nor do they think that such a position is morally tenable.

An ethic of risk requires, first and foremost, that one enter the fray. This is risky business for people who hold ideals and values that might be tested against difficult working conditions. This does not require the abandonment of ideals or values, but rather a contingent balancing against other ideals and values that are called into question and constant testing of the border between strategy and cooptation or capitulation. Such risk-taking should be tactical and informed. Failing to reflect on dangers creates the risk that lawyers may become inured to injustice, erode self-worth, and lose vision. This affects both clients and lawyers. Clients and lawyers who open themselves up to each other and are willing to consider their work together with a mutually respectful (and critical) eye can help to reduce some of the risks and can garner some of the benefits elaborated in the experiences of lawyers and clients reviewed in this book.

2

Why Talk to Clients and Lawyers?
A Grounded Interpretivist Framework

Broadly generalized, there are two strains of literature on legal services lawyers. One strain takes an explicitly normative stance regarding what outcomes, relationships, or processes are "good." Scholarship in this genre provides advice about how legal services lawyers should act in order to optimize the assistance they provide to their clients. They advise on everything from choosing cases and clients from disparate community interests to empowering clients and avoiding paternalism. Such literature is not purely instrumental, as much of it provides a rationale for the underlying values promoted. These authors share the espousal of value-based practice, even when they are grounded in the critical self-reflection of "lessons learned."

A second strain of research has its roots in the social sciences. This work focuses on legal practice without explicit reference to values or ideals. In contrast, it asks questions such as: why and how does this practice or narrative promote particular values in this particular context? Who does it disadvantage or privilege? The interpretivist social science framework emphasizes the meanings and perceptions of study participants.[1] It is less concerned with whether or not practices promote particular goals than how participants feel and think about the process and what it means for them, regardless of whether or not the outcome is "better."

Each of these approaches has its limitations. Some of the more instrumental literature obscures fundamental questions, such as who determines the values and goals that are to be pursued and whether they do further the interests they ostensibly promote. Even the more reflective literature is limited. Much of it, produced largely by clinical law scholars, tends either to be self-referential or to caricature practicing lawyers and clients. The literature fails to account satisfactorily for the daily experiences of legal services lawyers. It does not account for lawyers' self-reflection, nor does it explore the adaptations lawyers make so that their practice of public interest law is more compatible with other ideals or goals they embrace.[2] The dearth of studies that examine clients in legal services literature is particularly surprising because legal services practice espouses a vision that is grounded in respect for clients. While progressive lawyering theories are designed to foster certain qualities (such as autonomy) and achieve certain goals (such as empowerment) for and with clients, clients' voices are rarely heard in formulations of practice.

While much of the social science literature asks critical questions, it tends to be so removed from the realm of everyday practice that it is often irrelevant for practitioners. Its audience is chiefly other academics, which is reflected in where it is published, the language it employs, and the issues it chooses to investigate. Although much of it takes seriously the *perspectives* of study participants as research subjects, it does so largely without consultation with them as to the framing of the research, the questions that it asks, and the use to which it is put.[3] Like the normative instrumental and reflective clinical scholarship, it tends to be lawyer-centric.

Empirically grounded in the subjective experiences of both lawyers and clients, this study will allow us to better understand and assess the credibility of critical scholarship, and will be useful to practicing lawyers and their clients as well as to legal scholars. This study bridges the different perspectives outlined above. From the outset, I set the understanding of situated practice as an explicit goal of the research. I relied on the contributions of both strains of literature outlined here to frame the study and to inform my analysis. In each phase, I engaged with audiences both within and outside of the academy. I solicited client perspectives, interviewing more clients than lawyers. I have also attempted to give equal weight to the voices of each group.

In this chapter, I provide a framework for the study. Drawing on literature from a wide range of disciplines, I highlight salient features of lawyer-client relationships, with a particular focus on lawyers who profess a desire to work for social justice. I discuss some of the strengths and weaknesses of these approaches and explain how each of them contributed to this study and to my understanding of the data. The chapter concludes with a brief description of the study methods.

Professional-Client Relationships

In a variety of settings, professionals choose to work toward social justice. While visions of social justice and the best way to achieve it vary, these professionals often share the belief that their professional identity and the practice of their profession is shaped by this commitment. Professional tools and professional-client relationships are based on relations of power. Most clients turn to professionals because of the knowledge and related power that the professional presumably possesses. As such, to the extent that a professional's definition of social justice contains notions of equality, empowerment, and respect for client dignity and autonomy, tensions exist between social justice goals and the means employed to achieve them. These tensions are particularly striking when the working relationships require frequent and intense contact.

My questions are not new; indeed, there is a wealth of literature in a variety of fields that alerts us to the problematic nature of helping relationships. However, an understanding of situated practice is often missing from these important critiques and cautionaries. Theories cannot adequately address the day-to-day encounters and dilemmas professionals face. There is a gap between the theory and the practice of professions that may be most evident in assistance to those most socially marginalized, a field in which helping professionals must make difficult determinations about how to mete out insufficient resources.[4]

Self-flagellation has also been part of the intense reflection of "progressive practitioners" and the large body of critical literature that has problematized helping relationships generally, and lawyer-client relationships in particular. Such critiques have left many self-identified progressive lawyers at sea, with few guidelines for their work.[5] But perhaps more important, clients' voices are consistently missing from such discussions, even among critics who purport to speak on behalf of clients' interests. Many clients are in dire need of services that legal and other professionals provide, and have definite opinions about why they are needed and how they ought to be provided. To the extent that critiques exclude client voices, they run the risk of being uninformed, irrelevant, and perhaps harmful.[6]

This book is neither a valorization nor a condemnation of a particular form of public interest practice, although certainly many of the clients and lawyers in the study inspire admiration despite their admittedly imperfect practices. A situated perspective avoids neat categorization. It highlights the tensions that can be obscured by overly theoretical debates that may unnecessarily polarize or, alternatively, mediate contradictions by skirting true dilemmas. Tensions are difficult, but they are also opportunities. I hope this book will yield fruitful discussion of these tensions; I do not believe there are durable answers.

Professions and Hierarchy

Aspiring professionals master a specific body of knowledge in specialized institutions, often accompanied by a practice component. They undergo a socialization process to become conversant in the use of professional language and committed to professional norms.[7] At professional schools and in apprenticeships, professionals-in-the-making acquire specialized language as well as ways of thinking, reasoning, and defining problems to navigate their chosen world. Laypeople usually do not possess these skills and are often dependent upon them. The critique of lawyer-client relationships as unequal and disempowering rests on a conception of lawyering as a hierarchical professional practice on behalf of laypeople.

So-called neutral professional selection and training processes in schools and in employment have been implicated in perpetuating and reinforcing racial, ethnic, class, and gender stratification within professions and the broader society. Historically, professions have limited access to elites.[8] To the extent that individuals from groups that were once denied access enter professions, schools and professional associations socialize them into dominant values to ensure that the majority will work to preserve the status quo. These individuals are more likely to be *changed by* than to *change* the profession.[9] Socialization reinforces the division between clients and professionals.

Professions and professionals have the authority and the knowledge to decide what constitutes a legitimate problem or topic within their field. They can determine what circumstances or "facts" are "relevant" and thus worthy of consideration within the client-professional relationship. The parameters of relevance set by professionals tend to ignore the contexts in which problems arise and often fail to fully comprehend the range of factors that clients deem relevant to their cases.[10] Although many professionals act as though these parameters are clearly dictated by professional norms, the relevance of particular information, "facts," or motivations can be contested.[11] The ability of lawyers to set the parameters of interest, sometimes against the wishes of clients, is a symptom of, and can further exacerbate, an imbalance of power between professionals and clients.

Licensing and other gatekeeping practices help reinforce the distinction between the initiated and the uninitiated.[12] Professional codes of norms, often referred to as "ethics," prescribe or recommend behavior, setting out guiding values or visions of the profession.[13] These codes often reflect the notion that the professional has a higher-order obligation to others or to an abstract concept ("the poor," "the legal system," "knowledge") and a special ability and altruistic duty to carry out this obligation.

Some have mourned the loss of such higher ideals in the professions.[14] Others claim that the ethical/altruistic model of professionalism is a form of paternalism rooted in professionals' feudal sense of duty to others who are not their social equals, something that reinforces social distance.[15] In the legal profession, codes of conduct historically served as instruments of stratification. They were promulgated and used by white Protestant men of good social standing to regulate and stigmatize the limited practices available to immigrant, nonwhite, non-Protestant, lower-class or otherwise undesirable practitioners, such as contingency fee arrangements. Such within-profession stratification also reinforces the gap between professionals and clients from "outsider" groups, because aspiring professionals with gender, racial, and cultural demographics similar to outsider groups are either kept from the profession or marginalized within it.

Whatever their intention, professional boundaries place professionals in a higher social position than laypeople or para-professionals and enhance the power of the professional and the profession.[16] Existing status disparities such as level of education, gender, race, or class can exacerbate power differentials between professional and client.

Progressive Lawyering

Theories that examine the tensions between social justice goals and the hierarchical, disempowering aspects of lawyering and the legal process use different terms to call for a practice more compatible with social justice goals: rebellious lawyering, client-centered lawyering, collaborative lawyering, critical lawyering, and facilitative lawyering, to name a few.[17] In this study, I refer to this collection of practices and lawyering theories as "progressive lawyering."

Progressive lawyering encompasses elements shared by the other labels and it is one of the many terms that both lawyers and theorists use to describe these orientations in broad strokes. The term progressive lawyering is also identified with those who emphasize the complex interplay of social, political, and legal forces. For example, Nancy Polikoff emphasizes elements of inequality and oppression, using the term to describe "all those who use their legal skills to end poverty, racism, patriarchy, imperialism, and other impediments to social, economic and political justice."[18] Progressive lawyering also invokes Paolo Freire's distinction between social justice work that is "preserving" and social justice work that is "progressive,"[19] a distinction that is not always clear when working for social justice within deeply flawed systems.

Many progressive lawyering critics are or have been practitioners, and thus the critiques are often self-directed. These scholar-professionals generally do not call for abandoning legal tools but rather grapple with long- and short-term limitations of the tactics and practices that lawyers employ with and for poor people. Their critical scholarship often attempts to change prevailing practices using examples of how they or others have incorporated the changes they advocate. Some exhort lawyers to "listen" and work with communities in collaboration, taking their cue from community organizers or leaders or to work with grassroots organizations that may be involved in civil disobedience. Still others call for expanding the participation of nonlawyers, such as the use of lay advocates to accompany battered women through all steps of the legal process.[20]

On an individual level, lawyers have paid much attention to engaging in partnerships with clients, working to assure client-led decision making in the legal process. Certain legal practices, such as litigation, are viewed as particularly hierarchical and disempowering. Critics in this camp call on lawyers to enter fields that have been previously considered irrelevant to work with poor people, such as small business assistance. They advocate interdisciplinary legal practices. For example, lay advocacy draws on a peer assistance model, while small-business lawyering typically is based on a collaborative relationship between lawyer and client that draws on business knowledge as well as legal techniques.[21]

Beyond questions of efficacy, many progressive lawyering critiques are based on what others presume is the best interest of clients. But rarely do their proponents consult with clients or assess the broader framework in which lawyer-client interactions take place. How can a literature that purports to come from a moral stance of client dignity ignore client perspectives? Why do we not ask intended beneficiaries what they think of alternative lawyering strategies?

Despite the important role these critiques have played in expanding the progressive lawyer's toolbox and making traditional legal practice more responsive to client needs, they cannot erase what Lucie White calls "the tensions around the role of the teacher":

There is always going to be tension, in a community-based work that as-
pires to be both participatory and emancipatory, between the directive
role that an organizer, lawyer, leader, or teacher, must play to get the work
going and keep it on track, and the teacher's aspiration to draw out, rather
than dictate, the group's own voices. William Simon has referred to this
paradox as "the dark secret" of community-based poverty lawyering. You
need powerful leadership to get a community-based group together and
to help it undertake meaningful action. Yet with that leadership comes
the obvious risks of domination and exploitation.[22]

This paradox exists not only when the lawyer works with communities but
also in practice with individuals.[23] As the idea of paradox implies, many
of the same features that create the risk of hierarchical and dominating
power relations are also the sources for important social change. Communities and disempowered individuals seek lawyers and other professionals precisely because they are thought to hold the power to challenge
injustices. In fact, if the lawyer does not possess some type of knowledge
or access that the client or community lacks, then the client probably has
little use for the lawyer. How then do lawyers and clients tap power in
a process that minimizes the risk of further marginalizing clients and
communities?

There is no bright line between constructive criticism and paralyzing
rhetoric. The effective legal tools that draw fire as hierarchical and paternalistic must be balanced against remedies that would cripple their use.
This is what Louise Trubek has called "liv[ing] in the contradiction," in
her call for public interest lawyers to "learn to deal with the central paradox of our peculiar vocation: helping to bring about basic change and social mobilization while working within a legal system rooted in the status
quo and oriented towards professional decision-making."[24]

Many public interest lawyers do live the contradiction. Scholarship on
public interest lawyers, too, needs to pay heed to the improvisations and
understandings that lawyers and clients make from their practice. What
I found in this study is that the disciplinary knowledge that grows out
of theories of empowerment, autonomy, and collaboration, to the extent
that lawyers are familiar with them, leave lawyers with a set of tools and a
disciplinary language that inform their practice. However, when this language and the concepts it embodies fails to provide guidelines, or provides
guidelines that contradict with other, unarticulated values, lawyers are
confused. They find themselves unable to expand or change that language,

but they perceive their work in tension with some imagined ideal. For example, as I will discuss in chapter 4, when Pete makes a routine phone call for a suicidal client, he worries that he has not allowed her an opportunity to be empowered. Pete has a vocabulary for autonomy and empowerment, but his definition is narrow, centered on the professional legal relationship. Further, he has no vocabulary for other values that are clearly at play, such as caring and compassion, and thus he does not recognize their role in deciding how to act.

Lawyers do not act in a haphazard or unreflective manner even when they depart from the idealized practice notions of decontextualized theories. Instead, they develop their own ways of resolving problems that grow from their shared and accumulated experiences that are negotiated in a practice context with clients. It is up to practitioners and scholars to articulate these dynamic understandings so that they may be acknowledged and discussed. This study focuses on how progressive public interest lawyers and their clients grapple with the risks and potential benefits inherent in the tension of a professional practice for social justice. I explore the trade-offs and constraints progressive lawyers and their clients face as they attempt to provide and receive quality lawyering within a practice that may also be informed by conflicting ideals.

Law and Society Studies

Legal realism emerged as a response to scholarship focused myopically on "law on the books." Scholars in the legal realist tradition rejected this view of law as overly narrow and mistakenly dissociated from its application and interpretation, calling instead for a scholarship focusing on "law in action." They also viewed law as an important tool in effecting social change. Early legal realists shared with their predecessors a belief in the law as neutral, merely replacing the neutrality of legalism with the objectivity of social science, even as they expanded the scope of inquiry.[25]

Law and society studies have theoretical and methodological roots in legal realism. Nevertheless, they are less optimistic about the role of law as a vehicle for social change. In part, this is because they are less sanguine about the effectiveness of law for this purpose. It is also because they do not see the law as neutral but rather as implicated in power relations. The critique of legal realism is in many ways a predictable outgrowth of the legal realist perspective. Legal realism posited that the law could consciously be used for social engineering, and in many cases had been so used even if unacknowledged. As legal realism matured, those same insights were applied not just to the law itself but more broadly to the study of the law and the social engineering that legal realists attempted to implement. In examining the consequences of legal actions and the legal process broadly defined, it became clear to many that the law in action did not always produce hoped-for social amelioration, nor did it always act as predicted or as intended. The complex and dynamic relationship between the legal and the social also belies a unidirectional view of the influence of law upon society. Drawing on the insights of social constructionism, law and society scholars hold that the legal and the social are inextricably tied and mutually influential.[26] As a result, law and society researchers examine a broad variety of legal and extralegal tools and activities and focus on processes and practices, including the subjective meanings legal actors assign to their relationships and interactions.

Empirically grounded law and society research can illuminate the potentials and pitfalls of using the law as a tool for social change. Lawyering for social change cannot be pursued without entering into a particular economic, political, or social context not only of the larger society but also of the client-professional relationship. While clients and lawyers are constrained by their roles, they also exert power vis-à-vis one another and together in ways that challenge these positions. Awareness of the relevance of the relationship between clients and lawyers in addition to that of the legal process can help practitioners to mitigate or avoid some of the more disempowering or oppressive (albeit perhaps unintended) aspects of lawyering for social justice. To be effective, this knowledge needs to account for the expectations, desires, and experiential reality of public interest lawyers and their clients.

"Cause lawyering" is the term that sociolegal scholars Austin Sarat and Stuart Scheingold coined for all forms of lawyering in service of a "cause." While broader than the progressive lawyering that is the subject of this study (encompassing, for example, right-wing cause lawyers and pro bono practitioners), the growing body of cause lawyering literature enhances our understanding of the work of progressive lawyers. It has examined the way lawyers shape, influence, work with, and find professional and personal identity in causes. It has also examined the influence of practice settings and opportunities. However, it has just begun to examine how causes shape and influence lawyers.[27] By focusing too much on the influence of lawyers, lawyering, and legal discourses, cause lawyering analysis remains overly legal-centric. Failing to investigate client (and other) perspectives leaves cause lawyering only a partially realized project and underestimates important forces that shape the practice of cause lawyering.

By talking to lawyers and clients, this study seeks to situate lawyers not only within a practice setting, but in relationship to their causes and in dialogue with clients. But this study can only go so far. Indeed, any academic scholarship can only go so far.[28] To be relevant (and to be accurate), the scholarship of practice and professionals must acknowledge situated practice, which would include paying attention to all stakeholders.

Ideas of Power and Social Justice

Law and society research has been concerned with the concept of power in the law and the legal process.[29] There are many definitions of power, but one that many scholars draw on is the amorphous description(s) of power discussed by philosopher Michel Foucault, who viewed power as a dynamic current flowing through all relationships, its working most readily identifiable in the local and the specific:

> Power's condition of possibility, or in any case the viewpoint which permits one to understand its exercise, even in its more "peripheral" effects, and which also makes it possible to use its mechanisms as a grid of intelligibility of the social order, must not be sought in the primary existence of a central power, in a unique source of sovereignty from which secondary and descendent forms would emanate; it is the moving substrate of force relations which, by virtue of their inequality, constantly engender states of power, but the latter are always local and unstable.[30]

Foucault sought to understand what power is and how it works in given situations. Nevertheless, many assessments of Foucault focus on what his definition of power means for the possibilities of social change.[31] If power is enacted everywhere, including in personal relationships, the way we act, think, and make choices, then how do we combat oppression, how do we enter into relationships where power is not used to make others into objects, and where do we even begin? How do we resist power if it is in all relationships? An alternative perspective sees Foucault's conception of power as revealing potential for resistance. If power is everywhere, it can be challenged everywhere. If power is always moving and changing, then it is potentially malleable. It does not necessarily reproduce existing hierarchies; it may be used to challenge them. If power is in all relationships, then each relationship holds a chance for change.[32]

A second way to assess these insights is against their value in providing clues to detect and investigate the manifestations of power.[33] The notion that power is everywhere has been a source of a critical scholarship calling for an investigation of power at all points where its workings can be identified and addressed. If power circulates in and through all relationships, then any relationship that is examined for power must be viewed simultaneously within itself and within the larger context in which that relationship occurs. Power can also be sought out by examining resistance. Forms of resistance not only help locate the exertion of power against those resisting, but help to illuminate the dynamics of power in relationships when resistance itself is recognized as an expression of power.[34]

Local analyses of power shift the focus of the struggle against oppression away from bigger, often elusive issues such as legal injustices to the quotidian practices through which people and groups are categorized and constructed as social and political subjects. The client-professional relationship has drawn attention as a local manifestation of power deserving investigation.[35] Within this framework, challenges have been directed to all those working toward social justice to turn inward rather than focus only on an external "oppressor." Professionals (and their critics) who work to empower endeavor to bring power as they define it to another, often for goals that they believe should be achieved. Characterizations of marginalized people as "lacking power," "needing more power," or as targets for empowerment are all in some ways an enactment of power. This is not only true of institutionalized empowerment schemes, but also of more radical ventures and personal relationships.

Further, law and "law talk" as a means of communication has been implicated in reflecting and reinforcing power relationships through its largely rule-based and specialized form. The way that lawyers and clients focus on the importance of communication with each other and with the legal system they challenge together suggests that an examination of the dynamics of power within the lawyer-client relationship does not tell the whole story. Nontraditional legal communication can be a way for lawyers and clients to cooperate to challenge government agencies and the dominant ideologies that many of the policies and practices imply.[36]

This study draws heavily on the insights of power theorists in trying to understand the dynamics of the lawyer-client relationship. The interview guides were designed to elicit information about how lawyers and clients understand their relationships, and whether lawyers and clients viewed them as a framework of contestation and power and/or see themselves engaged in behaviors and practices that would mark them as such.

Critical Theorizing and Practice

The critical theorizing of lawyers and other professionals interested in working toward social justice challenges them to examine how they are themselves implicated in oppression and relationships of power on all levels, even as they advocate social change. It also alerts them to the dangers of thinking that legal tools are inherently neutral or can lead to social justice, however defined. As such, progressive lawyering demands constant questioning and contestation of identities and relationships on either side of the power differential. Although this may be an important step toward stocktaking and self-awareness, there are concerns about the implications of these critical arguments. Does this self-awareness lead to a paralyzing self-consciousness on the part of people who are interested in social change? What are the implications of these critiques for strategies that may be materially successful or have short-term benefits while perpetuating subjugation? Is it ethical to force people into particular client models? If a client prefers a strategy that she perceives to be the best for her own needs, is it ethical for her attorney to counsel otherwise even if she does not consider it the most effective strategy for her client or for an imagined community of beneficiaries?[37] Is self-scrutiny the best investment of the efforts of public interest lawyers and critical theorists? With so much to do, and limited resources, it is not clear that this energy is well-directed. Indeed, it may provide ammunition that better serves those who seek to further gut legal services programs.

It is disturbing that professionals purportedly working toward social justice may be implicated in oppressive relations of power. However, the flip side of this is that these same relationships also hold potential for resistance, change, and social justice—particularly if power is dynamic and potentially malleable. The danger and potential of lawyering for social change is brought into relief in what Everett Hughes called the "rough edges of work."[38] Progressive lawyering theories are negotiated in the daily, unglamorous interactions with actual clients with complex problems, in a context of limited resources within a social, political, and legal climate that is often hostile to the legal and moral claims that lawyers and clients make.

In their comprehensive review of the literature on lawyer-client professional relationships, Sarat and Felstiner found that most studies point toward relationships where one side wields power over the other and that the power holder is usually the person with the most resources.[39] More often than not, this is the professional. However, Sarat and Felstiner have criticized these views as incomplete, and claim that power is rarely, if ever, unidirectional or stable. In their extensive study of divorce lawyers and clients, they found that clients and lawyers engaged in dynamic relationships in which power was exercised in changing and subtle but often consequential ways. Without ignoring the unequal distribution of resources, they found that both clients and lawyers were engaged in struggles over definitions and meanings of goals, interpretation, and relevance. These were negotiations of power in which either side could influence the other and affect the course of the legal process.

Such power constitutes what Linda Gordon, borrowing from James Scott, calls "powers of the weak" to describe how battered women made creative use of limited resources, including social agencies, in order to extricate themselves and their children from abusive circumstances.[40] By Gordon's account, the "weak" are limited in the powers that they can invoke and may also have little control or certainty regarding the full consequences of invoking them. While these powers must be recognized as exertions of control and resistance, it is also important that the localized study of power does not obscure structural or systemic forces. Localized study need not be at the expense of examining larger forces, but rather is a way to gain insight into how relationships are enacted within, around and against larger structural forces. As John Gilliom points out in his study of the everyday resistance of Appalachian welfare beneficiaries against state surveillance, we must subject this type of resistance to the same type of scrutiny that we do any other political strategy.[41]

Study Design

In interviews with lawyers and clients, I explored questions that seem particularly troubling to those who profess a desire to help "disempowered" people even as they are self-conscious about the implications of helping work. If assistance proffered to another of unequal social standing is never devoid of paternalism, how should would-be do-gooders proceed? Should people seeking assistance be turned away for their own good, or be transformed from clients to collaborators—against their will? Should all methods that may disempower be jettisoned or radically modified? How can professionals and clients weigh the risks and benefits of such decisions? Is there a way to mitigate the imperialistic or paternalistic nature of the process? Regarding these questions, how should we assess the opinions of those who are the intended beneficiaries of aid?

In light of our paltry knowledge of professional-client relationships in legal services work, I sought a method that would allow me to learn from study participants. Too often theories are imposed by outsiders, or are developed by practitioners who are captives of their own experiences. In the spirit of grounded theory, I tried to understand lawyer-client relationships by paying close attention to how lawyers and clients described themselves, allowing conceptual connections and relationships to emerge from the data through ongoing analysis.[42] Although no researcher can extract or neutralize herself, I consciously tried to be led by the participants and the data as much as possible.[43]

As a result of my interest in the subjective perceptions of the participants, the study relies on interviews that were guided by very broad topic areas. I asked lawyers and clients to explore these areas freely, occasionally reining in the conversation with specific queries that aimed to clarify their logic or meaning. I also encouraged lawyers and clients to talk about whatever they deemed relevant, which allowed them to raise issues that I did not foresee. My literature review and pilot interviews indicated that public interest lawyers are aware of the risk of disempowerment in the legal process and have found ways to come to terms with their own practices in an imperfect world. Levels of awareness and modifications are likely to vary with years of experience, exposure to academic critiques, and the political era in which the lawyer decided to practice law. Thus, while it was not necessary to be too circumspect in raising these issues with lawyers, I chose my words carefully. I tried to avoid language referring to concepts that have become catchphrases, or "hot-button" issues, such as the word "empowerment." If such terms came up, lawyers or clients were asked to explain what they meant by them.

Clients' views about justice and the legal process are colored by their prior experiences with bureaucracies and/or legal institutions. This might be expected to change to some degree over the course of a good or bad encounter with legal services providers.[44] For this reason, I asked clients about their prior encounters with the legal system. Further, clients and lawyers often have discrepant perceptions of the legal process and its outcomes and different expectations of it. I expected that, together, clients and lawyers must negotiate a working relationship that contained some shared understanding or compromises. To examine this, and to make a more nuanced, composite understanding of the problems that lawyers and clients face, the sample is comprised of sets of lawyers and clients who worked together.

Because the lawyer-client interaction is different when observed than when retold, I wanted to observe lawyer-client dyads to supplement the interview data. Despite the cooperation and access granted from the research site, this was not possible.[45] Potential safeguards, like those used in Sarat and Felstiner's study of divorce lawyers and clients such as agreement by attorneys and judges in their research jurisdiction that they would not press for or accept the presence of study observers as grounds for a waiver of lawyer-client privilege, were neither possible nor appropriate.[46] This was largely because of the high level of vulnerability of most clients and the size and complexity of the legal system in Northeast City.

To minimize any effects of organizational differences in this research, I recruited all participants from one legal services organization. I chose a site that has a staff large enough to accommodate the sample size (assuming that only some attorneys would participate) and that focuses on client representation rather than high-impact work such as Supreme Court litigation or lobbying. The differences between these types of lawyering for social justice have been discussed at length in the literature and will be discussed in greater detail throughout this study. For the purposes of this book, the focus on individual representation means that sampled lawyers have much more frequent contact with a large number of individual clients.

Recruitment

After identifying NELS as my preferred research site, I contacted the director. Following internal discussion, the director sent a recruitment letter by e-mail (attached here as appendix A) to all NELS attorneys together with her endorsement of the project. Most lawyers were recruited by responding to the e-mail post. One expressed an interest in the project when interviewed for another project and had given me permission to contact him again. I interviewed seven attorneys and most of the clients they referred during the first eight months of data collection. After that, NELS's director sent a second e-mail recirculating the recruitment letter and updating the organization on my progress in recruiting lawyer participants. In her second posting, the director noted that confidentiality would be observed, but suggested that attorneys who had already participated in the study speak to colleagues. Pete, a NELS attorney, responded to that posting in an e-mail to all the staff attorneys with a copy to me. Although the language is tongue-in-cheek, responding to the need for confidentiality, the sentiment is clear:

> Without revealing identities, the experience of participating in this study is thought to be interesting and thought-provoking for both the attorneys and clients involved. It is thought to be a good opportunity to critically reflect on what we imagine we are accomplishing for and with our clients and how we go about doing that. It is thought to be highly recommended.

Three of the eleven attorneys who agreed to participate did so, at least in part, at the prompting of this e-mail and of other colleagues.

I asked lawyers who participated in the study to refer three clients whom they believed were satisfied with their representation. I assumed that lawyers would in any case be likely to refer satisfied clients (and satisfied clients would be more likely to agree to be contacted), so I made this an explicit criterion. I also believed that clients would report some dissatisfaction, tension, or difference of perspectives that would shed light on the concerns of disgruntled clients. However, as data collection continued, there was little or no report of tensions or differing viewpoints. Lawyers expressed an interest in learning from dissatisfied clients and a willingness to refer them, although they remained skeptical as to whether such clients would be willing to speak with a researcher or even return phone calls. When the first lawyers who recruited clients informed me of this, I modified the selection criterion to include clients who could shed light on the topics discussed in our interviews.

The Sample

SAMPLE CHARACTERISTICS

The recruiting procedures outlined above yielded a sample of eleven lawyers (out of approximately 40) from eight of NELS's nine divisions. Five were women, six were men. Six worked in NELS's neighborhood office and five worked at the main branch. All but one were white. They had worked at NELS for anywhere from several months to 26 years, with representatives along the whole spectrum between.

All but the most recent entrant to the profession and to NELS successfully recruited at least three clients. Four of the initial referrals did not result in interviews. Of these, one client was in the process of moving out of town, one ill client suffered further health problems, and a third informed me that he had no interest in participating in the study. The fourth client was one that I declined to interview due to concerns about the nature of her consent.[47] In these few instances, lawyers referred additional clients. I completed interviews with three of each referring lawyer's clients, resulting in a client sample of 30.

Three of the client participants were men and the remaining 27, women. Lawyers told me that this was fairly representative of most of NELS's divisions, with the possible exception of the employment and Social Security Disability caseloads.[48] Four of the clients were white, 24 were African American, one was Indonesian, and one was Nigerian. Client participants ranged in age from their early twenties to their eighties. Many of the clients or their close family members had significant health problems. One client with lupus was bed-ridden and breathed with oxygen support; another had advanced kidney disease; and one client was caring for two of her grown children in her home, one with schizophrenia and another with developmental delay. Many clients also had extended family or friends living with them, or they were themselves living with relatives or friends.

For some clients, the experience with the referring lawyer was their first encounter with NELS or even with the law; for others, it was one case in a long history. Many clients expressed surprise at the quality of services they received from NELS lawyers.[49] When asked to elaborate on this, they often responded that they thought "you get what you pay for," meaning that they expected free services to be substandard.

POSSIBLE SAMPLING BIASES

My sample may be skewed in several ways. It contains only lawyers who were still practicing public interest law at the time of the interview. It misses lawyers who left this practice due to the stress, frustration, and dissatisfaction it can entail. Thus, I believe the study's attorney participants were more likely to report job satisfaction and be less negative about the practice of public interest law than would be the members of a random sample of all attorneys who practiced public interest law during the study period.

Also, the Northeast City public interest law community perceives itself as unique. Public interest lawyers at NELS and in Northeast City in general consider themselves highly skilled, and the organizations can afford to be selective in hiring attorneys. These lawyers work within an unusually collaborative community and they enjoy high levels of support and prestige from within that community and the private bar. These factors may enhance job satisfaction and contribute to their ability to deal with job-related stress. They may also influence lawyers' assessments of what they are able to do with and for clients.

Clients may also be unusual. All seemed very satisfied with their lawyers, which may be a result of the lawyer referral. However, most of the lawyers interviewed felt that the large majority of clients they serve are pleased with the assistance they receive. This may be due to NELS's client selection process. All lawyers noted that due to limited resources, NELS does not represent clients whom lawyers feel NELS cannot assist. Receiving "client" status in the first place means being chosen from a larger pool of applicants and is likely to engender some sense of satisfaction. On the other hand, NELS does not engage in "creaming" in the sense of taking "easy cases." In fact, most lawyers enjoyed the challenge of difficult cases and felt that these clients were often in greatest need of legal services. The low expectations that most clients have of "free legal aid," noted above, also likely contribute to their satisfaction.[50] Because most clients were so satisfied, it was often difficult for them to recall (or perceive?) possible instances of conflict or tension with their lawyers, although I did probe for this.

Finally, NELS is an example of an urban legal services practice that exhibits all the "best" features of critical lawyering in that the process and means are highly compatible with the goals of equality and social justice.[51] NELS enjoys benefits that come from a thoughtfully crafted practice based on community engagement; mutually informing individual and impact work; ties with the local bar and law schools as well as national networks of public interest lawyers; and high-quality representation. If the dilemmas of progressive practice persist here, they are likely to affect lawyers and clients working with legal services programs that do not (or cannot afford to) engage in such "best practices."

3

Working for Social Justice in an Unjust System

I think very few lawyers can say that they've really made the world a little bit, in a teeny way, better. Most lawyers are really not engaged in that pursuit at all. And so I consider myself very lucky to have a decent-paying job where I feel like I'm doing positive things. Not earth-shaking things. But bringing a little bit of justice into the world.   —Ben, a lawyer in the consumer law division

If you have [Ben Silberman] on your side, you're fine. If you've got [Dora Mercer] on your side, you're fine. But the justice system, I would not take them on alone . . . And both of them, well [Dora] in the courtroom with me and [Ben] in the court with me for the bankruptcy, so I knew I was going to get a good deal. I had good lawyers.   —Elinor, a client of the consumer law division

All of the lawyers in this study shared a commitment to social change. Many were troubled by how their commitment has played out in work with clients over the course of their careers, particularly in the conservative political climate of the 1990s and the early twenty-first century that is at best apathetic and at worst hostile to poor people's claims. Clients were less direct in their discussion of social justice. While most felt dissatisfaction with the "system," they (understandably) focused on their immediate needs. Although their narratives reveal visions of a more equitable legal system, these are often clouded by the need to act strategically in order to solve pressing individual problems.

Whatever they think of the legal system or the government, individuals come to NELS with private concerns rather than in pursuit of social change. Lawyers and their clients must work within the legal system even if they are using it to challenge laws or rulings or legal processes. When they choose to work within the legal system, lawyers and clients must play by its rules and acknowledge its role as the arbiter of their claims.[1] However, lawyers and their clients do not really view this as a free choice. Clients and their allies rarely have viable alternatives to the legal system, particularly if they have not chosen the forum or initiated the dispute, as in child welfare cases.

Lawyers and clients view the prevailing political, economic, or social context in which they work as inhospitable or downright hostile to their goals. Lawyers and clients have managed this dilemma in part by constructing an understanding of the strategic need to work within existing systems. They tolerate this understanding by holding on to an alternative perspective and working from that perspective in various ways, as best they can. Lawyers in this study viewed work with individuals as a central component of social change that must be pursued even when the historical context is favorable to systemic changes. Ultimately, justice is measured by its impact on people. This chapter examines how lawyers and clients view their work within a legal system that, in their ideal visions, would be radically different.

Social Change as Vocation

Motivation

Without exception, the lawyers in this study chose the legal profession as a means to promote often amorphous notions of social change. At a basic level, lawyers believed they provide needed access to clients. They were troubled that although the law provided remedies for some of the problems their constituents faced, they did not (or could not) invoke legal remedies. One respondent said his constituents' problems were not so much that they were poor or had needs, but that they had no access to the legal system to assert claims for assistance. Liz, a lawyer working with the elderly, expressed similar feelings:

> You know, it's hard to say without it sounding like a cliché. We've talked about . . . wanting, trying to make— make it more fair out there, you know?

I mean, it's just really awful the way that people don't have access to things simply because of information or simply because they don't have someone to counsel them and simply because you know the bank or the nursing home or the hospital has other high-powered resources that they can bring to bear on the situation that puts the person who becomes my client at a disadvantage. Hopefully, only until they become our client [laughs].

Perhaps more compelling than the perception of need that drew lawyers into the pursuit of social justice were their own values and sense of obligation. Vicki, a recent graduate of an elite law school (and an elite college before that), put it this way:

If I'm at this point then it's my obligation and my duty to then look back and make sure that I'm doing something for people that are trying to come the same way or that, um, haven't been given the same advantages or the same privileges. 'Cause I, I totally consider it luck that I am where I am, and that if someone isn't given as, the same kind of luck, that I use my luck to help them out. . . . And that's the fundamental core of, 'cause I'm not a religious person and so I think that's sort of my religion . . . I think it's a tiny redistribution of resources is how I see it. That I have a huge amount of resources invested in me and so I want to go invest it in other people as well.

Vicki's motivation to practice public interest law was more of an internal push—in her case having led a privileged life—than a response to an external stimulus such as her perception of others' needs. Lawyers in this study chose careers in public interest law out of both motivations, often simultaneously.

Why Law?

For some, the choice of law seemed natural from the start. Jeff, a starting lawyer, explains how he selected his placement for a year of work through a Jesuit volunteer program that he participated in after college:

You list your top ten choices. And my choices happened to be legally based only because that's sort of the direction—only because I'm not good at math, basically [laughs]. I can barely add for Chrissake! Um, but I think I knew I wanted to be a lawyer. My father is a lawyer and my brother is a lawyer. I guess I have lawyers in the family, so. I knew I wanted to be a lawyer and that was sort of just waiting for substance to fill its sails and take it in one way or another.

Unlike Jeff, most lawyers' career choice was secondary to their commitment to social justice. Some recounted eye-opening experiences in high school or college as a result of contact with poor or disadvantaged people that led them to experience their own privilege. Ben was shaken by teaching in a prison as a college student:

> I was teaching in prison, which I had started while I was an [Elite College] undergrad . . . After I graduated, the school board hired me as a teacher to teach in . . . a maximum security prison. . . . The experience in jail was . . . a massive growing experience. I grew up in the suburbs in a fairly protected world and it was a real shock for me to sort of, sort of confronting the humanity of society's damned. And I had a lot of good relationships there and felt very engaged. I can remember when—I was a philosophy major at [Elite College], which was sort of at the opposite end of the world I guess in some ways, I mean very, very remote by definition. And I remember being in a panic at the end of college feeling that this is all wonderful and exciting and fun but I felt sort of disconnected from the world like I was floating around in summer camp for privileged children. And so the experience in jail kind of, was a really wrenching, sort of grounding in the realities of the world.

Joanne's career choice evolved over time. Always hoping to effect lasting change in people's lives, popular culture and personal trauma honed her focus on a legal career:

> It was really a wake-up one day . . . It was a combination of . . . I had been date-raped during my senior year of college. And although I really wasn't dealing with it yet, in May of that year I'm sure it was in the back of my mind. But I also had spent most of college watching *LA Law*. And a lot of my friends in college were going off to law school and it just occurred to me that that's really the path I wanted to be taking. So a year later when I really started dealing with the after-effects of the date rape and I was in grad school for biology and was very, very unhappy, that's when I kind of decided what type of law I wanted to do, which is not at all what I'm doing but I wanted at that point to do, to prosecute criminal law. And I left grad school and eventually applied to law school.

Joanne went on to explain her decision to move from prosecution to defense work and, later, to legal services work as a desire to address what she saw as root causes rather than later manifestations of dysfunction, thus enhancing the potential impact of her work.

> I thought that I was a true-bred prosecutor and I'd check out the defense side just to see what it was like and maybe get some pointers on how to be a better prosecutor. And I really discovered that I didn't like the attitude of prosecutors, that they were very self-righteous and that just wasn't who I was and who I wanted to be. And I loved it there. I liked doing the defense work. I liked helping out people in that one-on-one way. That was something I wanted to get out of biology but you're so far removed from the people you're helping when you're doing biological research that I never felt that, and I was feeling that with the defense work. But it also felt like I was just patching up problems . . . That's what led me to apply to civil legal services . . . feeling that that was a better place for me to be helping people do something better with their lives.

Marcia, Pete, and Suzanne initially pursued social justice in nonprofessional capacities in the nonprofit sector. When it became clear to them that their abilities to effect change were limited, they opted for professional careers as lawyers. They were not committed to law per se; lawyers like Suzanne saw law as a profession that was prestigious and flexible and could be leveraged to pursue social justice:

> I realized that the work that I did had some sort of importance to me personally . . . So I started working for a nonprofit organization. And then I realized that just having a BA, you know being at the bottom of a rung in a nonprofit can be a really horrible, frustrating experience [laughs]. So I needed an advanced degree and then it took me a couple more years to sort of think, like, well maybe law was the way to go. And part of it quite frankly was I didn't want to take the GREs because of the math and I realized that like the LSATs were sort of easier and that you only had to learn one trick to do [laughs]. And law also seemed more flexible. Like you get the JD and you don't necessarily have to practice. Like I wasn't sure I wanted to practice when I went in but I thought, you know, it's an advanced degree. It's a really—relatively prestigious advanced degree and I can sort of take it off in different directions depending on what kind of public interest I wanted to do.

Lawyers took stock of their relative strengths and weaknesses, often after considering different careers that they regarded as more promising avenues for social change such as journalism or community organizing. Marjorie taught before settling on the law:

> I taught for a couple of years and I thought I wanted to be a teacher because I thought that's really what this world needs is effective teachers, and I learned that I'm not the most effective teacher. So, I mean, but it was really I think kind of looking at what I could do to help people with my skills.

As Marjorie's comments make clear, many lawyers view other career choices as potentially having greater impact or serving a greater good. However, like another lawyer who joked about having an "unfortunate aptitude" for the law, Marjorie believed she had a special talent for legal practice compared to other career choices. "I wanted to go to law school because I wanted to save the world [laughs] . . . So I didn't have good abilities to become a doctor or become a teacher, so it just seemed like a good fit for my capabilities." In all cases, lawyers looked for means to maximize their personal efficacy in a way that would best fit their social justice agendas and the constituents they desired to serve. Even those who knew they wanted to be lawyers from the outset, like Martin, acknowledged a long-standing interest in social justice and were drawn to legal services work from the beginning of their legal careers:

> I mean actually it was a nice fit. I was always interested in social justice and social change and when I went to law school the first semester they had, you know, four different lawyers come in from different kinds of legal practices and talk to us about it and someone [who] came in was an attorney at [Northeast Legal Services]. So it just struck me right away that's what I wanted to do.

Later, in the same interview, when asked about job satisfaction, Martin noted: "I do like my work a lot. I tell anybody who will listen that if I couldn't be a legal aid lawyer I wouldn't be a lawyer. I don't know what I'd be, but I wouldn't be a lawyer."

Shaping Public Interest Career Paths

As a result of funding cuts, which have caused legal services programs around the country to be gutted, jobs have become scarce. At the time of my interviews (2002–03), NELS had been in a hiring freeze. All new positions during that time were funded through various foundations or the private bar. As most of these programs require that the attorneys and public interest law organizations wishing to participate submit proposals together, flexibility of substantive specialty is often crucial to landing a job at NELS and other public interest law organizations in Northeast City.

The difficulties of staying committed to a career in public interest law through law school and then obtaining work in this field are well documented.[2] Like most of the lawyers interviewed, Vicki hoped to stay at NELS, but she was employed via a fellowship sponsored by a Northeast City corporate law firm. A condition of her fellowship was that she join the firm at the end of her year at NELS. She saw this as her only opportunity to pursue public interest law:

> One of the measures of a law school is how many of their graduates have jobs. Finding a public interest job is much more difficult than finding a corporate job so of course [her top-tier law school] is going to track people into corporate. And I think one of the things that I benefited from was knowing what I wanted right when I walked in. . . . But even so it was still hard for me to stay committed. Um, it's so much easier to find another kind of job. And really it was a compromise to say, "Okay I'm going to go to this firm in order to do public interest work," when public interest work was probably what I really want to do. And yet to be able to do it, I'm going to have to go to a firm. So I think, I think it's hard to keep the focus on that as you're going through law school. Mostly because at the end of it you have all these loans and you're like well, I'm going to need a job [laughs]. And where am I going to find this job? It's going to be easier to find it in the private sector.

Vicki's experience is telling. There exists a lack of funding for legal services and a corresponding scarcity of legal services jobs. Legal education and legal career norms also work against careers in public interest law, setting a hierarchy of jobs according to client prestige and income that begins from the first year.[3] Further, the expense of law schools and dearth of scholarships make it difficult for students to accept lower paying legal services jobs, which may also be less secure due to the vagaries of funding that may or may not be renewed from year to year.

Funding considerations not only make it more difficult to be hired into and accept public interest law jobs, but they also infuse employment practices in subtler ways. At the time of the interviews, NELS could only hire new attorneys through sponsorship. It therefore needed to either cut legal services to clients or shape its hiring practices to increase their chances to obtain competitive funding. This meant choosing candidates from nationally recognized top-tier law schools. All of the recently hired attorneys who came to NELS via sponsored positions had attended top-tier law schools. Pete found such elitist hiring practices anathema to the norms and values that guide lawyering for social change. As discussed in chapter 2, such patterns reinforce existing power differentials and hier-archical practices within the profession as well as between lawyers and clients.[4] Lawyers from these schools are less likely to be drawn from the communities they serve or to resemble the members of those communi-ties in even superficial ways. Marcia, who served on NELS's attorney hir-ing committee, agreed with Pete. I asked her whether NELS had tried to recruit students from more diverse law schools or local law schools. She told me that only students from top-tier schools received fellowships, and NELS's attempts at diversifying their attorney workforce had disastrous results for NELS and its clients:

> We've tried it the other way 'cause I was on the attorney hiring committee and I was really pushing for that to happen. But the foundations just won't take these folks. . . . I convinced the attorney hiring committee at one point to try some other folks. And then you know when we didn't get an attorney that year, *boy*! I mean you know, I was . . . you know, I've changed my mind. Because we really need those attorneys . . . and it's a self-fulfilling prophecy.

Thus, NELS is caught within a system of financial support that reinforces existing power relations. NELS has ascertained through trial and error that in order to remain viable and balance other commitments (chiefly its mission to provide clients with legal representation), it must conform to these exigencies. The trade-off, a conscious decision by the organization, leaves attorneys feeling compromised.

Due to the difficulty of obtaining public interest law jobs, lawyers' flex-ibility about their particular specialization once they ascertained that they in fact wanted to pursue social justice using the law often paid off. Many decided on a career in civil (as opposed to criminal) legal services, but did not have a preference within that. Joanne got to her substantive specialty through a process of trial and error, although once she decided on a career in civil legal services she was willing to be flexible in order to work at NELS:

> I knew that [NELS] was one of the best places to work in the country for legal services. And I thought I was going to come here and do like welfare work or something and I didn't even know that dependency, the work I do, I didn't know it existed when I started [laughs]. They just kind of put me [where] they needed so many people in so many slots [so] it's where I ended up.

Lawyers like Ben and Marjorie had an interest in criminal defense and disability rights, respectively. Due to the opportunities available in the job market at the time they were looking for employment (Ben in the '70s, Marjorie in the '90s), they ended up at NELS, both in the consumer unit. Ben said of this:

> While I was in law school I had pretty much focused on the criminal justice system and I expected that's where I would be headed . . . Due to just the vagaries of how many people from [Neighboring State University] had applied to the [Northeast Defense Attorney's Office] or [NELS] or who knew who. A professor friend said that there were kind of too many [NSU] students who had done internships at the [Northeast Defense Attorney's Offense] why don't I go to [NELS]? And I was fine with that idea. But it's not like there was a lot of planning for me to become a consumer specialist at [NELS]. It sort of just developed over time. I came here, I was doing family law for two years and there was an opening in consumer and I was getting drained in Family Court and decided to make a change. And I've been here, well this coming September it will be [over 25] years, so I mean it's a long time.

However, lawyers' choices were not only a result of constraints and flexibility. There were those who were able to decide among a number of public interest jobs and different kinds of legal work. Lawyers with such options followed a process of "trying out" various types of legal work. As law students, Liz and Suzanne used clinical or internship programs to investigate high-impact work and found it too far removed from clients to be satisfying. Steve had a similar experience doing death penalty work, which he found too esoteric and all-consuming.

> I ended up in civil legal services but I had always wanted to do death penalty—ever since I was in law school I wanted to do death penalty work. And then about five years ago the opportunity came to do it. So I did. And I would have regretted it if I had not done it. It turns out that very quickly I determined that the particular, that work was not what I wanted on a day-to-day basis. It had nothing to do with my belief system. It was more to do with my temperament and sort of the day-to-day grind of what I was doing.

More than the workplace dysfunction that he noted, Steve disliked the long hours and the lack of client contact. His realization that such work was not for him brought him back to bread-and-butter legal services after 11 months, when a job opened up at NELS.

> Partly it was an office that was not entirely functional. And I didn't want to give them 20 hours a day . . . it was too much mental stress. Ironically not because my clients were going to get killed by the state, which sort of was not what was going on. But it was all this just, it was very sort of, visceral. I didn't, you know, didn't want to go to work. I didn't want to be sitting at my computer writing all day. It was a lot of sitting, isolated at my computer, writing. Just was not what I wanted to do. So I got lucky and got this job. Sort of lucked into it when someone went out on maternity leave [laughs].

As I have described, lawyers in this study chose careers in public interest law in order to pursue social change. They found their jobs through persistence, their willingness to be flexible to secure public interest jobs, trial and error and, sometimes, luck. What were their thoughts, having engaged in the practice of public interest law, about their attempts to bring about social change through the law?

The (Im)Possibility of Systemic Change

Assessing Law as a Tool for Social Change

Many lawyers, particularly those who had been practicing since the 1970s, saw the law as a means of tapping into power. Their initial optimism, nurtured in a political and social climate that inspired hope, went largely unrealized. Some spoke of having far less impact than they imagined when they started out. For lawyers like Ben, who continued to practice public interest law despite the disappointment, this did not lead to absolute disenchantment with the law.

> I viewed my becoming a lawyer as being somehow at the cutting edge of social change, which I think in a lot of ways made sense given the early 1970s, '60s. I mean it was this little blip in legal history where the courts were actually a vehicle of social change as opposed to their historic role, which has now been reestablished as keeping order on the plantation . . . I certainly don't have any illusions any longer about my role being in some sort of vanguard or cutting edge of social change. At the same time, I don't feel disillusioned at all.

Lawyers who began practicing in or after the 1980s started out with more cynicism and were less sanguine about the potential of the law (or any other tool) for social change. Their initial expectations for broad social change were lower, but they seemed equally committed and passionate about their work. Steve began practicing in the late 1980s. While attending college, he worked as a residential tutor for disadvantaged children brought to live in a wealthy school district and attend public school. During this time, he attended a conference where he experienced a proverbial "aha" moment: "I . . . was attending a conference on racism I think and so I'm in the middle of this conference—the light bulb went off in my head that the revolution was not happening and that the best way for me to attempt, in my highfalutin way, to effectuate social change is to become a lawyer."

Steve's explanation reveals an assessment that adds political and social context to lawyers' calculations of their own strengths and weaknesses. His appraisal of the opportunity for revolution within his political and social milieu was pessimistic. Given this particular sociohistorical context, he felt that a career in public interest law was the best contribution he could make toward social change. Unlike some other colleagues, his clear-eyed strategic realism apparently left him few misgivings or doubts about his career decision:

> I mean, am I changing the world? No. But the revolution still isn't happening and at some basic level, this office, legal aid programs, and myself

personally make a difference in people's lives on basic bread-and-butter issues. And yeah, we're still playing at the margins in terms of the social, I mean we're not changing the political/social system, but we make things less worse for people. Which, and you know, there are people in this office who have a lot of trouble with what we do—not in terms of they don't like their jobs but it bothers them more that we're playing at the margins, that we are not fermenting the revolution. And we're not. We're not. We really are not. And that's fine. I mean, I can live with it. But no, I love this job, this is a great job. And we do make a difference, both individually and on issues that affect our client population. And *but for* the work we did, things would be considerably worse for our clients.

Steve's initial expectations were quite different from Ben's. He did not expect to be able to effectuate the broad change that Ben had anticipated. In fact, he chose a law career as a result of his estimation that no broad social change was on the horizon, and he indicated that if he believed otherwise he might be out there "fermenting the revolution" rather than tinkering or sniping at what he saw as a "fundamentally flawed" legal system. Steve was not alone in his outlook. When there is no hope for social change, work with individuals becomes even more important. This supports Tremblay's assertion that, contrary to what many of the critiques of legal services lawyering allege, the chief limitations of legal services work are structural rather than personal and professional:

> I suggest that experience teaches us that poverty lawyers are generally good, energetic lawyers committed to social justice and to lessening the pain of poverty. No doubt there are poverty lawyers who are oppressive, paternalistic, mediocre, or unfeeling bureaucrats. This, however, is not the problem with poverty lawyering. Rather, the defects in poverty lawyering are structural, institutional, political, economic, and ethical. Teaching poverty lawyers to change their attitudes may be critically important, but those attitudes and the resulting behavior are largely products of the conditions under which poverty lawyers work.[5]

Joanne, a lawyer working in family advocacy, expressed pessimism about the ability to sustain systemic change over time. Her pessimism was less a result of changing political and historical tides than a general skepticism about systems change. Her experiences in Family Court, notorious among Northeast City lawyers in the public and private sector alike as a deeply troubled system, made her doubtful of the long-term effects of any systemic change: "I've been doing a lot of task forces here. And I'm at the point where I think that there's nothing I can do to make global change [laughs] in this work because I see what I've done and I see that somebody else has done that before and it doesn't make any difference."

Clients Assess Systems for Social Change

In contrast to lawyers, clients rarely speak directly about notions of social change, although many expressed dissatisfaction with government agencies or the legal system. Clients who did say that the system needed to be changed spoke generally. Explanations of what needed changing were often diffuse and without any expectation that change would come or that they could instigate it. This was in part because they often lacked knowledge of how things work and thus how they could be changed— although lawyers may not necessarily have greater success in figuring this out. Their experiences (in many ways like that of the lawyers) have also taught them not to expect social justice and to doubt their potential for bringing it about.

Denise, who successfully fought eviction proceedings with the help of the public housing unit, complained that the public housing authority was not held accountable for its poor treatment of clients:

> It sucks. I really did, I really—the law sucks as far as public housing, dealing with [the Local Public Housing Authority], Section 8. You know? How they got that ran. . . . It's like no care in the world, you know? And people take good time when you go down, you know for an appointment with the Housing Authority or Section 8 . . . The whole system is very nasty. And that—somebody needs to be looking into how [LPHA] and Section 8 run their establishment and how they treat . . . their tenants, the clients, whatever we are to them. You know, come on! 'Cause I mean it's not right. It's not right. But, hey, the whole law needs to be changed, to tell you the truth.

Most critiques were characterized by clients' sense that the agencies they worked with were unresponsive, disrespectful, discriminatory, and/or provided them with erroneous information (or no information). Eloise sought Social Security disability benefits for her grandson, Tarik. She was discouraged by the attitude of the people working at the Social Security office. Despite the desire to help her grandson, she was put off from seeking assistance: "[T]hey were so nasty. It was no fun down at that Social Security place. Um hmm. Some of them is nice, some of them just crappy, you know?"

Eloise lost her case. Marcia, her lawyer, believed that her claim was unfairly denied and wanted to appeal, but Eloise was disheartened. Like many NELS clients, Eloise was coping with numerous problems. She was raising several grandchildren after two of her daughters died within a month of each other about ten years earlier. Twelve-year-old Tarik's severe behavioral problems made caring for him difficult and magnified the difficulty of caring for other family members. Eloise's job at a local mental health institution ended when the institution closed. She is past common retirement age. For Eloise, the difficulty of getting to the Social Security Administration office was compounded by the logistical effort required to amass the necessary documents from a number of sources. The emotional effort of facing hostile or unhelpful claims officers felt Herculean. Once denied, Eloise was not sure she was up to the task of appealing. She explained:

> I'm just undecided whether to try it again or whether just to leave it go. Um, yeah, I got to go back through all that again . . . Yeah. So I don't know, I'm undecided . . .
>
> Corey: So what does [the decision] make you feel about the Social Security Administration?
>
> Uh [drawn out]. Kind of rough. Kind of rough. Well, I guess everything is tight now, a lot of stuff have changed and it's not easy to get these children and people on, you know, disability now. It's kind of rough out here. Nobody wants to give up nothing . . . That was the second time. So I said "Oh, well" [in a resigned, tired voice]. I'll wait, maybe I'll build myself later on and try it again but I don't think I'm ready to go back through all that hustle and bustle to get the papers.

Unlike Eloise, some clients were cynical, not resigned. They saw the government in all its branches as a monolithic and self-serving "system." Another client of Marcia's, Arlene, sought and received (in part) benefits for her disabled son. Arlene's son has severe behavioral problems and she did not understand why people with behavioral problems are not eligible for the kind of assistance that would not only benefit them but society. When asked about the Social Security Administration, the agency she was applying to for disability benefits, Arlene complained:

It stinks, you know? It really stinks. And for my child to be disabled, then you wonder why these kids the way they is today and when they turn into adults become murderers and serial killers and all this other stuff. Then you all wonder why the parent tried to get help, but then you all didn't want to help them at that time, you know what I mean? Taking away from them and this and that. It's crazy, the system is crazy. The system is just all screwed up. The system is just for the system, for them. It's just for the top dogs that's up there in them courts. That's up there in the White House. That's up there doing—you know, it's just, it's they stuff. You know what I mean? That's how I feel, it's they stuff. Because we got a lot of sick people that's out here. A lot of sick people that you got on the street that these people that come to court and they go to Social Security, ask for help, and deny these people!

Arlene's assessment of why there is not enough assistance for parents who want to help was consistent with that of some other clients in this study who, like Arlene, put forth a diffuse idea of power elites. In this appraisal of the state, the government branches are run by, and work in the interests of, those who have power. There is no hope of getting meaningful relief from government because it is not set up to serve people in need but to protect the interests of those in power.

Lest Arlene's contentions be dismissed as uneducated and paranoid conspiracy theory, she is in the good company of C. Wright Mills, whose theories widely contributed to sociology and political science.[6] In fact, theorists of American social welfare have asserted that most benefit programs are designed to encourage (low) wage labor by creating and maintaining welfare programs that stigmatize their recipients and distribute meager benefits under aversive conditions designed to discourage potential applicants.[7] As Sharon Hunt and Jim Baumohl observe in their study of Social Security disability benefits applicants: "A welfare claim is not undertaken lightly. While programs vary in their administrative particulars, application processes are by design invasive and often protracted, particularly in the case of disability claims. The modest benefits to be won at such a cost reinforce the greater desirability of wage earning."[8]

Clients also protested government agencies' lack of accountability. Irene, a client of the family advocacy unit, complained that the child welfare agency did not follow its own rules. The agency decided that the complaint against her was unfounded, but rather than return her child, they went on to investigate other areas of her life.

[T]hey took him from me for nothing. Right? They found the case un-guilty, so that means return the child back home. . . . I don't understand it. So, I just got on the point like I'm just like just fed up with them. I'm so tired of them . . . I think this case, I think they doing it for nothing. I think they don't have no right to do—now I could see if they found me guilty, and I understand they got to protect other kids just in case some-thing did happen in the house or, I understand that! That's not what I'm saying. I'm saying that you all going to have to back up when a mom is doing what she's supposed to be doing.

Although clients thought that government institutions were unresponsive to their needs and those of others like them, they were not entirely dis-couraged about achieving results for themselves. Many clients had already been helped or were somewhat optimistic that they would be helped. But this, they thought, was largely due to the fact that they had enlisted a competent lawyer. Most clients see the system as unresponsive in its insti-tutional form—but do see the system as responsive to particular individu-als: those who are represented by competent counsel. Elinor worked with two lawyers from two different legal services programs and was satisfied with her outcome. Her quote serves as an epigraph to this chapter:

If you have [Ben Silberman] on your side, you're fine. If you've got [Dora Mercer] on your side, you're fine. But the justice system, I would not take them on alone . . . And both of them, well [Dora] in the courtroom with me and [Ben] in the court with me for the bankruptcy, so I knew I was going to get a good deal. I had good lawyers.

Elinor does not say here that she received justice, but rather "a good deal." This is not because she thought that her claim was unjust or because she was trying to cheat the system, but rather because she did not expect jus-tice from the legal system. It is not a place to seek justice. Individuals can (sometimes) achieve just outcomes if they are competently represented, but it is indicative of their ability to work the system at the individual level as a result of having a good lawyer rather than an indication of broader social change. Just like Steve, Elinor notes the need for a lawyer precisely when systems are otherwise unjust and set up hurdles for those who are relatively powerless.

Clients are understandably more interested in resolving their immedi-ate needs than they are in engaging systemwide reform. This may be one reason that clients' analyses of government institutions do not explicitly address social change (or revolution). However, clients paint a clear and coherent picture of bureaucracies that are uncaring or even hostile. Their critiques go beyond blaming individual providers or bureaucrats and instead target agencies and systems. Government agencies do not meet the needs of the clients they are meant to serve. They act capriciously and are unresponsive to outside criticism. They appear accountable to no one. Clients' descriptions of systems resistant to change parallel those presented by lawyers. Victories, if they are achieved, are likely to be at the individual level. While client narratives make it clear that they would prefer to encounter systems that are respectful, responsive, and helpful, in the meanwhile they must cope with institutions that are none of these.

Making Sense of Their Work

Resisting Attempts to "Keep Order on the Plantation"

Clients' and lawyers' appraisal that systemic change is unlikely provides the context to understand their perceptions of the work they do together and the choices they make. For most lawyers, this centers on framing their work with clients in a way that squares with their understanding of limitations and possibilities. Lawyers in this study saw legal services practice as a venue where at least a modicum of justice or relief could be achieved. They viewed it as necessary to stem backlash. They also felt a moral imperative to stand by those who are marginalized and to stand in accusation of "the system," which is also a powerful political act. Lawyers and clients alike sounded these themes when they spoke of what legal services means to them.

Most lawyers found that sheer client volume meant that given scarce resources, they chose to take on less so-called impact work than they might prefer. Regardless of their tenure in the profession, lawyers grappled with the scope of their work's effects. Their deliberations reflect complex and sometimes contradictory notions of what constitutes social justice and what kind of difference is meaningful. These questions play out in different ways, depending on the context. One line of questions concerns the breadth of change—how many people are helped and to what extent changes take root in society. Another addresses the effect of legal remedies on the lives of particular clients.

All NELS lawyers have a lot of leeway in determining the composition of their practice. Most of those interviewed had practices that were largely individual client cases, with some "impact" work consisting of class action suits, representation of and collaboration with community groups, participation on various committees or task forces in their fields, legislative and administrative advocacy, and/or educational outreach and training.

Some lawyers saw their individual service-oriented work as having important ramifications for communities. Ben explained:

> I work in systems that, before I was a lawyer, the poor had absolutely no rights whatsoever. For example, a lot of my work deals with mortgage problems and homeownership and preserving homeownership. Before we came along, if you were behind in your mortgage and you're poor, you lost your house . . . So we came along and sort of figured out that people shouldn't lose their houses and there's ways of protecting their ownership and keeping them in and developed a legal practice that essentially didn't exist before. . . . in the trenches, primarily in the context of individual cases but also in the context of taking on the systems as a whole, we have managed to alter the balance of power fairly significantly, I think, at least in this little geographic blip.

By fighting against existing consumer practices on the individual level, he and other lawyers made broader changes by expanding the fields in which poor people could seek relief. Individual housing-related actions also have a specific societal role. In assisting individuals to remain in their homes, Ben also fights the stripping of wealth from local poor communities, as most poor peoples' financial capital is tied to their homes. In this way, he sees the preservation of individual home ownership to have a community economic effect that goes beyond individual beneficiaries of his practice.

Progressive lawyers in conservative times tread dangerous grounds. This is particularly true of impact work that may have broader policy implications. Unlike Ben, who sought the broader ramifications of individual or service work, Marcia indicated that she preferred individual work to impact work because the legal context was at odds with her vision of social justice:

> Now I'm not sure I made the right decision [to become a lawyer] . . . I'm just disappointed because now it's really dangerous . . . When I first graduated

> I was working for the Public Advocate in [a neighboring state] and that
> was a cabinet level departmental position and I did right to habilitation,
> 'cause my clients were mentally retarded, class actions in Federal Court.
> And then [laughs] now, like if you could stay out of Federal Court on a lot
> of issues it's better. It's safer to stay out.
> Corey: Because? The law—
> Yeah, the decisions are just so conservative.

On further reflection, Marcia reassessed. Lawyers are important in conservative times, but for different reasons than they are in progressive times.
Her assessment implies that no legal arenas should be abandoned.

> Oh, no. I actually, I don't really wish I hadn't [become a lawyer] because I
> think it's all a matter of keeping the pressure on. And even though I think
> we're in a really conservative time, the pendulum, you know people talk
> about it swinging back, it won't swing back if there's not a whole bunch of
> us working for it.

Lawyers who describe their work as primarily defensive, like Marcia, were
frustrated that gains they imagined possible seemed unattainable (and in
some cases gains made were reversed). At the same time, they saw their
role as a progressive voice in conservative times as crucial. To leave the
arenas of social change wide open to conservative influence without a
presence pulling in the other direction is perhaps more dangerous.

Decisions about whether to engage in impact work (and what kind) are
complex. Lawyers took account of strategic contingencies, not the least of
which is the inability to predict favorable outcomes. The balance was not
the same in all cases. Variations depended not so much on philosophical
outlook but rather on the perception of the arena for change, including
the receptivity of the players in that arena to social change and to the relevant group of clients.

On the more extreme end, several lawyers had experiences where the
arenas, as Marcia suggested, had been or were perceived as hostile and
unreceptive. The dangers involved in mounting systemic challenges have
not entirely deterred lawyers from impact work, but it has given them
pause, alerting them to think carefully about strategic choices. Both Ben
and Marjorie recounted one such example from their consumer practice.
The legislation of a Northeast City ordinance aimed at predatory lending practices was overridden by state legislation that not only cancelled

the local gains, but made the situation for victims of predatory lenders worse than it was before the City ordinance. This led Marjorie to believe that the most practical way to assist clients in the present legal climate is through individual representation. She saw the legal system as set up to privilege individual over collective challenges, thereby making broader change much less likely:

> When I think about just my area of law and that there aren't good regu-
> lators out there to protect little old ladies from door-to-door salesman
> scamming them and from big banks scamming them. And there's basi-
> cally no regulation and our view is that the laws are actually designed
> to, for the lawyers to be the regulators . . . The only way we can do that
> is to sue them. So I think to some extent the only way to really effect
> change in our area of the law at this point is to sue. Otherwise, well, to
> sue and educate people, but, I guess they go hand in hand. But, you know,
> I don't think, unless you could fully educate everybody you'd still need to
> sue people to enforce the laws . . . Well, we did get legislation passed in
> [Northeast City] and then the industry came in and got better legislation
> passed in [State Capital] that sucks. Or better legislation for them. So—I
> mean [the State], just like trying to get new laws passed seems like such
> a losing battle. So suing them is like the only way, or empowering people
> not to enter into loans.

In discussing her experience with the predatory lending regulations, Mar-
jorie identified another source of pessimism about the value of law as a tool for social change. She observed that the root of the problem is outside law and that law can only go so far in accomplishing social change:

> But on a deeper level, no, I mean this world needs education and hu-
> manitarianism and money [laughs]. That's how you're going to empower
> people. Or, you know, I think a lot of the scams that happen in our area
> are based on prejudice. That like banks would not be able to scam white
> people the way they scam black people and that it's just okay for them to
> do it because there's this like really innate discrimination going on.

As long as attitudes that stem from a combination of greed and preju-
dice persist, the law can only serve as a tool to help those individuals lucky enough to be able to mount challenges against individual perpetra-
tors. According to Marjorie's understanding, broader societal changes are

necessary to challenge the attitudes and values that give rise to the problems that poor people encounter. Law can only help ameliorate some of the symptoms for some of the people some of the time.

Although at times there has been optimism that legal changes can bring about changes in norms and attitudes, the depth and scope of those changes has often been less than hoped for, as the examples of school and housing desegregation are frequently used to illustrate.[9] Law is not separate from society, and it is likely that many of the conditions that Marjorie suspects contribute to the problem of predatory lending also influence legal institutions. If this is the case, the courts and the legislature reflect the same societal attitudes as do the practices and institutions that lawyers and clients challenge. They are therefore unresponsive to advocacy for systemic changes that might obviate the need for individual representation.

As illustrated in this section, lawyers' experiences lead them to be pessimistic about the possibility of systemic change, despite their expectations when they chose to enter the legal profession. With some important exceptions, lawyers believe that at best working systemically helps to stave off changes that detrimentally affect their clients in a conservative political climate. They worry that, at worst, systemic work is downright dangerous and wonder if the best tactic might not be to "lie low" and avoid raising issues in forums that provide opportunities to further curtail their clients' rights and benefits. Even more optimistic lawyers like Marcia, who see themselves as keeping the proverbial flame alive until the "pendulum swings back," have moments of severe self-doubt.

Clients Make Sense of "Just-Us"

Clients' attempts to make sense of the impossibility of social change centered more on formulating coherent explanations for why government institutions acted in ways that might seem capricious or hostile. Irene, in trying to understand the actions of a child protective service agency, drew the conclusion that the child welfare agencies must have a financial incentive to hold onto children under their auspices:

> I heard that . . . they hold the child for so long, after a while they don't get paid no more . . . So I'm thinking that they trying to draw out their money . . . And it sounds like it makes sense to me. 'Cause if I was getting paid for holding a child for so long, that's how I made my money, I'm going to hold them until I can't get that money. 'Til the state stops paying

me that money and then I'll either return them home or take them to the thing. So by me trying to hold him, I'm going to take the parent through this. They going to have to go to court, they going to go to parenting classes and then take up all their time. I know that's what it is. 'Cause they don't have no other reason to take a child.

While Irene's conjectures are relatively extreme, they are rooted in her observation that service providers have little incentive to declare that clients do not need their help or that the interventions they provide are not required. This puts them in an adversarial relationship with clients, even clients who have complied with their rules or whose investigations are unfounded. Irene's suspicions were compounded by the fact that although she wanted to sue the agency for mental distress, her lawyer told her that they enjoyed immunity (and that NELS does not take those kinds of cases, although she would refer her to a private lawyer). From Irene's perspective, the changing and unexpected demands on her as a parent and her lack of recourse "teach" her that the agency is all-powerful and that at best it can be navigated and placated (with the help of her lawyer), but certainly not changed in any way.

Others echoed Arlene's and Irene's assessment that government agencies and/or the court system look out for themselves, or serve the interests of those in power. For some this also translated into discrimination. Dara was one of three clients who used the term "just us": "Sometimes it's 'just us,' it's not always justice." When asked what she meant by "just us," Dara thought about it: "Um, let's just say—all right, let's just—it could run along racial lines, it could run along lines like let's just say people discriminate people because people, you know, because people are homosexuals and stuff like that."

And later:

Let's just say Hispanics and blacks, right? Let's say there's a Hispanic or black and they both commit the same crime, well they probably get the same time. A white person could go and commit the same crime that they committed and get lesser time. Like they could get 25 or 30 and the white person would do the same crime and get five.

While many accusations of discrimination centered on race, two clients (one white and one African American) felt that they were treated unfairly because they were women. A third client, Janet, experienced discrimination as a recovering drug addict. She thought that this discrimination could not be successfully addressed, that it was something that just "is." She encountered it not only in her attempts to seek benefits from the Social Security Administration and the courts but in the medical establishment as well:

> Being a drug addict even if you're clean or not, tends to make things a little more difficult, I feel, on you. You tend to get like a name . . . It's almost like you're discriminated against . . . [Drug addiction]'s a disease, just like cancer. And they don't discriminate against someone who has cancer, but yet they would against someone who is, you know, is an addict or an alcoholic. So I don't think that's fair. I don't know what could be done about that really, because I just think that's something that is. I've found that, well not through my personal doctor, but I've found that when I've had to go into emergency rooms and you are discriminated against.

Even clients who engage in attempts at systemic change are skeptical of its value. Lilly is a self-described activist. Despite her work on political campaigns and advocacy for the elderly, she too was cynical regarding any kind of systemic change, having seen others thwarted in their attempts to bring it about:

> I think the whole system is who—what dollars and who dollars. And it's not a happy thing. There are good ones. There are people that spin their wheels trying to do good. And I think a lot of people get very upset and they even leave the system because they can't do anything.

One client was not surprised to learn that the "system's" attempts to thwart poor people extended to legal services. When I discussed funding cuts for legal services with Lorna, she laughed. On reflection, she thought it perfectly logical that legal services programs underwent funding cuts. If the government is structured to discourage those who would challenge it, it made sense to her that there would be attacks on legal services: "Well, you know, if the government keeps us from finding out ways to fight the government then they won't have to put out as much money. I mean, you know, that's a rational reason to cut them [laughs]! You know, these are the lawyers that are fighting to help the poor."

As we have seen, both lawyers and clients express great skepticism about the legal system and its potential as a source of social change or even minimal justice. As Elinor's perception illustrates, to the extent that the legal system is responsive to the claims of poor people, it is only because individuals and their lawyers are successful in making it work for them. Lawyers and clients concerned with social justice must reconcile working within a system they view as fundamentally capricious or unjust. The chief way in which they do this is by understanding the importance of the individual work they do, and by casting this work in a subversive, system-challenging light.

Situated Practice in Conservative Times

The examples above bring out a tension that has been discussed in progressive lawyering circles since at least the 1960s.[10] Individual or incremental work is viewed as a means of alleviating immediate suffering and is sensitive to individual clients.[11] But it has also been criticized as insufficient and possibly dangerous. It is insufficient because the limited resources available to the marginalized have never been, and probably never will be, enough to meet all the needs of low-income clients. It is inefficient because it addresses only symptoms, so the problems recur not only for the client served, but for others. Individual work can be dangerous because it fails to mount challenges to the status quo—it works within systems rather than against them. By working within the system, the players need to acquiesce to the rules and the legal process, including the lawyer-client relationship, which reinforces existing relations of power. It also confers legitimacy on the system, even if that is not its intent. Pete explained the reason why he and Erica, a client who participated in this study, often argue:

> Because no matter what I've tried to demonstrate and what I've tried to do on her cases, she will still from time to time come to the conclusion that I'm on . . . the welfare office's side. And she may be right in certain respects. And the respect in which she may be right is I've already boughten [*sic*] into a whole set of rules that I'm then operating under when I'm giving her advice, where she's much more interested in completely circumventing or subverting the rules . . . So I sometimes try to take a firm line around issues around fraud and nonreporting and stuff like that and people will view that as being, well, you're just like them, then. Are you on my side or are you on their side? You're telling me I got to report this income and I can't live and you're acting like them.

Systemic challenges, on the other hand, purport to raise challenges to the premises and assumptions underlying the systems being contested on behalf of large groups of people, and in that sense expressly censure those systems. Systemic work is also considered by some to be more glamorous and intellectually stimulating than individual work. On the other hand, it is criticized because it tends to be divorced from (and sometimes inimical to) the interests of the clients it intends to serve.[12] It can also be at odds with values of empowerment, autonomy, dignity, and equality that are viewed by many as the moral and ideological foundations for social justice work. Systemic work generally focuses on the lawyer as the central actor, strategist, and decision maker, relegating the actual client or imagined beneficiary to the status of a bystander at best and a mere vehicle for the case or issue at worst.[13]

According to Marc Feldman, "An almost universally accepted and cherished idea in law practice for the poor is the dichotomy between service and impact." He laments, "Rarely do Legal Services lawyers imagine the possibility of abandoning the distinction of 'service versus impact.'"[14] Two advantages of a study of situated practice that focuses on the perceptions of lawyers and clients, rather than an abstract definition or prescriptive polemic, are empirical grounding and greater nuance. For this reason, I do not engage in a detailed discussion of academic differences between the so-called "impact" and "service" work, of which there is a voluminous literature. Rather, I draw on the study data to illuminate and challenge such distinctions in ways that may not neatly parallel the academic discussions.

Although they might not be broadly representative, lawyers' perspectives belie Feldman's criticism. As this section demonstrates, lawyers in this study were thoughtful about where the lines of so-called impact and service work blurred, suggesting that it is perhaps academics rather than practitioners who have trouble abandoning the distinction. Lawyers pointed out connections where their service work (as it would be defined by outsiders) was ongoing, important, transformative, and political. Clients' perspectives (and lawyers' consideration thereof) further challenge academic distinctions and assessment of the relative influence, costs, and benefits of impact versus service work.

Ben and Joanne, for example, challenged the notion that individual work is not systemic. As noted earlier, Ben explained how his work with individuals on predatory lending and other consumer-related claims affects the broader community. Joanne sees individual work as symbolically important. Joanne works with families, usually mothers, who are involved in dependency cases with their children:

> I guess one of the global, another global issue that we work on from an individual basis is just reminding people of our clients' constitutional rights. You know, just because they're poor and minority doesn't mean that they're not allowed to raise a family the way they see fit, and reminding judges of that, and through advocacy at the hearing and also through appellate advocacy.

Courts are stages that lawyers and clients can use to assert their views and to expose and challenge dominant assumptions, in this case about the ability to parent and the right to raise children. They are also a venue to remind judges, opposing counsel, government, and society of their obligations to poor people.

Even when there is a clear distinction between systemic and individual work, they can be viewed as complementary tactics, with individual work informing systemic work and vice versa. Ideally, this helps to combine the best of both and to remedy the pitfalls that each presents when employed singly. Despite the fact that all the lawyers interviewed focused on work with individual clients, all of them devoted some time to systemic work at varying levels and with varying degrees of optimism. NELS is an organization that allows lawyers the leeway to balance individual and systemic work, and this is a feature that has made it an attractive place for these lawyers to work. In an ideal situation, lawyers can link their individual work with their systemic work or that of others. Earlier we heard Marcia question whether she should have chosen the law as a tool due to courts' and agencies' generally inhospitable view toward legal services challenges. Here, she reflects on the enormous impact systemic work has when it proves successful, not only for leverage against the state but also for her morale:

> So NELS is one of the few legal services that I know that has sort of the national reputation that it can make—we can really make what we learn on the individual level have an impact . . . We had a lawsuit called [Plaintiff] that we won so it's kind of, we have their attention. And so they listen to us. . . . I think it would be much more discouraging for me if I only did individual cases and didn't have any connection with what was going on systemically . . . There's a real difference. I mean there are lawyers

here who just want to do that. Or just want to do legislative advocacy. . . . and I think one of our luxuries so far is that we've been able to get funding so that people can really do what they do well. And want to do.

Unfortunately, social change proponents do not always have the luxury of striking what they would consider an ideal balance in their work. Put another way, they do not get to choose the historical, political, or economic circumstances in which they effect social change and thus are not always able to optimize their use of both strategies.[15] While it is important to keep in mind the relative advantages and disadvantages of both approaches and to combine them when possible, choices also need to be understood as a result of the exigencies of practice in the current U.S. context.

As we have seen, many clients and lawyers make choices based on what they have learned from their experiences. The balance between individual work and systems change work is a logical outgrowth of their experiences with government agencies in a particular social and historical context. Here, the insights of political learning theory are helpful. In examining the apparent political apathy of AFDC recipients, Joe Soss's research with clients receiving public benefits underscores the importance of the lessons that clients learn from their encounters with government agencies, which are then globalized to other branches of government.[16] When agencies are perceived as unresponsive, hostile, capricious, and resistant to change (very much the way NELS clients and many NELS lawyers describe them), individuals have a lower estimation of their ability to bring about change. They logically infer from their experiences that any efforts at systemic change are likely to be futile and are thus they are dissuaded from taking systemic action.

The sense of futility regarding systemic change does not necessarily carry over to the ability to navigate or "work" (even if they cannot change) a given bureaucracy. Perhaps surprisingly, clients' assessment of their own ability to work the system is often heightened when they view systemic change as unattainable but have some success in getting what they want. This is an important survival mechanism; it is an expression of resilience. As lawyers and clients know, there are few alternatives to working the system as best they can. Many do work the system successfully, as did most of the clients in this study who enlisted the assistance of an attorney to gain leverage. Lawyers, too, feel that they are able to work the system for clients successfully even when government agencies seem all but impervious.

Legal Services Lawyering: Progressive or Conserving?

Most lawyers grappled with some sense of frustration over their inability to bring about systemic changes. The benefits they secure through legal processes can seem meager and inconsequential. Pete, a lawyer in the public benefits unit, was frustrated:

> Particularly in the setting in which I work, welfare stuff, the law only guarantees the most minimal level of safety net. So even if you're looking at things in terms of what is social justice from an economic perspective or what is the minimum kind of financial stability that you think any person who lives in an affluent society should have. The best lawyers here, in my practice, welfare law, are not going to accomplish anything approximating that. You know, if I do a great job on trying to get somebody who's being kicked off of welfare I've gotten them, let's say a single mother and two kids, $403 a month to live on. That's abhorrent. It's a joke, it's a farce . . . and we spend almost none of our time trying to advocate the grant level to be increased because we've decided it's a complete dead end. I mean, we're doing conservative work of trying to fight back even worse changes. So that's kind of the dilemma and the irony in all this. It's hard to figure out, well what am I doing, in terms of the broader vision?

Many lawyers, including Pete, coped with this frustration by keeping in mind that what they see as "farcical" changes wrought by the legal services encounter are nonetheless meaningful for their clients. Although some may view such rationalization as specious or self-serving, it was validated by the clients in this study.

Lawyers' and clients' varied understanding of their work described in this chapter is a far cry from acceptance of the status quo. It is better understood as a form of what Howard Lesnick calls "realistic radicalism"[17] in his explanation of how lawyers' worldview, including their rejection of the status quo, informs their practice and how this influences their work with clients. According to Lesnick, a radical perspective challenges prevailing legal, social, and economic structures.[18] While this distinction in orientation may not be expressed in public actions, we must be careful not to mistake liberal actions for proof that lawyers and clients accept the status quo. If radical lawyers only looked to radical tools, they might be paralyzed by the pessimistic assessment of the possibility for social change. Lawyers and clients who challenge the premises of the legal system are radical by definition, even if they choose to play by its rules when they perceive that as the best (or only) available strategy. In a hostile political and social environment, "realistic radicals" may adopt nominally liberal practices, but this is out of necessity. An examination of situated practice clarifies the meanings that lawyers and clients construct and provides a more nuanced understanding of the work they do together and the trade-offs they make.

As we have seen, the client and her lawyer often share a radical orientation in their characterization of the system as unfair and their desire that it be changed for the client and all others. Lorna's medical problems have helped her understand how insufficient medical assistance is for poor people who are ill, and she knows that her lawyer, Steve, agrees with her assessment:

> If you were faced with a terminal disease that somebody told you "we're going to take your medical benefits," how would you feel? How frightened would you be? Because that's my lifeline. That's all there is. There were no other services available to me. I wasn't on Medicare yet. Now I'm on Medicare but that doesn't pay for prescriptions until I'm on dialysis, and then I'm even sicker . . . Once I'm end-stage renal, Medicare covers all that . . . I'll be half-dead by the time I am, but it doesn't matter to the system that medications—I kind of never understood what the older people used to talk about their health care. I never truly understood that issue until I was faced with it. And I feel like them. I feel like there's not enough being done for those without medical benefits. And Steve sees it the same way I do, of course. And he has let me know that, I guess.

A liberal practice infused with a radical perspective calls for a strategic assessment of available resources coupled with compassionately informed assessment of client needs and desires. This respects clients' and lawyers' choices of individual over systemic remedies, even when problems are understood as structural or systemic. While this orientation should not be confused with a liberal perspective that not only uses but also *accepts* dominant norms and values, it can be hard to imagine how this difference might play out in actual situations and what it means to the participants. As we will see in the coming chapters, it is central to the way that lawyers and clients interact in that it is informed by a respect for client autonomy and dignity and a sense of equality and desire for collaboration.

Sanford Schram's "radical incrementalism" stems from a view similar to that expressed by clients and lawyers in this study in its pessimistic assessment of the possibility of far-reaching changes.[19] It seems to accept the impossibility of deep structural change and to recognize only the possibility of fleeting incremental change. Yet, it is also based on a realistic assessment of the pressing and immediate economic needs of poor people who can not wait for response until fundamental changes are realized. To forgo available but imperfect avenues of action would be to ignore people who experience need in pursuit of some imagined theoretical integrity. This would not serve integrity at all, but a theorizing devoid of ethics. Thus, we need a constructive framework for criticism that does not vilify or immobilize individuals willing and able to provide legal assistance.

The more radical piece of radical incrementalism is its purposeful challenge to the system within which change is sought. Francis Fox Piven and Richard Cloward's crisis strategy for overwhelming the welfare system by urging clients to claim individual benefits in record numbers served as the exemplar of Schram's radical incrementalism. This strategy was intended not only to provoke an immediate crisis that would lead to incremental change, but to expose the inadequacies of the prevailing system. So, too, public interest lawyers working for social change seek to challenge the legal system by exposing the gap between substantive justice and procedural fairness. Such challenges are not only to the system in its relationship with public interest clients, but to the legal system as a whole. Its claim to legitimacy rests upon such ideas as equal justice and neutrality.

Both Lesnick and Schram theorize what participants in this study practice. For caring individuals with a radical perspective, working within existing systems is dangerous but necessary. This is not only a tactical consideration. More fundamentally, it is ethical in that lawyers engaged in situated practice recognize the immediate needs of marginalized people and groups that cannot (and should not) be ignored, even as social change seekers work toward a more perfect system. This is the view of Steve, a lawyer who relishes opportunities to snipe at the system:

> My view of social justice in my job is getting as much as I can from a system which I think is fundamentally flawed. I think the welfare system's terrible. Um, it may be more or less terrible than it was five or ten years ago, but it's still fundamentally wrong. However, my clients have to live in it. And what I view [as] my job, in terms of social justice, is getting the best or the least bad deal I can for my clients out of that system. Because I have concluded, and it's probably a combination of (a) I don't have the

strength and skills to revamp the system, and (b) I don't think it's happening. And the best that I can do is work to try and reform it at some level incrementally but realize, you know, give me break. And at the practical level work within its framework to manipulate it as best I can to get the most I can for my clients. That's what I do.

Clients sense that lawyers are not judgmental of them or their plight; clients and lawyers create shared narratives of responsibility and injustice that legitimate clients' grievances and indict oppressive and unfair systems; and lawyers and clients seek to make systemic change when and where it is possible. The incremental changes wrought in this process can be meaningful for clients, improving their lot materially and validating their perspective, giving them a sense of vindication. According to Liz:

> I feel like if this person gets a little more power on an individual level, you know, to me there's social change in creating confidence for someone who has been living a very difficult . . . kind of life. So hopefully there is this perception that even someone with limited education, with limited money can go to [thumps on the desk] legal services, can get some help and get a problem resolved and that gives them connection, a feeling that their society is serving them . . . I don't know if there's a lot of social change in [individual relief], except for a sense of, in the person that, yeah, you know, the government thought that, I mean this whatever it was, you know, the corporation—whatever—thought that they could just roll over this person and then the person got some legal assistance.

Even in the best of times, premises that valorize systemic change are questionable. Systemic challenges can be long in coming and may not be lasting, even if they are successful. This should lead us to question what we mean by success. Measured by whose standards? According to which timeline? For the client who wants a home today for her children who may be grown (if not dead and buried) when there is a constitutionally recognized right to housing, the most successful and compassionate tactic might be to persuade the housing authority that she should be eligible for public housing. These challenges apply with greater force when, as we have seen above, the systemic work that would alter relations of power (for example between predatory lenders and their prey) is perceived as futile or even detrimental.

Reflective Lawyering as a Safeguard of Situated Radical Practice

In order to serve as a vehicle for social change, lawyers and clients who practice radical legal work within a liberal paradigm must be cognizant of the dangers inherent in using the "master's tools." This is at the heart of Lesnick's definition of liberal work that is infused with a radical perspective. Schram takes this further, and is perhaps more sanguine about the radical prospects of incrementalism:

> Radical incrementalism challenges the existing constraints on the politically possible, recognizing that the changes forthcoming will be in the form of concessions at best. Yet, such concessions can improve the lives of the oppressed and marginalized and create the conditions for further incremental challenges and improvements in the future.[20]

What distinguishes radical lawyers from liberal lawyers (and radical incrementalists from liberals) is not the form of their practice but their orientation. There is always the risk that working within the system will lead to cooptation or to becoming inured to alternative visions of more just systems. To maintain a radical practice while working within the system, public interest lawyers desiring social change must adopt an "attitude of critical consciousness"[21] toward the potential and risk of their professional role and must work toward expanding the boundaries of the possible and challenging descriptive and normative presumptions wherever and whenever they can.

Radical public interest lawyers need to weigh the risks and benefits of any social change tool or strategy and assess its ability to get us closer to social justice. A critical theory that pays attention to practice highlights the importance of self-awareness in carrying out this task, whatever route we decide to take. Scholarship informed by ethics and grounded in the lived realities of clients (and their lawyers) must be concerned with how visions of social justice and tactics of social change are played out in the contingent realities of everyday lives. To ignore this is to risk further injustice, even if intentions are good. It is only when we interrogate ourselves and our methods, and attend to the details of the goals we strive for and the means we employ to achieve them, that we can engage in the ongoing process of working toward social justice.

4

Did Someone Say Autonomy?

I guess without legal service, getting Ben . . . I wouldn't be sitting here. So I'm really grateful for that. That was like a load of pressure—you can't imagine—off of me. I couldn't deal with anything else until, you know, until that assurance. Life's still going on, that was the biggest weight on me, you know? I needed a lawyer, somebody to represent me or to speak for me.

—Cecilia, a client working with the consumer unit

When we feel like we're empowering [clients] . . . and they end up making a decision that would be bad, we ultimately don't want to see them in a bad result. But the thought [that] basically disempowering them and manipulating what their ultimate decision would be is somewhat sickening to us [laughs] . . . You know, and to some extent I feel like I have really good intentions and you know I feel like . . . I really do have altruistic views and perhaps among the best that you could possibly have because we don't have to deal with making money. We're just in a fortunate position that way. But at the same time it's like, well it's really supposed to be your decision.

—Marjorie, a lawyer working in the consumer unit

Autonomy is both a value and a goal espoused by most theories of progressive lawyering, which are rooted in the presumption that most clients are competent and entitled to make informed decisions. Progressive lawyering literature calls for attorneys to practice in ways that foster rather than impede client autonomy. Indeed, autonomy often is seen as a component of respect for clients. It is also an expression and affirmation of the belief that clients and lawyers are equals, a form of resistance that seeks to challenge dominant notions of the hierarchical relationship between lawyers and clients, particularly between low-income clients and the lawyers who serve them.[1]

The concept of autonomy in the lawyer-client relationship contains tensions. Should lawyers force clients to make their own decisions and act in a manner that the lawyer considers autonomous, even if the client is reluctant or explicitly refuses to do so? "Mandatory autonomy" is inherently contradictory, as it represents a paternalistic or "best interest" view that forces even reluctant clients (for their own good) to make decisions that they might not want to make.[2] Further, a strict understanding of autonomy in the context of poverty lawyering raises a double standard that both lawyers and clients in this study noted: Should autonomy be used to deprive clients of the type of services they expect from a lawyer, services that no paying client would think twice about demanding?[3]

Some reject mandatory autonomy due to the inherent tensions between paternalism and autonomy in the mandatory view. Those who subscribe to "optional autonomy" allow that clients should have the autonomy not to act in a manner that a lawyer may consider autonomous. Lawyers at the extreme end of this spectrum would respect clients' complete abdication of responsibility for decision making, even when those decisions involve aspects of clients' lives that may not fall exclusively within the purview of the professional's expertise. This view, too, is fraught with its own contradictions in that it would allow clients to shed entirely all aspects of autonomy in the name of autonomy. It also raises the concern that client agendas, values, and decisions may be submerged or lost in relationships that reflect existing hierarchies, even if neither the lawyer nor the client is aware of all the ways in which their own socialization and status bears upon that relationship.

It is clear that either version, taken to the extreme, is easily dismissed. However, it is much more difficult to provide fully satisfactory answers to the legitimate concerns raised by both perspectives.[4] Lawyers in this study believe in the value of autonomy, although they are not always able to articulate the source of their commitment and its importance. Some have read progressive lawyering literature that they believe supports autonomy. Others identify a desire to foster client autonomy as consistent with respect for clients. Lawyers in situated practice struggle with a desire to foster client autonomy because an autonomy framework seems insufficient to inform their situated practice with clients. We will see later in this chapter that clients themselves have a different perspective that they likely convey to lawyers which also complicates a focus on autonomy to the exclusion of other ideals or of context. As a result, lawyers were often at a loss to explain why autonomy mattered to them, or how they interpreted and worked toward autonomy in the context of practice generally, and in the context of particular cases. Pete struggled with how to encourage clients to make their own decisions while acting as their lawyer:

> I don't have the view that I would never advise a client as to what I think is best. I think poor people like rich people have a right to a lawyer's opinion. And when people can afford to go out and get a lawyer, they ask the lawyer, what do you think I should do? and they ask a doctor, what do you think I should do? So they have a right not to decide, also. And uh, but you know I try to encourage people to make their own decisions. I just like pointing out the possible advantages and disadvantages of different options.

Most lawyers staked out a middle ground formed in response to the individual client and the problem at hand. They lived with the necessity of making these types of assessments in order to function on a daily basis and negotiate their working relationships with clients. As with everything else, lawyer and client resource constraints entered into these assessments. Vicki said that with problems that are likely to recur, it made sense for clients and lawyers to work together to enable clients to learn to advocate for themselves to the extent possible.

> The people who work here have such—have had experience with so many people who are going to face these issues again. You know, our clients, we have so many clients that come back for very similar issues. Or they have to deal with . . . one agency in this case, and in the next case it's going to be another agency, but the processes are going to be very much the same . . . For them to be able to advocate for themselves is the best way for them to go about dealing with all of these issues.

As noted in chapter 1, like most legal services programs NELS struggles to serve its client base with limited resources. Thus, scarcity is always in the background of any discussion of client autonomy. Despite the role that resource allocation plays in thinking about autonomy, in my conversations with lawyers this was not their chief focus or concern. Lawyers were concerned that their actions and words may intentionally and unintentionally influence client decision making. More troubling was how to reconcile the ideals of autonomy that permeate their understanding of the lawyer's professional role and the empowerment goals of poverty lawyering with clients' needs, desires, and assessed competencies. They questioned what that means for the larger values of respect for clients and of client empowerment.

The Rationale Underpinning Autonomy as an Ideal

Issues of autonomy can be lost in the pressing crush of day-to-day interactions. When questioned about their legal practice, lawyers in this study seemed to be keenly aware of what some viewed as the "problem of autonomy," even while they had trouble articulating the contours of this problem. Most had not questioned exactly what they meant or understood when they talked about autonomy, and precisely why this was a value they held.

Carl Schneider's description of autonomy helps to illuminate the dilemmas professionals face by looking at value bases underpinning the autonomy ideal.[5] Three of the underlying (and closely tied) values behind the valorization of autonomy are relevant to this study. The first is the "prophylaxis argument," which states that the inherent power differences in the professional-client relationship create a hierarchical framework that works against autonomy.[6] These power differences are exacerbated when other social and economic hierarchies, such as gender, race, class, education, and/or disability, combine with the gap in knowledge and status between any layperson and a professional. To guard against this, professionals must take a strong view of client autonomy. Lawyers in this study often noted such power differentials. Pete's criticism of his colleagues' and his own tendency to let their expert knowledge influence the way they treat clients was shared by other lawyers.

> I think that there is a large degree of thoughtlessness on the questions of who is our constituency, who are our clients and what are we doing in order to be sure that we're, that we know what they want. And that we're in touch with them. And . . . I guess there's a strain of arrogance. That's where talking to someone like [a NELS lawyer who did not participate in the study] would be good, because he epitomizes that. . . . I'm a big fan of his, but you know, he's kind of one of those people you have to take

the good with the bad. The bad is that the . . . arrogance about like—"I've been doing this work for 30 years, I know better than the poor person what works for a poor person."

Vicki, a recent law school graduate, echoed other lawyers when she noted that the tendency to take control is fed by client expectations.

We talked about a study in [my] professional responsibility [class] that says clients don't want autonomy. They came to you because they don't know what to do and they want you to give them some sort of advice and they want to follow that advice. I don't know that that's true, but I think that's one side of it, that maybe clients don't want this autonomy that somebody's forcing it upon them.

The false consciousness rationale for autonomy asserts that patients (or clients or students) are socially and culturally constructed not to be autonomous; thus, even when given the opportunity to make choices, they may not. Further, they may not even realize that they are ceding to professionals.[7] It is only through prodding and cajoling that client consciousness will be raised and they will learn to identify choices and take on responsibility. Clients should, and in fact do, want autonomy, they just may not know it or they may not trust their ability to make decisions. It is part of the lawyer's job to ensure that clients do make decisions even if they are reluctant to do so. Lawyers like Martin tried to explain to clients that they need to take responsibility for decisions that ultimately affect their lives in ways that their lawyers cannot fully apprehend.

As a rule, if my client says, "What do I think you should do?" I respond back, "You have to make this decision yourself." Um, and try to force them to make the decision. If they still won't decide or if they ask my opinion after that, I will give them my opinion but I once again try to stress that it's ultimately their decision, I mean it's their life. They're the ones who are going to have to live with the consequences of the decision. I may not be happy about the options that I'm offering, but they really have to make that decision.

The false consciousness argument, rooted in Marxist philosophy, offers an explanation as to why clients may remain compliant in the face of degrading or well-intentioned, paternalistic treatment that may run counter to their unknown or unacknowledged wishes or interests. Many clients come to legal services after experiencing interactions with government agencies and the broader society that "taught" them to be cooperative and to expect ill treatment or at best a lack of interest in their wishes.[8] This socialization process is conducive neither to client exploration of their own interests nor to their development of tools to evaluate expert advice on the basis of considerations relating to their own life, values, and agenda.

False consciousness can also provide at least a partial explanation for the satisfaction that most clients experience in their encounters at NELS, despite not fully achieving their intended goals. Complacency and satisfaction were not necessarily viewed by lawyers, nor should they be viewed by outsiders, as measures of successful representation. Rather, they must also be viewed, at least in part, as measures of oppression and the suppression of expectations, which both engender and are then facilitated by clients' false consciousness. The strong view of autonomy requires that practitioners counter false consciousness, even against the expressed wishes of their clients, precisely because clients need to be led or forced out of the false consciousness that suppresses their buried wishes and interests.

The third rationale for autonomy that bears on this study is the moral argument.[9] As human beings with the capacity to reason and make decisions, we must act as agents in our lives. To push this responsibility onto professionals is an abdication of that responsibility and a breach of moral obligation. This view respects the dignity and abilities of clients (often at the expense of their stated desires). It takes that respect one step further, construing it as giving rise to an obligation to take responsibility for decisions that affect one's life. Not only are human beings capable of being autonomous, but they must be so in order to be fully human.

While this argument was not voiced among the study participants, it is an undercurrent in American society that enters into their relationships.[10] It was reflected less in the imperative directed at clients than in lawyers' discomfort with "taking over" responsibility for what they viewed as decisions more properly made by their clients. Their hesitancy comes both from the respect they accord their clients and from their reluctance to behave paternalistically even if the client explicitly wishes them to do so. Lawyers' reasoning about this discomfort is often couched in vague moral terms not fully satisfied by the prophylaxis or false consciousness explanations. Again, Pete's remarks display a critical thoughtfulness and insight.

Let's take, for example, a client who comes in and makes it clear they don't want [to problem solve]. Say I don't—this happens all the time, I'll say, "Did you call the case worker's supervisor?" "No." "Why?" "They never answer the phone. They never return my calls. That never works." And I'll say . . . "You're in the legal right and I can give you that advice, you know, you're on the right track, your instinct was right, you're being treated unfairly. The law's on your side, you don't need a lawyer though right now. Deal with this yourself and then call me if that doesn't work." "I don't want to do that . . . You're a lawyer, you do that. That's why I'm calling you." I think it's perfectly appropriate for me to say no. I'm not going to help you. And part of it, and a piece of it is, this time management thing . . . and that I don't want to work on this thing. . . . But part of it is the empowerment thing and I'm not going to enable you to not have the experience. So it is paternalistic. I'm not going to enable you not to have the experience of being able to solve your own problem and learning from it. Because I think that, I guess I can't really frame it in a nonpaternalistic way. So that's just paternalistic and I'm not sure that just because something's paternalistic it's wrong.

As Pete's depiction of client expectations suggests, there is a tension between the autonomy and notions of what is the proper role of the lawyer. According to Pete, lawyers should provide advice and opinions to clients, but they should not make decisions for them. Lawyers should act where clients need them, but where clients can act on their own they should be encouraged, perhaps even forced, to do so. In practice, the distinctions between these functions are not always clear and they may be contested. In the next section, I examine lawyers' concerns as they flow from situated practice with clients. In the section that follows, I examine how client experiences and their expectations of lawyers and the lawyer-client relationship challenge traditional conceptions of autonomy in public interest lawyering.

Why Do Lawyers Worry?

Lawyers in this study were troubled by their ability to manipulate clients. They seem to understand manipulation in the broad sense that Ellman employs the term, that is, to include "even well-intentioned, or seemingly modest, interferences with client decision-making."[11] Lawyers' worries about the reasons for such interference can be broadly grouped into two categories, although the line between the two is sometimes unclear. The first is composed of structural factors and professional constraints that impede client autonomy, such as resource constraints, agency directives, or professional strictures. The second category consists of values or ethical concerns such as compassion for clients or a desire for what lawyers consider "good" outcomes on behalf of clients. We start with an examination of professional and structural impediments.

Ben engaged in long-term cases against banking institutions. These cases can take years, but the action on them is sporadic and only necessitates client contact every few months or less.

> Settlement negotiations are, I find them to be somewhat difficult because it's like you know you haven't heard from me in two years and now we have a settlement proposal from the other side and they want to reduce the mortgage to this, and it's like, generally, it's like, "Well, whatever you think is best." "Well no, this has got to be your decision and why don't you come on in and we'll talk about it." And a lot of it is me making, giving them my assessment of what I think is a good deal. But also, frankly, it's, one of the sort of sometimes stated but more often unstated elements of the conversation is, "I got a hundred other clients, this is a really good solution, I think I've solved your problem. I really need you to say yes now because I need to move on to something else."

When questioned further, Ben was also clear that he would not recommend a resolution that he did not feel was to the benefit of his client:

> I mean, I've advised clients to say no plenty. That happens all the time. "I think we can do better than that. I mean I'm ethically obligated to pass this on to you but I'm asking for your authority to call him back and say go to hell, is that okay?" So that happens all the time.

This problem is characteristic of litigation of the kind Ben handles, which does not involve ongoing client contact and thus does not foster ongoing working relationships. However, Ben also noted the undercurrent of resource limitations of which he assumes clients are aware. It is clear that the manipulation or pressure on clients that worried Ben is more subtle in that he exerts it (even though he would prefer not to) in those cases where he feels that his advice is both for the benefit of the client and for the benefit of his caseload. Ben's knowledge of this potential for manipulation often sways him to take the prophylactic approach when clients attempt to abdicate responsibility:

> I work for the client. And I say that. You know, "This is your case." "Do whatever you think." I say "No, I'm not going to do whatever I think because this is your case and you got to understand what the proposal is, you got to understand what my recommendation is and we got to make a decision, we can't, you know this is your life. I'm not, I'm just—I'm your lawyer."

Ben tried to provide legal advice while not abdicating his professional obligation to help the client understand the settlement and make the decision. Ben wanted clients to see him as their lawyer, but also to understand that he is *just* their lawyer. It is clear from the conversation cited above that this is not an easy balance to strike. Ben understood that he shapes clients' decision making not only in explaining the legal situation and advising, but also through the mutual understanding that he is a legal services lawyer with limited resources.

Other lawyers are also troubled by what they perceive as professional or institutional constraints that hamper their ability to carry out client wishes.[12] Pete, who works closely with a welfare rights group, felt that such constraints hampered his choices. The example he provided was when he did not acquiesce to the request of a community organization, with which NELS has a long-standing relationship, to help with an action aimed at disrupting the Olympics one year:

> [A]n institutional constraint is we get funding. Our funders do not fund us to disrupt the Olympics. They fund us to help people on welfare who are getting their benefits cut off by the welfare system. . . . And we have much fewer institutional constraints than all those other legal services organizations that have congressional restrictions that are imposed upon them. Which they can't do some of the very things that Lucie White and Gerry López say they *must* do. They can't do organizing, they can't do administrative advocacy, so that's sort of institutional constraints.

Pete's inability to represent his client as that client saw fit was a source of tension between him and the client and led the client to question his commitment. It was also in conflict with his desire to empower clients and allow them to make decisions about their representation. The assistance and choices he could provide were circumscribed not only by his clients' willingness and ability to make decisions about their cases, but also by his professional and institutional identity. This underscores a limit of client autonomy inherent in the lawyer-client relationship.

The lawyer's professional role is a double-edged sword. In order to provide the very legal assistance through NELS that Pete's client deemed of critical importance, such as representing a group member in a benefit hearing, Pete must refuse to engage in other types of representation and political activities requested by that same client.[13] These might jeopardize his effectiveness as a lawyer. Although he considered himself committed to his clients, he nevertheless felt compelled to maintain a certain professional distance to be effective in the ways that his profession allows.[14]

Ethical or value-based impediments arise even when structural or professional hurdles did not work against client autonomy. Lawyers also worried because they often come to legal services work wanting to help people, and many can become deeply invested in the clients they serve. Even when there is fleeting contact, as Liz describes below, lawyers are eager to respond to concerns that they flag. Lawyers are frustrated when clients reject assistance or advice that they believe will be beneficial. Liz related:

> People who get into this line of work I think naturally have an instinct as part, you know, someone might describe that as a social work instinct that, or a social work kind of orientation, that you know we want to solve problems, we want to make people's lives better and sometimes I find myself, as a client's talking to me, like already thinking about what could be done. But then I really try to say to the client, at the end of the story, well what would you like me to do? And sometimes what they want me to do isn't really like the full scope of what I think could be done. Or yeah, they realize that this is a problem, but that's not the issue they want me to work on. Even though I think I could. And fix it!

Liz gave an example of a situation in which she attempted to convince a client to address a problem that she viewed as important and easily resolvable in addition to the tax problem for which he sought her help. While she referred the tax problem to another lawyer, she wanted him to work with her to address the other matter, and in fact followed up with the client to try to persuade him to let her handle it. It was clear from the detail and tone of her description that she found this frustrating, although she knew it was the client's choice and not her own:

And I really didn't think [the tax problem] was going to be that big an issue. I figured it was discrete, they could find someone to work with him on that. This other thing was going to be able to put money in his pocket like within a couple months and—[He] didn't want to deal with it . . . I actually referred him to the other lawyer who followed up with him like a week later even and said, you know, "Okay, we've referred your case to these other lawyers to help you find someone to help with the tax issue. Now could we talk about this?" And he said "No. I really [laughs] want to get this other issue resolved."

Liz cited her "social work orientation" as responsible for her trying to convince clients to heed her advice. Because she cared, it was difficult for her to be apathetic about the result of this client's exercise of his autonomy, which likely led to his failure to take advantage of important resources for which she thinks he is eligible.

Vicki, who was still mulling over how her education related to her evolving practice, explicitly questioned the valorization of autonomy.

I just wonder whose idea it was that client autonomy was so important. Not that I think it's not, but I sometimes wonder if someone in academia is thinking, like, "Clients need to be autonomous and we need to give each person their individual autonomy and so this should be a tenet of um, you know, the kind of lawyering that we want to head toward."

Her suspicion that these concerns originate in academia implied that they may be out of touch with what she knows of her clients' lives and desires, and she continued later to question whether the way she had been taught to conceptualize autonomy in her professional responsibility classes may in fact be too narrow or off the mark in some way. Vicki was interested in what my conversations with other lawyers and with clients might yield, and she wondered aloud:

Do we think that our clients are feeling autonomous when really they're not [autonomous]? Because it's something that we've decided, "Oh yeah, they're fine." Like I'm dealing with them on an individual basis and I'm giving them the choice to make decisions and so that's autonomy. And so . . . when you talk to lawyers and they say . . . "Yes I think my clients feel some sort of autonomy in this lawyer-client relationship" [it might be] just that we have the wrong idea of what that autonomy would be.

Lawyers like Vicki attempted to reconcile professional conceptions of autonomy with what they learned from practice. When the two clash, as they often do, they are a source of tension for lawyers and a point of negotiation in the lawyer-client relationship. Most lawyers bracket these questions and instead resolve the tensions ad hoc, usually by trying to assess and balance what clients tell them about their particular needs, abilities, and desires. The negotiation takes into account the legal structures and bureaucracies in which the lawyers and clients act, and the circumstances of clients' lives.

Why Clients Seek Professional Help

While clients were reluctant to make decisions independently, they were less likely than the lawyers to perceive their reliance on lawyers' advice (rather than just neutral information) as undermining their own decision-making power or as a form of manipulation. This might be because many clients were in situations where their previous lack of knowledge and the difficulty in obtaining information from government agencies led to the problems that brought them to NELS in the first place. Clients saw lawyers as a resource to help them make better decisions not only about the legal issue that brought them to legal services, but in other matters as well. In describing how she chose between options for handling her housing situations, Virginia said she would solicit her lawyer Martin's opinion before making decisions:

> I would ask him, how would he go about this? And he would tell me his point, but he would also tell me that you don't have to do this. You can go by your mind, you know, but I—and I always use my mind—but I like to hear how you feel about it, so maybe I could make my decision right, but I don't want to make the wrong decisions [laughs].

Many clients, in fact, expressed strong beliefs that navigating the legal system without a lawyer is not something they would attempt if given the choice. They viewed others who did do so as naïve or foolish. Dara, who works for Northeast City in community service, told me about paperwork she had recently received related to her legal problem. I asked whether she had looked through it herself:

> No! No. 'Cause I knew I couldn't understand, I knew I couldn't understand none of that stuff, that's why. If I know I know what to do—I do

community service and social work. I don't climb, I don't fish . . . I just think that when you got certain stuff that you're not clear about, you get a professional to handle it, so that is what I did.

When I asked whether she could handle it on her own after having been through the process once with a lawyer, Dara responded firmly:

> No. No, it's no way because the deal is, is that there is some things that you need to be able to observe, and you need to know professionally what it is you're looking for.
>
> So it's not something that laypeople—?
>
> No, not at all. Not at all, not at all.
>
> So is the language on the forms really complicated or it's just technical, legal or—?
>
> It's the process. I mean, it's a process that's not a familiar process for most people. And it's something that a professional should handle. There's no way in this world I would go and file legal proceedings and not know what I'm doing.

Dara stated explicitly what many other clients intimated: Lawyers have access to "the system" and know the ropes in a way that laypeople do not. Clients perceived some (but not all) lawyers as better able to work the system. Not any lawyer can and will help: only lawyers who are both competent and care enough to use their expertise to go to bat for clients. When I asked her about justice, Martha illustrated the importance of having a good lawyer through the examples of a friend and a nephew, who had both been involved with the criminal justice system. For her, what made the difference in these two cases was the quality of the legal representation.

> The law can work for you or against you. In [my friend's case], it worked for him. I've seen the law work against a person, too. If you get an incompetent lawyer, you're in trouble. My nephew, he got picked up for, he was messing with drugs at the time. Now, they locked him up. They gave him a public defender.

Martha knew that the public defender was not doing his job, and she exhorted her sister to speak up and demand better representation for her nephew. To do otherwise, in her opinion, was to court the risk of having the law work against her nephew. "In that instance the law worked against him. Against him in the sense that he had, there's no other way to put it, an incompetent lawyer. Or a person who just didn't care. And [her nephew] didn't speak up for hisself. It just rolled over him." The lawyer's incompetence, coupled with her sister's and her nephew's failure to speak out or attempt to seek better representation, led to what Martha viewed as an unjust outcome.

Martha also saw the component of caring as an important feature of good representation. Noreen, too, emphasized the importance of caring to the quality of representation in relating an incident where her lawyer, Joanne, chastised her for talking abusively to a paralegal. Noreen explained that while she regretted speaking angrily to the paralegal, she did so because she was frustrated that Joanne would not be representing her at a meeting for her case.

> I had an appointment at [the child welfare agency] and the paralegal could come and I think at that time, it seemed like things were going downhill, or I don't know exactly what's going on, I just felt that the paralegal couldn't go in there, couldn't go in there and fight for me like [Joanne] would. I just felt that it was different. . . . I was probably out of line, but I just felt the [paralegal—I'm] not saying that she didn't have as much passion, but . . . I just felt like if it comes from Joanne it would just be different. I just thought it would be different.

When hearing this story, I assumed that Noreen thought "it would be different" because as a lawyer, Joanne would command more authority than the paralegal. Noreen clarified, however, that her concern centered on her relationship with Joanne and Joanne's feeling about her and the case.

> I think it was [pause] think it's actually because [pause][Joanne] believed me. I'm not saying that the other lady didn't believe me. But I just felt that, I'm not saying that she doesn't take all her cases personally but I think she acts like—I got the impression that [Joanne] took it, the case, very personally and—she was genuine and I just felt that [Joanne] could get across more than [the paralegal] could.

In seeking competent and caring representation, clients did not abdicate responsibility for decision making, but took charge of their cases and marshaled resources as best they could. Martha's criticism of her sister as well as Noreen's insistence upon representation by Joanne at the risk of engendering bad feelings with the paralegal and Joanne's short-term displeasure are similar to stories told by other clients. They indicated that clients believe it is a person's obligation to seek the best assistance she can, and not wait for justice to find her. This is the kind of autonomy and initiative that makes sense to clients. Theories that fail to account for these exclude client perspectives that shed light on how public interest lawyering works (and does not work) for clients. They may also gloss over the source of some of the tensions that lawyers experience but find hard to articulate. Expanding definitions of autonomy to include a broader perspective would respect client experiences and provide a broader vocabulary and conceptual toolbox to critically examine situated public interest law practice.

Clients like Virginia, Dara, Martha, and Noreen view reliance on lawyers' advice and assistance (even beyond what a progressive lawyer might find comfortable) not as abdication of agency but as increasing their options. It increases their leverage in and against the legal system and the other bureaucracies with which they must deal—even if their autonomy is not maximized in the immediate context of representation. Discussing and sometimes even handing a certain set of problems over to an attorney is a strategy that helps them make better decisions.

Folding this understanding into the existing concept of autonomy in the client-professional context is critical to understanding situated practice. This involves a contextualized appreciation that takes into account clients' lives and not just the particular issue that brings them to seek legal assistance. The relationship with the lawyer is but one part of the larger whole of a client's life; its value must be assessed in that context. This may be easier for clients to understand than it is for lawyers, for whom the lawyer-client relationship is generally their only window into the lives of clients.

Knowledge, Power, and Navigating the Legal System

Even seemingly independent clients can be hampered by limited knowledge of the legal system. Knowledge is a prerequisite to informed decision making and, as discussed above, both lawyers and clients perceive lawyers as professional interpreters of the law. Some of the lawyers in this study noted that their specialty involved particularly complex navigation of the legal issues or relevant bureaucracy, thus impeding extensive client input into the handling of their cases. Ben claimed that lawyers as a professional group tend to mystify the legal process, but that he himself was uncomfortable when clients thought that he would "do the magic." At the same time he found that many clients neither understood, nor wanted to know, the detailed explanations of the legal or financial minutiae that made up much of his work. Although all of the clients I interviewed said they understood their lawyers, many did not seem to know or care about the legal arguments or even necessarily what stage their case had reached. Understandably, most clients were more interested in the bottom line or the outcome of their case: Will I get my children back? Will I be reinstated for public housing? Will my disability make me eligible for Social Security benefits?

Lawyers spoke of attempting to communicate with clients in language that is clear and understandable. Several kept their clients abreast via written documents even if they spoke to them on the phone or in person. They did so for the client to have a record, but also specifically so that clients could review the information as often as they liked and would have time to think about it, discuss it with family and friends, and formulate questions. They tried to explain simply without "dumbing down." Several lawyers told me that when clients did not understand the legal situation, they believed the fault was with themselves and their inability to communicate rather than with the client's inability to grasp the problem. Martha said of communication with her lawyer, Martin:

> He didn't use legal language that I didn't understand. . . . He explained it in such a way that anybody could understand. No, it was no big technical things that needed to be explained, you know. And if it was, he didn't put it to me that way. He put it to me in such a way that I thoroughly understood it even when he wrote the letters. . . . It's not a whole bunch of "whereas" and you got to break down words and whatever.

Like Martha, most clients thought that their lawyers explained things clearly and to their satisfaction, often decoding incomprehensible documents that came to them from a variety of government agencies.

In many cases, it is not the lawyers at NELS who are "responsible" for the legal smoke and mirrors, but the agencies that either refuse to explain, or mislead, or make things difficult. Virginia, also a client of Martin's, described a notice she received in her ongoing battles with a public housing authority:

[W]hen I don't understand I say right away "I don't understand that, can you explain that a little better to me." So he really explains it pretty good. He explains things where I can understand. 'Cause a matter of fact, I had got this paper, you know? And Housing, instead of writing my paper out—that's what really made me go to [NELS]. . . . They was trying to put me out and I didn't understand the reason because the way they'd written it only a lawyer could understand it. And it was *a mess*, I couldn't understand none of this stuff. . . . I was like "what is this? What is they done?" I know it got to be something but I don't understand this stuff. I took it in. . . . "Yeah, they was trying to get you." They tried to . . . put so much stuff in there that I couldn't understand.

As noted in earlier chapters, many clients find that agencies will not listen to them, even when they are armed with information provided by their lawyers. Carolyn asked her lawyer Suzanne to accompany her to every conference regarding her child, including school meetings. When I asked if that made a difference in the way she was perceived, Carolyn responded: "Definitely, yeah! Because people take you more seriously. Because when you're by yourself, you're just a parent. When you're a parent with a lawyer, they listen [laughs] a little bit more, so. That's definitely a plus." Even when NELS lawyers and clients work together to empower clients with knowledge, there still may be little that they can do to change the systems for their clients, much less for other beneficiaries who do not enlist their help. In fact, some clients like Leslie understood that the systems were so unresponsive and impervious to change that even their lawyers had trouble getting through.

I really don't see how any individual can deal with these people by themselves. . . . And they wouldn't even call Liz back sometimes. And they would change people in midstream so you wouldn't know who to call. And so [Liz] would just keep calling and she would write letters and make sure she had copies of the letters that she had sent. They're very difficult to deal with.

Although NELS attempted to work with the bureaucracies that serve their clients, as described in chapter 3, these attempts did not carry over to other institutions, nor were they generally widespread. Nearly all clients mentioned misinformation, lack of information, or incompetence on the part of various agencies or complained that written documents they received were unintelligible, incorrect, or not sent in a timely enough way to allow them to comply with instructions.

Some clients also report being dissuaded from working with lawyers. Ruth had initially contacted a child welfare agency for assistance when she discovered that her children were being abused by her brother. When she later found herself in a confrontational situation with the agency, she attempted to resolve the problem on her own and was frustrated because she felt that the agency was hostile and refused to consider her perspective and the needs of her children. At the time, she had been working with Kendra, a lawyer at an advocacy agency for homeless people. Initially, Ruth only met with Kendra because she was required to do so, but they developed a good working relationship. Ruth turned to Kendra in desperation when she encountered difficulties with the child welfare agency, and Kendra referred her to Joanne, who specialized in child welfare cases. The child welfare workers then tried to dissuade her from working with a lawyer:

> I just needed help at the time, I couldn't afford to get an attorney that would cost money. And so I tried, you know, I just asked Kendra for her assistance in that 'cause I needed somebody bad.
> So you had tried to talk to the social workers before you got help from an attorney?
> Yeah. See my children w[ere] away from me—and they just treating me like, you know, "screw her." And they just didn't care. So Joanne stepped in and they tried to make it a big thing about me hiring Joanne in the first place. That I didn't need her; that they're just there to help me and I'll play an important role. And they was just feeding line and everything like I was stupid 'cause I was homeless at the time. So she helped me a lot, she really did. 'Cause if it was not for her I wouldn't have my children back.

Ruth fought for legal representation by standing up to case workers who tried to deter her from working with a lawyer. In the child welfare context, any confrontation with child welfare workers is likely to result in "Mom" being labeled as "uncooperative," a label that can carry severe implications for the outcome of the case. Many mothers are understandably intimidated and afraid to risk involving a lawyer for fear of retribution. It can take great courage and resourcefulness to find and work with a lawyer in this situation, so Ruth's insistence on legal representation can hardly be seen as a reflection of dependency, passivity, or lack of responsibility. Amy Sinden, a practicing attorney and critic of informality in child welfare proceedings, argues that legal representation in such contexts does not necessarily impinge on client autonomy. In a system unresponsive to clients, legal representation may give weight and legitimacy to the client's position that agencies or courts might not accord to the unrepresented.

> [W]hile proponents of informality insist that representation by an attorney disempowers participants by disabling them from speaking in their own voice and on their own behalf, I suspect that having an attorney speak on one's behalf can also be experienced as empowering, giving a parent a sense that she does not stand alone, that her position has legitimacy, and that it commands attention and respect from the judge.[15]

In an ideal world, clients would not need lawyers to be heard or to legitimate their positions. Clients in this study, however, bear witness that such is not the case. Having a lawyer gives them leverage and an ability to navigate the legal system more effectively. It is hard, then, to view obtaining and relying upon legal representation as abdication of autonomy, even though there is certainly loss of control and the danger of manipulation of which attorneys and clients must not lose sight.

Situating Legal Representation within the Lives of Clients

Lawyers want to maximize client knowledge about their legal problems so that clients can make informed decisions. Some also believe this serves client interests, should clients encounter legal problems in the future. However, many clients (rich or poor) find legal troubles highly stressful. Poor clients often have the added complication of coping with other simultaneous difficulties. Lawyers are keenly aware of this. Steve, who handles Social Security disability claims, noted that although the legal work he did was the most pressing issue for *him*, for many clients it is not. He generally prefers to do as much of the work on cases himself as he can:

> ['C]ause that way I know it gets done. And I don't mean that in a blame sense. 'Cause there's lots of, sometimes it's that there's blame, but most of the time it's like, yeah, of course it doesn't get done because there's six million other things going on in the client's life, and why should this be the most important thing? It's the most important thing to my relationship with the client because I'm not helping them with their eviction and their homelessness and their—all of that stuff. That's not, you know, so

for me this is very important, but for some of my clients it's not critical and so when you're in crisis only that gets done which absolutely has to get done.

Clients prioritize activities for the same reasons that lawyers do: resource constraints. If a client can shift the burden of one problem to the lawyer, this frees her up to cope with other problems. Although this is a logical allocation of resources in the context of clients' circumstances, it fits uncomfortably with ideal notions of their autonomy in relations with lawyers.

Many clients also come to NELS in states of extreme stress that make it difficult to process information. All of the clients I interviewed (or their family members) experienced a combination of problems (e.g., physical disabilities, homelessness, or mental illness). In addition, many described palpable physical symptoms of stress such as chest pains, difficulty sleeping, headaches, and crying that led them to seek assistance from NELS. Denise, who sought reinstatement of eligibility for public housing, described nearly a year and a half of moving from one temporary situation to another throughout Northeast City with her teenage daughter while trying to keep her job (and her furniture). "It was so sad. It was sad. A lot of times I was just like, I just broke down and cried, [my daughter and I] both cried together and I kept telling her you know, things going to be okay. . . . [Sighs] Oh, it's stress, it's really stress."

When I asked Martha why she sought assistance from NELS, she replied:

I was hoping they'd get these people off my back. . . . I was really up against a wall because I was paying an awful lot of rent considering my income. . . . And when I went over there to try to help those people see that it was something wrong with the amount of rent I was paying and my income, they told me that they couldn't change anything. . . . My daughter is a schizophrenic and my son is autistic and they're adults. So I have to stay home with them, I can't work. So, it was like, you're between a rock and a hard place. And these people had me with nightmares, and they weren't going to do anything, "We just want our money."

Clients seek lawyers to help them deal with discrete problems in order to relieve stress and to free them up to deal with other aspects of their lives. They enlist professional help for legal problems to increase their life choices and minimize harms to which they and their families are exposed. By marshalling resources, clients like Cecilia enhance their sense of self-efficacy by feeling more in control of situations that had previously felt overwhelming and baffling:

> I guess without legal service, getting Ben . . . I wouldn't be sitting here. So I'm really grateful for that. That was like a load of pressure—you can't imagine—off of me. I couldn't deal with anything else until, you know, until that assurance. Life's still going on, that was the biggest weight on me, you know? I needed a lawyer, somebody to represent me or to speak for me.

The Retainer Model

When we examine the assumptions of a narrow view of autonomy, it is clear that we hold poor clients to a higher standard than we do paying clients. Further, the morality argument which holds that autonomy is an expression of our full humanity belies the notion that poor clients should be subject to stricter autonomy standards than wealthy clients.

Perhaps the most blatant contrast between our attitudes toward paying versus nonpaying clients becomes evident in the "retainer model," whereby lawyers are available to clients for consultation on an ongoing basis. Both lawyers and clients viewed ongoing "lawyerly advice" as a luxury that paying clients demand. Maryann joked that she felt comfortable talking with her lawyer about any problem that arose and that their relationship is reminiscent of the relationship that the rich people she sees on television have with their lawyers. "It's like he's a family lawyer or something. A family friend/lawyer. Like . . . some kind of legal show or something, and this family has this lawyer, like that they're totally like coming to their gatherings, and they're friends as well as professional."

When I asked Maryann how she made decisions about her benefits, she marveled at her good fortune in being able to call her lawyer:

> I always call Pete and ask him. 'Cause if I'm not clear about what I'm going to do, I do! I just like call him right away. You know, like, if I feel as though I come up to a situation where I think that I have to choose and I don't know if I'm going to make the right choice or something, I'll definitely call him. I mean, that's real. It's real. 'Cause sometimes it, it's like, damn, this is like kind of too good to be true!

In our follow-up interview, I asked Pete about this type of ongoing relationship and he was more ambivalent. Unlike some lawyers at NELS, he does not subscribe to what he called the "retainer model" of legal services. He suspects that it promotes client dependence. Pete had applied for another job (and has since left NELS) and he wondered how the clients who have grown accustomed to calling him for advice would fare if he leaves. He also worried that Maryann and other clients use him as a first resource before solving problems that he believes they could handle on their own. As an example, he mentioned Bette, who turned to him for help finding an apartment:

> She went to family court and the court ordered that she could take all the possessions from [her husband's] property, anything she wants in there she can take, whether it's hers or his. But she had to move within, I forget what it was, I think it was 30 days. It was a very short period of time. And she called me up that night, stressed out. "I really need your help, can you go on line and try to do some apartment searches for me." And I told her, "No, I can't do that. Go to the library." And I actually did a couple of searches and said here's some good websites. And part of it was I'm not doing that for her, but part of it was also, you know, I'm trying to fight her instinct of having to turn to someone from the outside to help her get through this because she's capable of doing it.

In addition to Pete's concerns for client dependence, he also told me that the retainer model is not feasible given existing resource constraints. This is where the similarity between the "rich persons' retainer model" and legal services breaks down. The reality of limited legal services often gives rise to hierarchies of needs that legal services lawyers and theorists commonly refer to as "triage."[16] Lawyers and theorists find triage troubling and debate its value. Debates about whether and how to order priorities can be highly contentious. NELS sets policies about which clients they take and which legal services they provide, but relies on staff lawyers' input in creating these priorities. In practice, the policies allow broad lawyer discretion. Discussions of autonomy with the lawyers in this study made clear that many employ a form of triage at the level of case handling. While they might not consciously employ guidelines, in many of the interviews lawyers revealed consistency in trying to tease out just how they mete out the level and kind of services they provide to individual clients.

As a counterpoint to Bette's case, Pete presented an example of a suicidal client for whom he offered to make a phone call about what he viewed as a minor matter that required absolutely no legal expertise. Pete treated the suicidal client differently than Bette, whom he viewed as savvy and capable. Their requests for extralegal assistance might be similar; their circumstances and abilities were not. Pete's suicidal client was overburdened and not up to confronting complexity or hostility. Pete sensed that a phone call to the government agency was one burden too many. It is of clients like these, and all others whose situations fall closer to this end of the spectrum, that Martha Minow speaks when she cautions that self-reliance should not be our chief criterion of autonomy:

> [S]elf-help, even when supported through expert assistance, should not become the driving vision behind lawyering for people at the margins. Most poor people have to negotiate for themselves daily, maneuvering through social and economic frameworks where they are systematically disadvantaged. Sometimes, the best way to honor the dignity of disempowered persons is not to expect them to advocate for themselves, but instead to ensure their representation by the toughest, most high-powered lawyer available—just as a wealthy corporate client can expect.[17]

Clients have different levels and arenas of capacity and incapacity, making it even more difficult to consistently categorize degree of need. This means that when clients and lawyers formulate the terms of their relationship and the scope of assistance, they must assess and negotiate whether the client can and should handle the problem(s) on her own. As Vicki explained:

> I think a lot of times what I'll end up saying is, and I think again it's that individual client assessment . . . I have a client right now who is having to run around and do all sorts of different things to get paid for something that should have just been given to her right up front. And she's another one that I feel like I have, again a vested interest in because, really, she shouldn't have to be doing that and sometimes like I think I could do it better because she's just so tired and so frustrated . . . and that because I'm not personally involved and I don't need the money as desperately as she needs it and I haven't run around as much as she has that I feel like I can do it better. And so I think it just depends on the clients and so for some clients I will do it. And other clients I'll say, "You need to go do

this." And really it just depends on how much the client's dealing with and how well you think they can, they can do it.

Appraisals can be complex, and lawyers' assessments include their understanding of a client's capacities, her circumstances and her ability to communicate them, the nature of the problem (including whether the client and lawyer understand it to be a legal problem), and the lawyer's caseload and priorities.

Just as the clients cited above wanted to consult with lawyers in order to make better decisions, lawyers also felt a tension between wanting clients to follow their advice and fostering client autonomy. Most lawyers had confronted situations in which they believed that their client was making a bad decision, although nearly all of them said that they felt obligated to comply with their client's decision. Marjorie noted that many clients of the consumer unit focus (understandably) on the short term to the detriment of their long-term interest:

> I'm trying to think of situations where clients want to make a decision because it's going to change something right now, but in the long term it's not the best thing for them. But when they come to us they've already done that [laughs]. They already made the decision about getting into a loan that was a good thing at that time but in the long run it was a really bad decision.

This makes lawyers skeptical about the ability of clients to make what they consider good decisions when a client's wishes conflict with their lawyer's judgment. Martin, a lawyer in the public housing unit, described how he handles such situations.

> [I]f the client has clearly said that's what they want to do, then that's what's done. I mean, you have to respect the client's wishes. . . . If I feel extremely strongly that the client is making a decision that's going to have significant harm to them, I tell the client, "This is your decision to make; it's not the one that I would make." I would explain why I would make a different decision. I would tell, make it clear to the client that regardless of the client's decision that I will respect that wish, and I would probably put it in writing, that I'm advising you to do this; however, if you choose to do something else that's what I'm going to do.

Martin explained that although he bases his advice on his experience as a lawyer, it is clear to him that the client must make the decision not only because it impacts her life, but also because his predictions may not be borne out.

> I have on occasion had clients tell me that they want to do something that I think is totally foolish, in terms of their case. It still has merit but it is just not the best way to go. And quite frankly, we took that option and they did just fine. Now it didn't turn out quite the way one would expect, but that was their decision and they made it. And it worked, so I can't say that just because I recommend something, even recommend something strongly, that's there's a hundred percent guarantee that what I suggest is going to come to pass.

While Martin expressed his desire to enhance client decision making, he clearly felt that it was his duty as a lawyer to inform clients when he "felt strongly" that they were making a poor decision. However, this was tempered by his example of the client who rejected his advice and fared well nevertheless. Nearly all lawyers had an example like Martin's.[18] These are cautionary tales that lawyers tell to themselves, and sometimes others, not only to encourage clients' decision making. They also function to reassure lawyers in cases where they have more than a little trepidation about the results that may come about when they implement clients' decisions.

Marjorie provided an example of a different kind of lawyer-client conflict over the course of the case and illustrates where triage considerations can further influence conceptions of autonomy. Unlike the example provided by Martin, this was not a matter of strategy informed by a lawyer's imperfect ability to predict an outcome. In Marjorie's example, she viewed the legal claim that the client asked her to present as flat out wrong and rooted in a complete misperception of the law. Marjorie was concerned because she felt the client disbelieved and mistrusted her. She was also concerned that putting forth a clearly erroneous position would be a waste of time which, if dedicated to this case, would necessarily mean that time was not utilized to the benefit of other clients. Marjorie also considered her own reputation and that of NELS before the court. Still, Marjorie was unsure what to do. She did not want to discontinue representation and vacillated about whether she could (and should) put forth the client's argument.

I've already opened the case. I've entered my appearance on it. Do I try to get out of representing her because there's no way I'm going to do it, like I'm wasting my time going to a judge on this case? You know, it's so clearly they're in the wrong and she has to pay the mortgage back. I mean, there are other things we can do, but as far as whether she's legally obligated, she is.

So you can't even start with a negotiation on that point?

No. I mean she's just wrong. But, you know, she really wants her day in court and it's, well—do I, you, do I represent her for her day in court even though it's completely wrong and do I put a lot of time and energy into a losing case? Probably not. If it means that I'm not going to take another case.

Marjorie is torn by her desire and training to act according to the client's wishes and her understanding of herself as a legal services lawyer who must spread her resources as equitably as possible among too many clients. She also considered her professional reputation for herself and on behalf of the clients who might benefit from respect accorded to her and to NELS. Marjorie's compelling commitment to autonomy and agency is apparent in the fact that she remains troubled by this relatively extreme case, one that would seem easily resolved given the mix of factors we have examined in this chapter.

Limitations of the Professional Relationship

Lawyers' professional responsibility to engage in zealous representation and the adversarial system exacerbate the tension between client autonomy and the achievement of desired outcomes.[19] Steve displayed perhaps the most zealous attitude, declaring unabashedly that he does not let concerns of client autonomy get in the way of desired outcomes. For example, he told me that he warns clients that if he thinks it might bode well for their mental disability claims, he might induce them to cry at a hearing, even if they might not want that. When I asked him whether he'd ever had a client ask him to withdraw a case, he responded:

I typically won't let clients do that. I make it very difficult for clients to withdraw their cases. If I have a client that I believe is disabled and the client says I don't want to pursue this anymore, unless they really, really give me no choice, I'm not going to let them drop a case.

So how do you do that?

I ignore it initially. I then, I really push and push and push and say well you know you have to do that in writing. And then [noise] most of the time by the time I get to the hearing they're fine and they'll do the hearing. Totally paternalistic. It doesn't happen a lot. This is not a common occurrence. I mean, one client says, "I don't want to go to the hearing." I say, "You have to go to the hearing." Now, of course she doesn't have to go the hearing, but I don't tell her that. . . . So they go. Which is somewhat disingenuous, 'cause they don't have to go to the hearing, they could just not show up. But I'm not going to tell them that. We had one client [laughs] who's very, very mentally ill [and] we finally got her to apply. She signed all the releases. She comes back a week later and says "I want to take them back." And we said, "Oh you can't." Of course she can! She can go down to Social Security, but we don't tell her that!

Although Steve used this story to highlight his somewhat cavalier attitude toward autonomy within the lawyer-client relationship, it was clear from this and later discussions that for him this type of strong-arming only happens within certain parameters. These were cases in which the client initiated representation. Most of his examples are of clients affected by mental illness to a degree that he questioned their competence. Further, they were all cases in which the client articulated the initial and overarching goal of obtaining benefits, which Steve described as an "all-or-nothing" prospect. Thus, the decisions that he manipulated from his clients were all within the framework of this goal, and often revolved around his assessment of the best legal strategy. What differed markedly about his presentation of the issue from that of other lawyers, though, was his apparent lack of concern for the effect that the process has on the client and her sense of empowerment or autonomy.

It was also clear that Steve's paternalism does not extend beyond legal strategy. Personal choices, including how to use money that a client may get from an action that he pursues on her behalf, were unambiguously decisions that are the client's alone. Fond of dramatic examples, Steve illustrated this point with one of his first cases as a lawyer, which he described as "a cautionary tale that [he] tr[ies] to keep in mind."

Now, I killed my first client. I think about that one. A woman, an alcoholic, got a big check. At that time they weren't giving representative payees to alcoholics on Social Security. That was fifteen years ago. And

whereas before my representation she couldn't drink enough to kill herself on the monthly check that she got, when she got $10,000 in back
pay,[20] within six months she drank herself to death. A bit harsh. I mean
that was a—you know, could I have done something in retrospect? Probably. I could have sort have been all over her about doing something else
with the money. I didn't think anything of it.

Although poor choices by clients trouble him and he tries to persuade a
client to act differently, he would not manipulate clients or take actions
on their behalf outside of the legal arena. Asked what he might do now
with a client like his first one, he said "I would have a discussion with the
client, and if the client—but ultimately I would probably do nothing."

For Steve, it was clear in most cases which decisions are strategic legal
decisions that justify his manipulation of a client. Other lawyers who were
even more troubled about personal autonomy gave examples where it was
clear to them that they should not even offer the client advice. While they
might provide information about the ramifications of client choices, they
refused to take responsibility for decisions that were personal ones, even
if clients requested advice in these matters. Pete provided one of these
examples.

I had a case recently in which somebody had to figure out what to do with
the welfare office related to who the father was of her child. And she was
a prostitute and she was living with one of the possible fathers who said
he was the father. She started the relationship with him shortly after the
child was conceived. And then she stopped prostituting. You know, it was
a dilemma, so whether she wanted to pursue a welfare action or just give
up on the thing because the costs of pursuing it might be that he might
learn that he might not be the father and I'm not going to make that decision as to what she should do about that—that's too fundamental.

In Joanne's family advocacy work, these lines are even less clearly drawn
because legal issues are inseparable from intimate personal and family
issues and because the representation is generally both long-term and
intensive.

Does it worry me that we're going along fine and then suddenly my client's using drugs obviously and screwing up her case? Yeah, that upsets
me a lot. And then I have to sit down and say—well, drugs are a different

issue but when a client, say, is not visiting [her child or children], I have to sit down and say, "She's making that choice." I have done all I can to figure out why she's not visiting. Does she not have tokens? Does she not know how to get there? Does she not know when the visits are? If I fixed all those problems or assessed them all, made sure they're not problems, and she's still not visiting—I mean, you know.

Joanne had to remind herself that some choices are the client's alone, even if they affected the outcomes of the case. If she had determined that there were no strategic or legal issues to address, then she must recognize the client's choice, painful as that might be.

In response to my probing to understand the source of tension surrounding issues of autonomy, Marjorie shared the following insight.

I think because . . . the tension is that, like I really take seriously that this is your case and you make the decisions. And ideally, you know, our view and probably typically the view of NELS attorneys or at least public interest attorneys certainly beyond that is that you want to empower clients to help themselves. So theoretically we should be able to empower clients by giving them all the knowledge and spending time educating them about why a certain thing is good or bad and then they're going to make these decisions that we would make. And when we feel like we're empowering them or trying to like give them the knowledge that they need and they end up making a decision that would be bad, we ultimately don't want to see them in a bad result. But the thought of then basically disempowering them and manipulating what their ultimate decision would be is something sickening to us [laughs].

Marjorie was aware of the contradictions posed for her by the value of autonomy and self-determination and her desire to see clients "better off." When she felt her clients made "good" decisions, there was no conflict; autonomy and her desire to see the client better off were served. However, when clients' decisions resulted in bad outcomes vis-à-vis their own declared goals, she was faced with a dilemma that derived from her status as a professional who viewed herself as charged with helping clients make "better decisions."

While lawyers' perceived notions of client best interest sometimes complicated their understanding of client autonomy, lawyers had less trouble walling off the interests of other parties. I asked Suzanne whether she was ever concerned that successfully helping a client regain custody of her child may hurt the child. She told me that while others often asked her about this and seemed troubled by it, it was not of major concern to her.

> When I'm talking to people about my work . . . once you tell them that you, you know legal services lawyer, they think that's good [laughs]. Um, "What do you do?" "You work in dependency court?" And then, once you explain that you're representing parents but not children, usually people are always asking like "Well, you know, what do you do if you don't think the parent's capable of having the child?" And there's, there's always the public defender answer of like "You know, that's not my role in the system. The system's set up to give everyone a voice. You know, the children have plenty of voices. It's not my role to judge a parent. That's what [the child welfare agency] is doing, that's what the judge is doing. You know, my role is to represent the parent and try to get for them what they want." I think the system probably still does err on the side of too much caution. . . . I think it's much more likely that kids, that parental rights are terminated rather than not terminated to the detriment of the children and the families. You know, and the system's so loaded against them that, you know, like I can't imagine that I'm a good enough lawyer to be able to sort of like sneak something by [laughs].

Autonomy Redefined

William Simon characterized the notion of client empowerment as "liberation from lawyers as much as obtaining leverage on the outside world."[21] As clients in this study testify, these can sometimes be incompatible goals. While autonomy is important, it needs to be understood differently if we are to employ it in a way that is relevant to the lawyer-client relationship in a legal service setting for the foreseeable future.

MacKenzie and Stoljar have promoted the term "relational autonomy" to serve as an umbrella for a diverse collection of feminist critiques of autonomy.[22] The concept of relational autonomy seeks to retain the values at the base of autonomy that can be sources of power for marginalized groups such as agency, self-determination, and respect. It seeks to place these values in context and to recognize that human beings are by nature social beings, dependent upon one another to varying degrees. It is not a sign of weakness or abdication of responsibility (or autonomy, for that matter) to rely on others to make better choices and to help us through difficult times. Indeed, the marshalling of resources, including professional advice, is an exercise of agency and self-determination that further enables clients to retain or regain control of their lives in difficult circumstances.

Lawyers and clients sketch the parameters of their relationships through a negotiated process that takes into account a variety of considerations. This includes the client's stress level, capabilities, desires, and current life circumstances. It also includes the agency with which the client is dealing, the client's experiences with that agency, the degree of receptivity that can be expected, and the complexity of the legal problem. Unfortunately, such negotiation is framed by the lawyer's workload, agency resources, and the needs and desires of current and imagined future clients. These factors may not be made explicit, although as we have seen in the examples cited above, traces of them are available for exploration by lawyers, clients, and others whose ears are attuned. Negotiations continue throughout the life of the legal issue and the relationship between the lawyer and client. The negotiated relationship may develop and change over several years and over a number of legal and other problems.

While we should not adopt a blind or atomized version of autonomy, we must not give up on autonomy as a concept that informs progressive legal work. Much as the prophylactic argument suggests, lawyers attending to the practical details and substantive balancing suggested in this analysis will more likely be attuned to client needs, desires, and life circumstances. A revised notion of autonomy that makes this balancing act explicit would call for us to continue to be troubled, hence thoughtful, and to encourage client autonomy in ways that make sense to clients and lawyers acting together in context. Lawyers must pay careful attention to autonomy concerns and discuss these concerns with clients even while they might, and I would argue should, be willing to balance the autonomy ideal with those of compassion and concern. Together with respect for the client's wishes and appreciation of the full context of a client's often complicated and stressful life, these form the elements of a contextually sensitive situated practice. An expanded, contextual understanding of autonomy would also recognize a broader range of client actions, including the delegation of responsibility that might otherwise be seen as inaction, as an expression of considered self-determination. Such a revised notion of autonomy will also lead to a revised notion of how lawyers and clients work together within the legal services context. I examine other aspects of these relationships in the next chapter through consideration of the theme of collaboration.

5

Collaboration

The lawyers can't get out there and do it by themselves. They need help. I'm a helper.
　　　　　　　　　　　　　　　　　　　　　　　　　　—Valerie

You do what you can. . . . And I've certainly had my share of cases where the client just didn't follow through in a way that was going to make it happen. But sometimes it works. And I think you got to give people a chance to do that. And maybe I'm being foolish about it but if you kind of give the client some consistent communication about how the system works, like making sure that they understand what they're supposed to do, even if they fail this time, maybe they'll learn for the next time.　　　　　—Martin

The previous chapter focused on the value of client autonomy. This chapter examines a technique of lawyering that has been called "collaborative lawyering," which is in many ways closely tied to notions of autonomy. Collaborative lawyering models portray lawyers and clients as "co-eminent problem solvers."[1] This term is rooted in a belief that both lawyers and clients can and should contribute knowledge and skills to the relationship, and that clients should make decisions and take actions. In this chapter, I briefly examine the basis for collaborative lawyering and advocate adoption of a broad definition of collaboration. Relying on that definition, I then explore collaborative work from the perspectives of clients and lawyers. Last, I discuss a number of ways in which lawyers and clients collaborate that have gone largely unnoticed in the literature, at least as examples of collaboration.

Exalting Collaboration

Progressive lawyering proponents advocate collaboration based on its value and efficacy. Value-based rationales for collaboration stem from the notion that clients and lawyers are equals. Collaborative practices seek to mitigate the hierarchical aspects of the professional relationship. Although lawyers may have formal training and greater access, clients are experts on their own lives and possess knowledge and problem-solving skills that are at least as important as attorney expertise to the "success" of the lawyering relationship. Collaborative lawyering has also been justified on more instrumental grounds. Engaging clients as much as possible in the representation provides clients with opportunities to learn from the process and develop tools to advocate for themselves and/or others, perhaps obviating the need for a lawyer in the future. This is a particularly compelling advantage when resources are scarce and clients cannot be assured of future legal assistance.

Collaborative lawyering models assume that clients desire participation in the legal process. But is this really what clients want? And if not, as discussed in chapter 4, there may be good reason for lawyers to honor client wishes despite their own notions of ideal practice. Many clients do not express a desire to understand the legal process or to achieve future self-sufficiency but instead seek to allocate one of the many burdens they bear. They seek lawyers as professionals who can resolve problems through the use of professional tools and as information providers who "know the ropes." This is often lost on progressive lawyering proponents. As Ann Southworth points out in a critique of Gerald López's rebellious lawyering, the call for greater client involvement in the legal process too often undervalues the contributions of legal expertise.

> [I]n defining his prescription for rebellious lawyering, López offers an excessively pessimistic assessment of the range and value of the skills that lawyers can provide. His alternative vision of lawyering imagines a relatively minor role for lawyers' specialized knowledge and skills. He urges lawyers to downplay their legal expertise and involve clients in lawyering work. But he does not adequately discuss circumstances in which clients might rationally prefer, and perhaps even benefit from, a stricter division of responsibilities.[2]

Clients in this study were not inclined to downplay lawyers' roles, and many clients rationally and prudently perceived such skills and experience as necessary to successfully navigate the legal system or relevant bureaucracies. As discussed in chapter 3, they believe that the legal system is stacked against poor people. There is little chance of achieving justice but, with a competent and caring lawyer, they might be able to prevail.[3] Clients were also more obviously and directly dependent upon lawyers than vice versa, particularly if the problems for which they sought assistance were immediate crises and if they had no other means of assistance.

Piomelli argues that critics of collaborative lawyering scholarship have not paid careful attention to differences among scholars.[4] Further, Piomelli claims that critics have attacked caricatures rather than trying to think about the rationales and values at the base of collaborative lawyering theories, which he sees as exemplified in the work of Lucie White, Gerald López, and Anthony Alfieri. This, he contends, is a consequence of insufficient attention to the work of practitioners that leaves much of the discussion of practice in the rarefied world of the academy. Collaborative lawyering theories can be fairly appraised only when they are examined together with knowledge gleaned from lawyers and clients engaged in practice. The work of theorists such as White, Lopez, or Alfieri should be viewed as useful formulations to be engaged by practitioners and clients.

If we are to understand collaborative lawyering in practice, we need to see it in an expansive form that includes not just a narrow definition of "legal" work, but the lawyer-client relationship in its entirety, as understood by lawyers and clients. Piomelli offers a definition based on aspects of different collaborative lawyering theories:

> At the theoretical level, these new visions share, to differing degrees and levels of sophistication, an understanding of the predominant lawyering activity. . . . They view lawyering as fundamentally a process of persuasive storytelling, in which the depiction or "re-presentation" of clients is central to obtaining desired responses from others. Framing who clients and other actors are, and what happened or is happening to them, is central to persuasion, and thus lawyering. For reasons of politics, ethics, and efficacy, these scholars believe that lawyers should encourage clients and their lay (i.e., non-lawyer) allies to participate actively in this framing.[5]

Consistent with the variety of collaborative practices found in this study, such a definition is compatible with an understanding that clients and lawyers have distinct roles, different areas of expertise, and many different opportunities for navigating different kinds of collaboration. It does not dictate that lawyers and clients take equal parts in handling the situation for which the client seeks legal assistance, nor does it imply that all clients collaborate to the same extent and in the same ways. Contributions may vary according to the legal issue, individual and organizational constraints on clients and lawyers, and the resources available to each, including time, money, expertise, and level of competency. Piomelli's definition invites investigation into the ways lawyers and clients negotiate the actual situations in which clients and lawyers find themselves. While no one theory can possibly account for all situations, theories can offer a way of thinking about the encounters and choices, provided they are open to the concerns and realities of situated legal practice.

Does Collaboration Enhance the Legal Process?

Lawyers' decisions about how much to involve clients and in what aspects of representation were often framed as a cost-benefit analysis within the context of time constraints. Investing the time to educate some clients would necessarily mean serving fewer clients. One factor lawyers weigh in determining how much to involve clients is the perceived efficacy of involving them, both for the case at hand and for future encounters with government bureaucracies. Steve, a benefits lawyer specializing in Social Security Disability Insurance, said that the process of determining and proving disability status was very complicated and thus he tended not to involve the client in those details. Moreover, these encounters are not likely to recur. Once a client's disability status is established, it is not likely to be revisited, nor is this process, in Steve's eyes, similar to any other process the client might encounter. Therefore, he saw little point to having clients understand the process so they would be able to negotiate it at a later time on their own.

Pete, who valued collaboration in theory, found it inefficient and overly resource-intensive in the context of a busy legal services office:

[W]e have a ton of work to do. I mean, it's absurd. And how few of us there are relative to the nature of the problem and we set up all these artificial ways to safeguard us from clients—like having nine hours of intake a week. But still, even with that, the time—the workload is unbelievable. And then that creates this problem of having to cut corners basically and not do educational or empowering work. There's a strain of the collaborative lawyering stuff that I think theorizes that it could be more efficient to do collaborative lawyering because you're garnering the strengths and the skills and abilities of the client also, who then are going to do work on their case. I don't believe that that's usually true. I think from my experience it's usually less efficient. There has to be a certain level of collaboration 'cause there's certain things that the client has to provide to you, but in most cases it's more efficient to just assume all the responsibilities and do it yourself.

Lawyers saw practical problem-solving, such as obtaining documents or strategizing about the practical contingencies that would facilitate or impede decisions or settlements, as an important and productive venue for collaborative work. Martin's clients possessed information and resources that he did not, and this information often was crucial to the success of their cases.

I like to talk to my clients about what I perceive to be the weakness in your case, because frequently they can problem-solve on how to resolve that weakness much better than I can. A good example was we had a client who is wheelchair-bound. He lives in a subsidized Section 8 unit, he'd been there for a long time but the place wasn't being kept clean. And most judges would say to that particular person you got to figure out a way to get somebody in to clean your unit. . . . So I talked to him about that. I said, listen, you know, if you can find somebody to clean your unit on a regular basis, and they're willing to come into court and say that they're going to do it, then I think you can succeed. Well, he went out and found somebody. I was not aware of any service that I could get for him to do that, but he did it. So the kind of talking to your clients about the weaknesses in the cases helps move things along.

Marcia echoed this sentiment. She represented children applying for disability benefits, and her clients' ability to consider themselves experts on the manifestations of their problems can often make or break a case. Thus she viewed her practice, particularly before administrative judges, as necessarily collaborative. It is her job to make the client feel at ease and understand what will happen at a hearing. This allows the client to do the work of telling her story, which is usually the crux of the case.

> I know the judges pretty well by now so I tell [clients] as much as I know. "This judge is really pleasant, but you know that doesn't mean you don't have to describe in detail what the problems are" . . . "This judge is an old white man and he doesn't hear well" and—I mean, I'll just give them as much information as I can and also help them relax. . . . Because, you know, "You're really just going to be describing what you know because it's what happens in your household and out on your sidewalk so you're the expert on that and you're going to do a fine job. . . . You are really the person who knows this and you know I'm going to provide you with an opportunity to really explain it to the judge."

Marcia found that by explaining the legal requirements to her clients, they could figure out what "stories" would help advance the case productively. Clients are the experts in the sense that only they have access to the stockpile of stories and experiences that make up their lives and the understanding of what such experiences mean. Marcia thought that client outcomes were better when she established open-ended and collaborative relationships rather than a more directive orientation.

> If your client is kind of in tandem with you rather than you're sort of telling the client what to do, they're going to be a whole lot better witness and so I definitely say, "This is what we're trying to prove. Now what stories [laughs] do you have so that we can prove it?" See, it's actually pretty simple—I mean my legal standard—so maybe it's easier for me in that regard.

It is notable that one reason Marcia thought that she could engage in such collaboration with clients was because she believed that the legal issues involved were rather simple and easily communicated. This position is starkly different from Steve's, although they both worked within the parameters of the Social Security disability regulations, and both of them dealt with the full range of physical and mental disabilities that can be hard to prove. In fact, Marcia's work with children had added complications. Marcia worked with minors, therefore her representation is complicated by questions regarding competency and, when the children are old enough to testify, the need to reconcile different perspectives. Further, young children cannot always describe and understand their illness, and many adolescents are embarrassed to talk about their problems. The difference between Marcia's and Steve's perspectives indicates that whether or not a particular legal issue is amenable to client collaboration may depend more on lawyers' assessment both of clients' capability and the legal complexity in a particular field rather than any objective measure of either of them. These assessments are likely based as much on lawyers' self-estimation, their estimation of their work, and their desire to retain or relinquish control as on their legal experience or their experience with clients.

Joanne provided a detailed example of the kind of collaboration that Marcia described. In response to a question about what she learned from her clients, she discussed how a client whom she viewed as a model parent won the case for herself.

> [The child welfare agency] said she chose her boyfriend over her daughter and got a restraining [order] and threw her daughter in care. And the thing that my client did that actually would make me a better parent and which I use as an example to help my clients be better parents is she went with her daughter in the car to the foster home. Then she said—it was a Friday—"You're going to spend a weekend with a friend of Mommy's, okay? Mommy has something else to do. And I need you to stay here and be a good girl and be taken care of." Walked her into the house, saw a fish tank, got her involved in the fish tank and left. When she told that story she brought the judge to tears. I mean he was like, [loud—in a voice of decree] "Child's going home! Today! Immediately!" You know it was just so clear that despite Mom's own trauma, despite whatever it is that [the child welfare agency] said she was doing or saying, she was putting her daughter's feelings first . . . I had never really thought about, to that point, using my client as their own best advocate. It was always me explaining my client up to that point. And allowing her to explain herself, and to be who she was, and for the people to see the parent that she was, was really good.

Joanne qualified the lesson she learned about collaboration, noting that this strategy can be "kind of risky, 'cause a lot of times Mom's not something that impresses the hell out of the child advocate." Steve also said that relying on clients can be dicey. This was one of the more difficult aspects of working with Janet, a client whom he referred for this study. Although she appeared capable and agreed to handle some aspects of procuring paperwork, she often did not "come through."

You had mentioned [that] Janet Palma was a harder client.
Oh yeah.
So what about her . . . what aspects of it were harder?
She lost paperwork. Repeatedly. She consistently overestimated what she
    could do. And it took me a while to figure out that just because she said
    she could do something it doesn't mean she could.

Steve found being disappointed by clients who he thought would come
through more problematic than working with clients who from the outset
said that they could or would not take on tasks. In those cases, he did
not rely on the clients but rather knew from the beginning that either he
would have to take on certain tasks or assume they would not be done.

Lawyers and clients must work together to negotiate the form and
scope of collaborative practice in a way that works for the client, for the
lawyer, and for the goals of representation. Steve described working with
a very capable client, whom he described admiringly as "uppity," so that
she could attend a welfare sanction hearing unrepresented.

The woman . . . has two big chips on her shoulder. Probably rightfully,
but you know, they get in the way of getting things done . . . Bottom line
is she was being threatened with a welfare sanction which is basically—
we're going to cut you all off for 60 days, the whole family. And we have
to go in and have a meeting with them about what to do about this. And
we concluded that because the person she was actually going to meet
with was fairly decent, it was better if I didn't go, 'cause sometimes having
a lawyer there just sort of ratchets it up. But I had this long counseling
session with her about how what she needed to go in there and without—
again I was very clear to make it, I'm not asking you say anything that's
immoral or wrong, but you want to go in there and be nice. And so we
had this whole long sort of thing about how she could go in and what she
could say.

Steve and his client made this into something of a game, and Steve rel-
ished working with a client whom he saw as unusually sophisticated, noting "it was great fun." The client successfully negotiated the hearing to
avoid sanction without feeling compromised.

It worked, it was great! She was great! This was a wonderful client, she
got it. She went in, the meeting was fantastic, this action went away. . . .

That was a fun one. . . . And she took care of it beautifully . . . and she was savvy and capable enough to do that all by herself. It was great. So that was a big success.

Some of the clients interviewed drew on lawyers as one among several resources.

These clients did not work on their cases at the same time as the lawyers, but instead collaborated sequentially. They worked independently to the best of their ability, and then called on a lawyer only when the problem surpassed their own significant abilities. These were generally, although not exclusively, more educated clients, several of them self-described activists or involved with their respective communities in some form.

Justin, a client of Pete's, explained that when he came to the United States, he applied for asylum *pro se*.[6] He relied on information he obtained from others and via the Internet. He then successfully applied to the Immigration and Naturalization Service to have his family join him through the reunification process. Justin also applied for medical benefits on behalf of his daughter. Only after she was denied the benefits, to which he believed she was entitled, did he turn to Pete for legal assistance. At the time of the interview, he worked extensively assisting other immigrants. He explained that in helping people, he goes as far as he can without drawing on formal legal assistance, calling on lawyers to assist him only when necessary. He saw this as a cost-saving device for himself and others.

> Well, from there I learned through Internet, INS.gov form and everything. The instructions I learned about. Of course, I look how to invite my family for a reunion. So I filled up a form, I730, then after about nine months my family invited by U.S. embassy in Indonesia so everything . . .
> So you did everything on your own, you didn't do that with a lawyer, you did that by yourself.
> Yes. Because it's free of charge. So I did myself. And I applied for my lawful permanent status myself. And I help my people so that the people who not go to the lawyer because the lawyer sometimes ask for money for his consultation fee, a fee that is really high for us. Then it's better for me if I have a very, very hard case to go to social lawyers like [Faith-Based Social Service Organization] either to [Immigration Law Organization] . . . because they charge a very low price.

Pete, Justin's lawyer, found Justin's resourcefulness helpful.

> I mean, you saw the level of organization that [Justin] brought to this case. I did very little work on that case. I did almost no factual gathering. I mean I just did the legal punches on it. He had—he was a great collaborator and I think he was empowered from the experience in the sense that he affirmed in his mind that if he's persistent enough and doesn't take no for an answer and ultimately he can prevail, and that sometimes it is appropriate when you've tried hard enough by yourself to call on your lawyer. He tried very hard by himself before he got me involved.

Lilly is a client who worked with Liz. She described herself as a well-educated activist who had seen "better days." Lilly drew on legal assistance only after attempting to solve problems on her own.

> I don't just, if I get something, just say, "Hey Liz, take care of it." I will do it as far as I can but when I get to the level that they do not pay attention, then I turn it to her. The thing that made [me] turn to her is when I said to the person at the welfare department, "That is not true, I do not have to go on welfare [in order to apply for medical assistance]." She said, "Oh yes you do!" I said "I do not. . . . " "Oh yes you do!" I said, "I want to talk to your supervisor." She called over her supervisor. He said, "No, she doesn't have to go on welfare." And that's when I gave it to Liz. With a full litany of exactly what was going on so that she could get right in.

Lilly viewed it as her responsibility as a client to do the most she could to make her lawyers' (she works with more than one) work easier and then drew on their resources and connections only when necessary. She, like Justin, viewed her own resourcefulness and knowledge of the law as an asset that was extremely helpful to the lawyers she works with. Lilly further explained that asking for assistance was hard for her to accept initially because of her own self-conception as a self-reliant person, but that she has learned to reach out for help as she has aged.

> When I was much younger I was very reticent and very quiet about it and so I did not go out to have others take care of it. But as I came to the point that my hair got gray enough that I could say what I thought, then I can go out and say, "Can I get this help? Will you help me with this?" Why should I spin my wheels?

For her, as for Justin and most other clients, it was important to take responsibility for whatever they were capable of handling. Thus, the boundaries of collaboration are often determined by clients' perception of the types of problems they experience, their own abilities to handle them, and the receptivity (or lack thereof) on the part of government agencies to their efforts.

Clients "Doing Their Part"

Many of the clients in this study thought that although their lawyers were professionals who have certain tasks in representing them, their lawyers could not work alone or without their assistance. Clients often had a clear idea of what it meant to "do their part" in order to advance their cases. Many underscored the importance of providing lawyers with crucial information and documents. Dara was satisfied with her lawyer. She acknowledged that while Marjorie worked hard, She had helped her own case by doing her part as a client. Dara understood that if she had not been able to secure the documents that shored up her claim against her mortgage company, Marjorie would likely not have been able to furnish proof that would convince the lender or the court.

> She really worked hard on my case and the outcome basically was a good outcome. And I guess when you have most of these documents and stuff that you need it makes it a little easier. And if you keep that kind of stuff then at least you have something that they can look at, that they can go over. 'Cause if I didn't have all that stuff, then she wouldn't have been able to find the discrepancies.

Maryann told me that she learned from her lawyer the necessity of keeping and sharing documents so that he could handle her case better. Pete's explanation of why she must retain written records made sense to her. She came to see this as one of her obligations as a client and one of the ways in which she could participate on her own behalf.

> If I'm sloppy or something like as far as not knowing where my papers and stuff is—[Pete] gave me this big envelope [laughs] and was like writing on "must leave in this folder for lawyer," "this is lawyer and your stuff" and like, like I could put all that stuff in there you know. 'Cause you know sometimes you have to refer to it or whatever and, I can't be telling him my problem and then like, "Oh I don't know where the paper is."

Nancy, another client of Marjorie's in the consumer unit, noted that clients must do their part not only so that lawyers could build cases on paper, but also so that lawyers could successfully challenge authorities by proving a client's commitment to her own case.

> She said "Nancy, bring this in," I brought that in. . . . And that was a
> help, too. If I couldn't bring her information that she asked for, be in a
> certain place at a certain time, because we're going to go to court and talk
> to the judge and I'm representing you and they're going say, "Well, the
> client's not here." Next second, "Oh the client didn't come . . . oh the cli-
> ent's not here." How could she help me and keep explaining to the judge
> that my client's not here? When they say, "Oh that client's not interested."
> Set another date, set another date. No—every time we had to go to court
> or something like that I met her down there, she asked me to meet her.

Nancy contended that lawyers cannot convey client commitment to others if the client herself does not demonstrate such commitment. As noted below, Nancy refers to Marjorie as a "mediator" and sees having a lawyer as crucial to having her viewpoint heard. However, it is also clear from Nancy's designation of Marjorie as a mediator that she does not view Marjorie as *replacing* her in the eyes of the relevant authorities, recognizing rather that each of them has a distinct and important role to play in the process of representation.

Client collaboration and the notion of what the client's obligations consist of varied with the client's sense of her own capabilities as well as the subject matter. Carolyn and Erica sat on two ends of the spectrum. Both felt that they have certain obligations as clients. Carolyn viewed herself as a collaborator in the fullest sense.

> Suzanne gave me a couple of ideas for making copies. Then after, myself—I
>   wanted to have, always have copies of everything. I kept a log, a journal
>   of what happened on a certain day or anything that was to do with my
>   daughter. My daughter's schooling, uh, testing of any sort, and sometimes
>   that would, we would sort of watch each others' back with things. If I didn't
>   know something, you know, Suzanne could tell me or I could tell her.
>   'Cause we both kept notes. So it kind of worked hand-in-hand together.
> And do you think that, I hear from what you're saying, it made a difference
>   in court and with the judge. Do you think it made a difference in the way
>   that Suzanne related to you or in your relationship?

Carolyn: Oh definitely, yeah. 'Cause we were in a relaxed kind of, um, status with each other. Where it was open and we could talk about things. And um, flip different thoughts back and forth together until we agreed.

Both Carolyn and her lawyer, Suzanne, viewed Carolyn as a client who "functions well." Carolyn took an active and informed role in advocating for her daughter, and, unlike many of Suzanne's other clients, had no difficulties with mental health or mental retardation. This made the type and scope of collaboration with which she felt comfortable much different than what Erica, another of Suzanne's clients, saw as viable. Carolyn's and Suzanne's teamwork went well beyond compliance or even amassing paperwork. They "flipped ideas" back and forth, engaged in strategic discussions of Carolyn's case, and helped each other think about the best way to move forward. According to Carolyn, she and Suzanne functioned as two sets of eyes, ears, and minds attuned to the issue at hand, relying on one another to catch what the other might have missed.

Erica also saw Suzanne and herself as a team but presented a very different picture of what collaboration meant. Erica characterized her obligation as client as following Suzanne's instructions.

I'm her client, I got to be the best client, you know. We got to work together, like a team. And it is work.
Yeah. So what kind of things do you do, like from your end, you know, of the team?
Okay. Well, if I have a problem and she gives me advice, I either got to take that advice or to deal with it on my own. If I deal with it on my own, it blows up in my face; if I take her advice, everything goes smoothly. That's what I mean by being a team.

For Erica, the essence of collaboration was compliance. This does not seem to be collaborative except in the broadest sense of the term. Compliance, however, was no simple task for Erica, who was described by both herself and her lawyer as volatile, impulsive, and moody, and who also suffered with mental illness and limited functioning and coping skills. It is also important to understand that Erica and Suzanne were working together in the context of the family advocacy unit (as were Erica and Carolyn). This means that many of the requirements that Suzanne presented to Erica came in the form of inflexible demands ("hoops she has to jump through") set out by a variety of child welfare agencies as prerequisites to various milestones, like visits with her children.

Suzanne and Joanne, lawyers in the family advocacy unit, saw Erica as typical of clients in their unit. In the words of Joanne:

> We really deal, in this unit, with the very bottom of the barrel as far as self-sufficiency. There are no other clients at [NELS] who have lesser abilities than our clients do.
>
> In terms of?
>
> Everything. They can't figure out . . . I mean, I have clients who will tell me on a Friday that on Monday they have an appointment at the doctor and an appointment at the therapist at the same time. That they can't miss. "What have you done about that?" "Nothing." "Did you tell them, did you tell somebody when they were making the appointment that you already have another appointment at the same time?" "No." These are people who don't realize that they need to send an excuse in to school when their kid is home sick. And so their kid has a long list of unexcused absences that looks terrible in the court. All they needed to do was write up an excuse. They're also people who don't know how to write an excuse or don't—I mean they're the ones who didn't finish sixth grade and got educated in [Northeast City] public schools and therefore don't know how to read and write. Actually, you can finish twelfth grade and not know how to read and write in [Northeast City] public schools, and I've seen that! Those are the people that we're dealing with. The ones who just have very little ability to get along in the world as the rest of us know it. And so it's hard. And they're the ones that make just terrible choices. Just every time they're faced with a choice, they pick the wrong one.

Suzanne also found it hard to collaborate with her clients on strategic behavior that can greatly influence the outcome of their cases. She, too, characterized clients of the family advocacy unit, particularly those who struggle with mental illness, as generally possessing bad judgment.

> I do think it's probably unique about this unit, is that I think almost all our clients have bad judgment. I mean, it's really an unfortunate fact.
>
> Well, like what? About their kids?
>
> Well, it's like, maybe like bad social skills? I mean like bad judgment about like what's a good idea. Like sometimes it's just like not knowing, like not knowing how they should properly discipline their kids or not knowing

how they should interact with their kids, or you know. But sometimes it's just not . . . understanding when it's appropriate to fight. . . . Understanding, you know, like, a lot of my clients have a huge problem with this idea of like, you know, look, you've just got to kiss some butt. You know? I mean, if you kissed some butt, everything would make it a lot easier. And they just, they don't, they feel so beleaguered that they, that that is not an option that they want to do. . . . I try to have conversations sometimes with clients about picking their battles. And a lot of them just don't, they don't really get that. And they're much more focused on what's immediately in front of them. You know, and trying to talk to them about the long-term goal of like getting your kids back eventually. That means you're going to have to suck it up with this social worker or let [child welfare workers] in your house or do this or do that. Um, and they also have trust problems, they're like, "Well, if I do this, how do I know it's going to work so why should I even do it?"

Other lawyers confirmed Joanne and Suzanne's characterizations of the family advocacy unit clients as a group facing extreme difficulties. Even so, nearly all lawyers talked about clients who demonstrated a range of ability and willingness to collaborate.

While Joanne and Suzanne were careful not to ascribe fault to their clients (blaming the public school system, mental illness, their beleaguered state, and justifiable skepticism and mistrust), this does not change the fact that they found it hard to collaborate. Whatever their source, the hurdles outlined above work against strategic and long-term planning. They also inhibit candid discussions and therefore discourage a trusting relationship in which extensive collaboration is an option.

Lawyers felt that these problems stemmed more from the limited abilities of the clients than from the legal circumstances, and most found that cases benefit from client collaboration even where opportunities for input are limited. Martin, a lawyer in the public housing unit, emphasized that even collaboration that is narrowly restricted by circumstances (as with Erica) can involve difficult decisions. In talking about Denise, a client whom he referred for this study, Martin noted her courage in making a very difficult decision that allowed her and a younger child to remain in subsidized housing.

A lot of times when people come to see us, they are obviously having some kind of a problem and the resolution of that problem frequently will require them to change in part their conduct and it's the clients who are the best at doing that in my opinion get the best legal results. And some of the things that we have to tell our clients are really very bad news and very hard for them to do. I mean, in Denise Hanson['s case] she had already done it in part but what I had to tell her was the only way you're going to get back on Section 8 is to make sure that your son never lives with you again. Not a message I like to deliver and not an easy thing for a mother to do for her son. But that was what she had to do. The clients who are less able to carry out and discipline themselves and do the kind of things that they need to do are the ones that get the poorer legal results.

Martin characterized Denise's ability to think through and carry out a difficult decision as the mark of a client who was not only capable and determined but one who also met her obligations for a successful outcome that she herself set. Martin further recognized that the legal work or advice that was his part of the team effort to keep Denise and her daughter housed paled in comparison to Denise's part of distancing herself from her son.

Lawyers and Legal Knowledge as Leverage

Clients recognized that lawyers had more leverage than they do, by virtue of their professional skills and their status. Justin explained how he collaborated with Pete to secure health benefits for his daughter. Justin felt that his own knowledge of the issues was helpful to Pete, saving him time and work. He consciously and strategically leveraged Pete's expertise in working with the system because he believed that the authorities would listen to Pete. In contrast, he was often dismissed because he was an immigrant, despite his knowledge of the relevant laws and procedures.

> Yes. It's very easy because I learned many things about the public benefits law so I can keep in touch very close, we can understand each other.
> So when you were, when you called Pete, what were you hoping that he could do for you?
> Well, I was sure that everything will be smoother because, you know, I am an outsider in this country even I am a lawful permanent resident here. Well, the person in charge like Pete will be better if he handles some things in this case, you know what I mean? To say that I'm nothing to the government people. As a newcomer maybe, maybe they will underestimate.

Claire, a client of the consumer advocacy unit, consistently referred to her lawyer, Marjorie, as a mediator. She said that without Marjorie neither the agency she challenged nor the court would listen to her. After Claire explained how she had been a conscientious client by fulfilling her responsibilities such as following instructions, procuring documents, and appearing in court on time, I asked her if she thought that she and Marjorie had worked as a team:

> Well, naturally she did it all. I wouldn't have known, uh, what do you call it? The *chain of command*. You know, I couldn't go to the judge and say, "Please judge your honor could you do this for me." The chain of command was my representative, my lawyer, my mediator. So she did a lot of work, too, as well. And found out things where she can get information through, "Hello, my name is Marjorie Donald, esquire." Like they wasn't going to talk to me.

Claire believed that even if she acquired the knowledge and could take the actions learned from her lawyer, the agency and the court system she dealt with would not respond to her because she is not a lawyer. As discussed at length in chapter 4, clients unequivocally testified to the importance of a good lawyer in a system that some viewed as arbitrary and others viewed as responsive only to those with competent representation. This can severely limit the scope and effectiveness of client collaboration.

Clients also gained practical skills from their encounters with lawyers, even if only learning when and how to use lawyers as an informational resource or for leverage. Denise felt that working with Martin has helped her cope with other problems:

> I'm trying, my nerves have been so bad. It's just so bad. But it's getting stronger now, 'cause you see now I'm knowing how to deal with them. Without getting angry, you know, I do, it's just go to the source, I'll just find out what's going on, when they send me letters I keep all my documents, you understand what I'm saying? Then I go find me a legal aid lawyer. And then the lawyer will deal with that. For real. It's, I mean, it's we'll be working together, you know, I ain't going to put all the work on them, but they be doing basically the work theirselves. But I still have to do my part, you know. I don't even get upset and uptight no more like I used to, because I was like on pins. I was on pins and needles, I didn't know which way I was going or coming.

Although learning when and how to use a lawyer may appear insignificant when compared to some ideal notion of collaboration, Denise certainly perceived her experience as significant in terms of her ability to manage stress, handle documents, deal with her public agencies, and enlist relevant aid.

Clients came through their experiences feeling better able to demand and receive service. After working with lawyers at NELS, some said they became more willing to challenge government offices without fear of recrimination. When I asked Maryann, who was active in a welfare rights organization, whether she was ever nervous about appealing or challenging the decisions of the welfare office, she responded:

> Not actually. No, because, because I know I had [Pete]. And then I know, like my organization does a lot of this, like looking this stuff up and we know our rights. So I know from the time they try to BS me, you know what I mean? I'd be like "that's BS" [laughs]. "I'm calling my lawyer," you know. Especially if they try to say you can't appeal.

Lorna contrasted her lack of knowledge in a previous situation with her confidence in making demands on the Social Security Administration after she began working with Steve:

> Well, I was like, you know, "This decision; I'm not satisfied with it." She didn't say well you have the right to appeal. I didn't even think about appeal at that time, I just, you know, "This isn't right, this can't be." But never did I get any paperwork that says you have the right to appeal this decision, here's how you appeal it, until after Steve got involved. Then, of course, they kept everything totally legal because they had no other choice. I mean, even today when I went, the woman said, "Oh your lawyer's not with you?" I said, "No, there's no need for him to be here. Unless of course you're going to try to aggravate me again" [laughs]. Yes I did, I didn't care.

It is not my intention to suggest that clients and/or lawyers learn to view these institutions as any less capricious or mean-spirited. I asked lawyers whether they thought that their intervention led clients to view the legal system or government agencies more favorably. Most hoped that it did not have this effect because they believed that these institutions are fundamentally inimical to the interests of poor people. As noted above in the section discussing autonomy, these institutions also remain intimidating, incomprehensible, and unresponsive to unrepresented people. Nevertheless, many clients were galvanized by their experience. While most clients did not speak of engaging in large-scale political or social action, many spoke of referring others to legal services or speaking publicly about problems which they had previously concealed. For many, this meant going beyond initial feelings of embarrassment or self-condemnation to an understanding of their problem as widespread or having a broader social context.

Counteracting Mistreatment

Lawyer-client interactions can be a significant counter-action to the demeaning experiences that clients have with the bureaucracies. When asked about her view of the law after her experience with the Local Public Housing Authority (LPHA), Denise complained about:

> How they talk to you, how they look at you, how they look down at you. You know, and I'm like, "Well why is you talking to me like that?" I said, "I'm human just like you are. . . . You want me to respect you, you got to respect me, too." I said, "If we didn't come into this office you all wouldn't get paid!" . . . I just can't understand. . . . They are very nasty.

Lawyers concurred with this assessment, and for many, like Steve, it underscored the importance of treating clients with respect and dignity:

> Typically our clients' interactions with the system are negative. The people are mean to them, bureaucrats are mean to them, they always get told no, and they're treated rudely and nastily. So I think it's extremely important that we . . . are respectful to our clients. And I think that's incredibly important because I think what, one of the worst things I think is that happens to poor people is they're dehumanized. And if I can treat my clients respectfully, that is not as important as winning their case, but it's pretty damn important.

In addition to the ethical imperative, treating clients with respect may also have broader political significance. According to political learning theory, bureaucracies teach citizens lessons about agency and their ability to influence the political process. In Joe Soss's (1999) research with beneficiaries of two different government benefit programs, Aid for Families with

Dependent Children and Social Security Disability Insurance,[7] he found that participants in welfare programs who were treated disrespectfully and arbitrarily had lower estimations of their ability to influence agencies and effect any kind of political or systemic change. These individuals were less likely to challenge caseworkers or lodge complaints and were less active politically as measured by voting behavior. To the extent that clients in this study perceived agencies as responsive to their claims after securing the assistance of an attorney, their experiences with NELS's attorneys may mitigate the lessons taught by capricious, unresponsive, or disrespectful agencies.

Creating and Sustaining Shared Meanings of (In)Justice

As discussed above, lawyers and clients were skeptical about the power of legal encounters to bring about systemic change or to "transform" or "empower" clients in a way that would obviate their need for lawyers. It would be incorrect to conclude that clients were passive, did not collaborate, or did not learn. Given the stressors in most clients' lives, initiating and maintaining the lawyer-client relationship demonstrates strong motivation, resourcefulness, and engagement. While some clients were referred to NELS by caseworkers or other professionals, many exerted significant effort in finding NELS and following through on their cases. Denise only heard of NELS after she went to her city council representative's office at City Hall and was then personally escorted to NELS by one of the secretaries in the office.

> I'm on Section 8 [housing], okay? And it got back to Section 8 and without them even coming to me asking me any questions they took the word of the other tenant [that her son engaged in violent behavior]! You know, and I'm like "how can they take her word when you all haven't even heard my side of it?" "Well it doesn't matter." I said, "No, it doesn't work like that." So that's when I went to [a City Council staff member]. I went to, I did, I use all my resources, all my, the ones that I put into office, that I vote for, I went to them trying to find out what can I do with this affair's going on. They was like, "Well they can't do that." Everybody kind of said, "They can't do it, they can't do—." But I had little short time to stay where I was at before I was put out so I'm like: "Well somebody has to do something." So that's why I went to [Councilmember] in City Hall and I spoke with one of his secretaries and she, she walked me over to Mr. Reynolds's office.

Other clients, like Denise, told of tapping into any organization that they could think of, explaining that they were not sure that NELS could help but that they were not going to give up until they had tried everything.

On an even more basic level, the clients who initiated contact with NELS showed an understanding that their problems might be legal problems, although for some this was a "shot in the dark." What William Felstiner, Rick Abel, and Austin Sarat refer to as "naming, blaming and claiming" is the transformation of troubles into legal problems, a socially constructed process that is far from obvious or inevitable. To use these terms, it was usually only clients who had already "named" ("perceived an injurious experience") and "blamed" ("attributed responsibility for that grievance") who went to NELS to assist them with "claiming" ("voic[ing] that grievance to the person or entity believed to be responsible and ask[ing] for a remedy").[8]

Many clients spoke of friends or family members who experienced similar problems but who did not take any steps to respond to them, despite urging, and as a result "allowed themselves" to lose a home or eligibility for desperately needed benefits. Clients who initiated contact with NELS already had some hope or expectation that NELS might be willing and able to assist them. This was in contrast to friends or relatives with similar problems who may have "named" and "blamed" but despaired of "claiming" due to a perception that this would be fruitless. Nancy told of what happened to a family member whom she had tried to convince to come to NELS for assistance:

I know a personal fr- well, a relative. I told this relative about what this person is doing for me. I said go to these people, if she helped me she can help you if you are in a similar situation rather than lose your house, and they lost their house! Yes they did. Lost their house, all that money they put into it and everything, they lost their house. And then I was—I said don't even, I don't want to hear it because I told you what to do, told you who to go to. Even if you talked to her and she gave you some type of information, a lot of people don't act out on things that they, information that is given to them. Information was given to me, I acted on it. I gave the information, spread the good news and the good word to someone else and they just didn't act on it. And then when they, the man go and knock on the door [knocks twice] and say the truck is outside, then they want to—"What did you say the woman's name was?" [imitates with derision]. Please. It's too late at that point.

And I can't feel empathy for you because, but sympathy at that point. Because I tried.

As Nancy's critique illustrates, NELS's clients as a group might from the outset have a greater sense of their ability to challenge the systems they encounter. Whether or not this is the case prior to representation, their encounters with lawyers reinforce clients' notions that government agencies should be accountable for their treatment of clients as well as for the assistance they are obliged to provide.

Even though most clients initiating contact with NELS may have named and blamed, their claims or attribution of responsibility were often tenuous or intertwined with a conflicting sense of personal responsibility. Their ambivalence was reflected in Lorna's apparently contradictory assessments of poor people like herself. Lorna was sympathetic to people whom she saw as compelled to break the rules due to the sheer impossibility of living on the paltry benefits of a stingy welfare state:

> Well when you're poor, you know what? You kind of know you have to find a way to make ends meet. You have to find a way to get your needs met. And you tend to be one of these survivors. One, usually when you're on public assistance, 90 percent of people on public assistance have been low-income their whole life. So they learn to manage a budget real close and know how to fight the system to get everything and anything. And sometimes the fight is hard. And sometimes you literally have to lie to get your needs met. Be really resourceful, we will find a way to get what we need. And it's sad that we have to go to the extremes sometimes. But it's good to know that people are still willing to fight for everything they need.

In apparent contradiction, Lorna more harshly judged beneficiaries whom she had earlier admitted were compelled by their circumstances to be rule-breakers in order to survive. She was hesitant to speak to her lawyer Steve about what to do with the proceeds from the possible sale of her home because she feared that he would see her as "one of those people" trying to "get over on" the system. Despite her concern, she consulted with Steve largely because she trusted him as someone who would not prejudge her or be suspicious. Her narrative reveals her attempts to distance herself from people who cheat the system.

I just decided that he was open enough and honest enough and very caring with me that he would see me as who I was and that my fears weren't really rational. That he would see me as somebody trying to mess with the system. Because a lot of people do. You know, they do. I have friends that are still getting over on the system and I'm like "you're the reason I'm still fighting so hard" [laughs]. But I don't say that to people's face, I'm not—but at the same time I do get mad at the abusers of the system because they have made it difficult for me to get what I need. And I blame that for the reason that I've had to fight so hard to keep my medical benefits. It's that there's so many people out there abusing the system that there's not enough services for those who truly need them.

Many clients took pains to explain that they are "deserving" or "faultless" (and that their lawyers saw them this way, too). Some of the clients' apparently contradictory assessments regarding their own and others' deservingness can of course be attributed to social desirability bias, that is, the desire to appear more positive or put forth attitudes that participants perceive are socially acceptable or would please the researcher. It might also be clients' assessment of a variety of people, some rule breakers and some (like themselves) deserving claimants.[9] The prevalence of client worthiness narratives indicates that there is more to them than a generalized desire for social acceptance in the interview context. Clients are aware of societal perceptions that valorize personal responsibility while ignoring the force of circumstances, attributing the problems of the poor largely to their own faults.[10] Clients' experiences with hostile and suspicious bureaucracies reinforce negative perceptions of poor people, making it all the more important for them to distinguish themselves from the stigmatized, "undeserving" poor. Like Lorna, even as clients understand themselves and others who are similarly situated as victims of an unjust or capricious system, they are careful to point out their own virtues, and in some cases, distance themselves from "troublemakers." Many clients explained that they were "good": they were wronged and not at fault; they secured documents; they were organized; they followed their lawyer's instructions; they did not cheat the system, despite the opportunity to do so.

Lawyers often shored up a client's conception that even "deserving" individuals can be wronged by institutions or agencies and provided hope for recourse. In this way, clients and lawyers collaborate to produce and legitimate legal claims. Lawyers reassure clients that they were indeed wronged. In cases where clients may have no legal recourse, or where the benefits they will eventually receive or recoup are paltry, lawyers commiserate with clients by agreeing that the benefits are meager, that the system is unjust, and that the rules are punitive and intrusive. In this way, lawyers may help to shape emerging or existing political consciousness.

Individual Clients, Systemic Challenges, and Community Work

Client-lawyer collaborations that produce and reinforce political consciousness for both lawyers and clients may also result in expanding individual claims to include more general or systemic indictments, even if their claims are unsuccessful in the courts.[11] Many clients come to NELS with problems they believe to be unique. Some put off seeking assistance due to embarrassment. Clients were often surprised and indignant to discover that others experienced similar difficulties. Not only did this knowledge lend support to their claims, but it also shifted their perception of the root of the problem. Martha, a client working with Martin in the public housing unit, did not know that her complaint against the manager of the public housing in which she lived was one of many until she came to NELS and her lawyer told her about a number of infractions against other tenants. I asked Martha about her decision to be a named plaintiff in a class action suit:

> I saw the advantage of pursuing. He asked me did I mind being a part of a class action suit? I have no problem with that. Because something has to be done about where we live. And I told him it would be fine and he told me my name would appear, and that was fine with me. And like I said, he didn't make the decision for me, he asked me. You know, would I consent? It wasn't like he was bullying me or pushing me or urging me. He just laid out the facts, told me what was happening, and would I like to participate? See, because I could have very well said well, I got what I want, the heck with everybody else. But as it stands, what could happen, I could get the recourse that I have now, but who's to say they won't come up with something else later? Because they had a lot of infraction down there.

Shoring up confidence in this way also encouraged clients to take on and sustain more active community roles, as in the case of Justin, who assisted refugees from his country. He gained this knowledge through his own experiences and by collecting information from government offices and the

Internet, calling lawyers for supplemental information or steering others to legal services and pro bono lawyers when necessary. While clients still remained dependent on lawyers in many instances, many were better able to know when and how to enlist their services and feel more confident that they could challenge recalcitrant institutions with the assistance or information provided by a lawyer.

Ben charted a similar process from the perspective of a lawyer. He described the evolution of his understanding of the way in which lawyers can learn of problems from clients and then, through outreach, create a public perception of the problem. This reinforces its recognition as a legal problem which can in turn drive demand for legal services. Ben's example of how NELS became involved in transforming the understanding of student loan scams is worth citing at length.

> For the most part, the clients have always been, you know, my share of the people who walk in the door. I mean, we have been largely a demand-driven program, which is not to say we're sort of passive 'cause actually one of the things I've learned is part of our job is how to identify issues and get the word out there. I mean, a lot of people, particularly the poor, don't recognize problems that they have as legal problems. I mean, if you get a lawsuit in the mail, okay, you have a legal problem. . . . In the early '90s the big issue was fraudulent trade schools and the student loan obligations of people who were being left with—not only they didn't get a job, but now they got [a] student loan [that] is going to haunt them for the rest of their lives. . . . We started getting people coming in describing this horrendous story, and a lot of it's very heartbreaking. . . . Someone without a high school diploma on welfare, they're on line at the welfare office and somebody gives them a flier that they can get a job and they go and it's this trade school, and the recruiter has them. . . . "Oh, you can become a medical assistant, try on this, try on this" and you know this white jacket and stethoscope. "How does that feel?" "That feels great, but how can-?" "Oh you can, you can, I can tell, you know here's a test, oh man, you're the best." And it's all just a scam to get the student to get the Pell Grant and the student loan money from that, off of that person and then just throw them out the door.

What Ben described was the trickling in of clients with information and stories; some were in a state of despair and requested some kind of help, but did not necessarily view their problems as legal. The individual stories touched the legal services workers upon hearing them, and they were then moved to find a legal remedy. NELS was motivated to address this area due to the sense that this problem was widespread and its true scope might only become clear through outreach on the part of NELS and community groups that would elicit client reporting of the problem. Ben also described how information gleaned from individual clients provided opportunities for moral entrepreneurship, which is the process of "mobilizing constituencies and developing network relations that reinforce and institutionalize their moral beliefs."[12] Ben's investigation of the problem, and NELS's decision to make student loans a priority, led NELS to devote resources to individual cases as well as to systemic work.

> Well, we heard a number of these stories and it's just heartbreaking and "God, we got to do something." At the same time, it was kind of happening in other parts of the country and you kind of get in these networks and you start figuring out things to do and start filing some lawsuits. A lot of times I'll file a lawsuit just to try to understand something. I know that it's a wider problem but I'll file a lawsuit and take depositions and dig into it and use it as an oppor- it's like research, almost. . . . I'm going to learn how are they doing this, why are they doing this, how many people are they doing this to. You do a couple of those cases and then you start realizing this is a huge problem and then you start getting reporters interested and you start giving speeches in the community and you start getting the word out and then what happens is a lot of people that have been victimized say "Oh my God, there's someone doing something about it and also it's not just me, I'm not like a bad person, I was wallowing in my sort of self-pity and, you know, I was just so ashamed of having been suckered that I didn't think that there are all these other people getting suckered and in fact there's this office that's trying to do something about it." Then you start getting a flood of people with student loans. So, you know, I believe that you can't be completely passive in what's coming in the door that you have to sort of play a role in almost legitimizing certain issues as legal issues and getting the word out.

Scholars have underscored the paternalism in moral entrepreneurship, in which elites often exert top-down influence.[13] Such tendencies, when they are top-down rather than constituent-informed, can be more moralistic than moral.[14] Lawyers like Ben combat such hierarchical tendencies by seeking client input, when possible. However, mechanisms for organized client input are few and likely biased to perpetuate lawyer-driven interests. For example, NELS has community representatives on its board. These are often recruited by NELS's staff members, and thus are more likely to be clients who lawyers already identify with. Another source of constituent input for NELS's moral entrepreneurship is what individual clients bring in to NELS. In the example that Ben provided, he viewed the aggregation of client concerns as the driving force for his work. He felt strongly about retaining a collaborative lawyer-client relationship to inform which problems NELS will address and how, even in its collective actions and organizational decisions.[15] Arthur, a lawyer who worked at NELS for over 20 years, explained:

> Unlike some public interest organizations, there is that constant flow of clients coming through the door. And that is keeping lawyers and paralegals acutely aware of the problems, the patterns and to the extent that legislation or litigation or administrative action is being taken it is informed by that flow of people that never is ending and it is not off in an ivory tower, it is not off totally unconnected or disconnected from the actual needs of poor people.

Another way in which NELS seeks collaboration with constituents is in its relationships with grassroots, community-based organizations. About half of the lawyers interviewed mentioned working closely with grassroots organizations in a way that helped shaped their legal work. Examples mentioned included assisting individual constituents, testifying in public hearings, providing legal advice, education, and outreach, and, as in the example provided by Martin, mounting litigation with them:

> We represent [a public housing tenants group—PTG], so for example in the early '90s [LPHA] had a huge vacancy rate. They admitted to at least 25 percent of their units being vacant and needing repair; we suspected it was more like 30 or 35 percent, which is a real crime. It's a waste of public money, people needed housing, the waiting list was years and years long and they weren't even adding people to the waiting list because it was so long. So in conjunction with [PTG] we brought a class action against the [LPHA] and HUD which really did, was very effective in terms of freeing up money and getting rehabilitation done and whatever work is being done now.

Martin explained that the relationship between the housing unit and PTG was ongoing: "If they perceive a problem, they call us and ask us to get involved, and if we perceive a problem and we think that they're a useful vehicle, then we call them, so it's a pretty wide open relationship."

Later in our conversation, Martin described some of the risks of collaboration with constituent groups. It can pressure lawyers and public interest organizations to limit the scope of work and it also may be at odds with the needs of individual clients or competing client groups or organizations.[16]

> Our public housing tenants, at least the resident councils that we represent, asked us not to undertake to represent anybody who's being evicted from [LPHA] based upon allegations of drug activity. So we respected that request and we don't represent those people. We refer them to [two other Northeast City organizations]. . . . So you know our clients have conflicting interests on this one, you know we don't want to see individual tenants put out, especially ones who really had no control over what was going on but by the same token our other clients are saying, "Listen—drugs, drug activity is a real problem in my development and I don't want you to do anything to make that any easier for drug actors to be there."

Martin went on to explain that he is troubled by such conflicts, but feels more comfortable acquiescing to the requests of NELS's partners knowing that people turned away because of this policy can find representation elsewhere. Sustained collaboration comes at a price; individual lawyers and NELS as an organization have to weigh the extent to which they will compromise and collaborate when the needs of individuals or partner organizations raise such requests.

Conclusion: Situated Collaboration

The mutually reinforcing process of creating a legal narrative with clients and with client groups is important for a number of reasons. First, as suggested by literature on ethnographic techniques that focus on narrative, the act of communicating a story that may have remained hidden because it is embarrassing or seems unimportant to a receptive audience can be in and of itself validating and cathartic.[17] Further, it can enhance a client's and lawyer's understanding of the problem through the perspective gained in discussion and mutual discovery.

Beyond these more personal benefits to clients, the examples provided by Martin, Ben, and Martha point to the attendant political ramifications of creating shared narratives of legal responsibility. The individual who is given an opportunity to express her experience to a competent and caring professional "comes to perceive similarities between privatized experiences and those of some larger entity."[18] Working with a sympathetic lawyer clarifies the link between what the individual sees as a private problem and a large systemic problem.[19] Besides the potential material and therapeutic benefits, once transformed into a legal issue, clients and lawyers assert the validity of their claims in the legal and political institutions where these experiences are given meaning. Not only does this validate clients' sense of having been wronged, but it also challenges the legal system to recognize their claims as legal grievances rather than as personal failures. Further, collaboration around legal work provides NELS with the opportunity to engage in conversations, informed by community input, about what problems to address and how.

One of the contributions of sociolegal scholars is their investigation of the role of the law outside of legal institutions, including its political and social impact. In his book on the role of law and rights in the pay equity movement, Michael McCann notes the importance of the law's "constitutive and strategic dimensions of most social movements. Indeed, the very emphasis on the indirect effects of formal legal action suggests that it is a limited and often secondary component of a larger multi-dimensional political campaign."[20] McCann's study shows that laws designed to bring about social change and conceptions of rights may be most beneficial outside of classical legal arenas. They influence the way people interact, including how they think and talk about entitlement. Workers use the language of rights and the law to make claims for pay equity in the workplace and in the public sphere. While claims may or may not be successful in courts (if they even make it to a court), mobilizing the language and the imprimatur of the law is often a successful tool for motivating self-interested constituents and gaining support from bystanders. The law can also shore up a sense of the right-ness of claims, and in some cases can do its work without having to invoke legal authorities. While few individuals have brought suit under the Americans with Disabilities Act, its enactment prompted many employers and employees to act differently. In their study of people with disabilities, David Engel and Frank Munger show how, despite limited use of potential legal remedies, the Act has perhaps been more significant in changing the way that individuals with disabilities and others perceive their mutual obligations.[21] These studies show how the law and legal tools shape our identities, consciousness, and the way we perceive our relationships with others and with the state.

In this study, clients' and lawyers' collaboration to shape client griev-ances as legal problems has similar political import, regardless of the sta-tus of their claims in traditional legal arenas. Valerie is a former union activist in her seventies and is a client of the consumer advocacy unit. Although she and her lawyer had taken no legal action as of yet, once she learned that she might have been the victim of illegal lending prac-tices rather than her own erroneous judgment, she was motivated to act. Once Valerie re-characterized her problem together with her lawyer, she saw it as systemic and a legitimate target for educational and political action. She had been interviewed about predatory lending by newspa-pers and appeared on television. Valerie has spoken about it with poli-cymakers and political groups such as Northeast City Council members and state representatives. She told me that she intended to speak out nationally, planning to attend a conference in Washington, DC. Valerie explained that she had taken on a role locally and statewide in speaking out about her experience with predatory lending because "The lawyers can't get out there and do it by themselves. They need help. I'm a helper [laughs]."

Although lawyers can do legal work, broad-based advocacy requires that clients speak for themselves and for other clients in similar situa-tions. Not only does client activism help to "sell" policy changes to legisla-tures and administrative agencies, but it can also encourage other people to come forth with problems they believed to be merely their own. Once people recognize their problem as something shared and, as such, sys-temic, they often lose some of the embarrassment that comes with a sense of personal failure. Valerie emphasized that this was another reason she has spoken out. Since her decision she had been approached by friends and neighbors who confided that they, too, are or were victims of preda-tory lending—and she directed many of these people to NELS.

[A reporter] asked me would I talk to the neighbors about [my experi-ence with a predatory loan]. And I knew every one of the families. I told him no. And the reason was because the first time I would go to some-body and tell them, "Hey, I know you were caught up in this stuff" and try to talk to them, then the first thing [they would say is], "How do you know about my business?" It's that people are private. Because like me, I was ashamed in the beginning . . . and I said "Well, I don't let nobody know that I'm all mixed up in this." You know? Until I thought about it and I said well this is your opportunity to speak on it so nobody, other people don't be caught up in it. So this is the reason why I start getting out there talking about it.

Valerie's advocacy efforts have helped lawyers, activists, and the media uncover the scope of predatory lending in Northeast City and elsewhere, to reach out to those who need assistance, and to put a face on the problem. This contributes to "selling" predatory lending as a problem that should be addressed by policymakers on the local, state, and national levels, rather than one that is left to individuals to cope with privately.

Like other forms of collaboration, the process of transforming an individual sense of wrongdoing into a legal claim is a joint enterprise shared by lawyers and clients and created out of the personal and legal material and frameworks with which they work. In all aspects of collaboration discussed in this chapter, clients' roles and lawyers' roles are not interchangeable. Each partner brings different knowledge and a different set of skills. The experiences of lawyers and clients demonstrate clearly that both are necessary components of the working relationship and are mutually reinforcing. The essence of collaboration is to draw on the skills and strengths of each collaborator in ways that not only enhance the "product" of the collaborative work but also strengthen the individuals engaged in the process.

6

Lawyer and Client: Face to Face

Well, it's certainly the lifeblood of the work. The reason you get out of bed in the morning is because of the clients. And it's the reason that I wouldn't trade my job for lots of other jobs that, you know, are available to people who graduate from law school . . . the everyday workaday kind of thing with the clients certainly acts as an inspiration.   —Jeff, a lawyer who works with elderly clients

Something happened and Jules, my oldest daughter, wasn't able to come here and I was crying. I was upset. And I called Suzanne, you know? 'Cause my reflex was not to call, and cuss them out. I go call Suzanne. She said, "Please Erica, you got to calm down. I understand how you feel. If you want me to I can get a court order." You know? She just calmed me down. She's like a friend.
—Erica, a client working with Suzanne in the family advocacy unit

Progressive lawyering literature stresses the importance of focusing on clients. The basis for client-centeredness is respect for clients, client autonomy, and decision making. Legal services lawyers and clients in this study reveal a complex foundation for a practice centered on the individual client: the often transformative nature of the client-lawyer relationship for both client and lawyer. This takes place when lawyer and client open themselves to each other, even within the limited context of their legal services relationship. Beyond the material assistance clients seek from NELS, empathy, respect, and a feeling of connection are deeply powerful and affirming for people who feel ignored, judged, or even abused by a host of legal and other government bureaucracies. While relationships with clients can be difficult, for these lawyers they are also a source of inspiration, challenge, and enjoyment. They provide feedback for the work that lawyers do in systems both clients and lawyers see as impervious to change.

Direct Representation

NELS is devoted to direct representation. This means that the bulk of its work involves client contact. Marcia enjoys contact with clients. She saw this as a temperamental preference rather than a value.

> I really actually like having individual clients and I know that there are people who don't. And so they're doing a class action and don't actually see their client hardly ever because it's an abortion provider—whatever— it doesn't bother them. Well, that's just kind of not how I feel. I really like meeting my clients; getting to know them.

Steve confessed that his enjoyment of contact with clients was due at least in part to his voyeuristic tendencies.

> At some point I determined that it was important to me to have individual clients. I mean, part of me still, I mean, I think I have this sort of ideal that yes, I'd like to be sitting in an office doing impact work, but I know myself better now. I always want to have clients. Because clients are fun. Part of it is selfish. I mean, I suspect there's some voyeuristic aspects to it in a sense that, you know, it's horrible, but hearing clients' lives and the stories is like—"Oh my God!" [laughs]

Steve found the difficult lives of his clients compelling. For him, as for Jeff, the complex problems that clients brought to his legal practice also provided him with exciting professional challenges. As Jeff said of the diverse problems his clients brought:

> When you're on intake, you have to get ready for just about anything to walk in the door or to call on your telephone. And that's sort of, it's that sense of, you know, there are lots of people out there that, you know, from all different kind of crazy backgrounds and stories and lives that are going to possibly walk into my office today and sit down and, you know, try to work through a problem with me. And so that's exciting and it's satisfying and it's probably why I'm here. [laughs]

Suzanne was also drawn to individual work because she discovered unexpectedly that she enjoys connecting with her clients "as people" rather than the legal problems they present. Involvement with the intimate details of clients' lives was particularly deep in the family advocacy unit due to the nature of the work: to help parents who have become involved in child welfare cases as a result of alleged child abuse or neglect.

> I also didn't think that I wanted to do family law . . . [W]hen NELS came to me and said well we have these two projects . . . and I was just like "ummmmmm [points arbitrarily] family law?" [laughs]. But it turns out . . . to be a really good fit for me because you're really dealing with the people, and their problems aren't separated from their legal problems. I mean, their problems are that their family is not working. . . . That's their legal problem and that's their personal problem.

Suzanne's fascination was fed not only by her admitted curiosity but also by her interest in relationships and her desire to get to know the client and possibly make "a difference." She tended to visit the homes of her clients, not only to get a feel for what child protective services workers might see, but also to enhance her relationships with those she represents.

> Part of me's just nosy, I mean, part of me I think is like a frustrated psychologist or social worker and like just seeing how people construct their lives and . . . getting to know people and getting a sense of what their social networks are and what their life is day-to-day is . . . really fascinating to me. And sometimes . . . I feel like I form some bonds. And it's limited 'cause I'm their lawyer. . . . And you know I like all of that. I mean sometimes there's a feeling that maybe I have made somewhat of a difference, but . . . you know, it's in little ways, it's not huge.

All of Suzanne's clients whom I interviewed described a connection with her that went beyond the professional. Carolyn explained that Suzanne not only represented her in hearings but also came to school meetings and home visits. She characterized their relationship as having a personal dimension, and she was particularly grateful to Suzanne for reaching out to her daughter, who was diagnosed with mild mental retardation and is very shy.

> Sometimes [Suzanne showed] just a little bit of empathy and sympathy. . . . And she also showed a friendship. It wasn't as much as like a

client . . . type of deal. We were close. We were on a friendly-term basis. And she understood what I wanted. And, um, we would get together
and one of the main things I found that is really great that she did, is
my daughter's very, um, at times can be very shy. And she is, um, MR,
mildly. And what she did was she gave her a booklet and explained all
about court. She took her on a trip around the courtroom one day and
she showed her how it doesn't have to be scary. And I think that was a really great thing. Because that really took the pressure off my daughter and
allowed her to be able to speak without fearing things.

The interest that a lawyer shows in a client can be an important dimension of the relationship. Suzanne's interest was helpful for Carolyn's case,
as it put her daughter at ease before testifying. Carolyn also appreciated
the caring and the investment in her family that Suzanne's involvement
conveyed.

Becoming a Client

For many clients, being accepted for representation by NELS was an
accomplishment. Not all clients need representation and for some, brief
advice can satisfy their needs. A supervising attorney at the branch office
noted it was difficult to ascertain the percentage of clients that NELS accepts, largely because it is not clear what it means to be accepted as a client. More specifically, she noted that while the consumer unit, for example, gives advice "on all mortgage foreclosures," they only represent about
10 percent of the clients.[1] It is likely that some proportion of clients who
are offered brief advice or referred elsewhere would prefer having their
cases accepted for more comprehensive representation. Cecilia, a new client in the consumer unit at the time of her interview, was discouraged by
her initial meeting with a NELS intake worker and one of the other lawyers in the unit.

> I had went to legal aid and at first I was like dissatisfied, distraught. I had
> one interview and it didn't sound real good at all. . . . Especially when
> they said they didn't even know whether they were going to take my case.
> I didn't know that that was a procedure they had, that they have a meet-
> ing and then they decide whether they will even accept you. . . . As far as
> I was concerned, they took every case.

Although Cecilia admitted her own lack of preparedness, she felt that the intake workers' treatment of her was unnecessarily harsh, likening it to her experience at the welfare office.

> I felt that they wasn't maybe as sympathetic as they could have been. I never been there before. I didn't know; she act like I was supposed to know what to bring. The first time, I didn't. And they didn't tell me. . . . I said, "They ain't going to never pick up my case." I came home really down. And, 'cause things was getting to the gun and I procrastinating, kind of drag my foot. And so I was like, they ain't going to help me, I don't have time to fool with this." Saying to myself. I said, "Oh, they ain't nothing but like the welfare office, you ain't nothing but another number."

While very few clients talked about hurdles and lack of sympathy as Cecilia did, her case is instructive because it highlights how the existence of a screening or selection process brings home to people that they are lucky to achieve client status. Other clients told me how they "lucked out" in receiving the lawyer that they did.

As Cecilia suggested, clients often do not know what papers to bring, nor are they familiar with the procedures governing intake. For many, their "selection" was a mystery. In Cecilia's case, the intake worker did explain to her that decisions to accept cases are made at Thursday unit meetings, although the basis for those decisions was not clear to Cecilia, nor was the timeframe. Cecilia remembered that the intake worker had assured her that if NELS could not take her case she would be told where else she might be able to receive assistance, but it was not clear to Cecilia that a referral would help save her home.

Cecilia was surprised when she received a letter from Ben several weeks after her intake interview indicating that he was taking her case. His letter (which Cecilia has kept) and her first meeting with him brought a flood of relief, coming at a time when the legal action against her was intensifying and her situation was becoming desperate. She had begun to seek private assistance that she could not afford as a low-income, single mother of two.

> So I really had gave up on them. I was going to try to struggle and put all my checks together and try to get me a personal lawyer and I got a letter from . . . Ben Silberman one day and it said, "I've decided to take your case,

please get in touch with me." . . . The day his letter came, I had got a letter from the sheriff's sale the day before stating some type of stuff and I was like. . . . And I called him, we set up an appointment . . . I was sitting there crying in his office. You know how stuff just come down on you? And everything, stress and everything. . . . So he's working on my case now, he's my lawyer. He wrote up all the necessary papers to send out to stop the judgment. So I'm really pleased.

Clients and lawyers indicated that stress relief begins in the first encounter. This may be due to the acceptance of the client's case, which may create the expectation that problems will be resolved. Most clients did not discuss the application process but focused on the quality of initial encounters with their lawyers. They identified these first meetings as helping to alleviate stress even if they were uncertain whether their case would ultimately be resolved. The aspects of lawyer-client encounters that bring relief seem to be characterized by a client's sense that the lawyer cares, has empathy, and provides some hope of recourse. More important, they do not judge them. Florence described her first meeting with Martin:

He introduced himself . . . he looked over some of the papers I brought. He explained to me what was going on with the other lawyers, what he could do. We sat down, he reviewed the information. Then he told me some of the things that [the manager of her public housing unit] had done wrong. And then he told me what he was going to try to accomplish. Which was to try to get them, you know, to lower the rent or do something and we [talked for] about maybe about a half hour, hour. And he really set my mind at ease. Because, not that I thought he was going to perform a miracle, but he made me feel better about the situation I was in. That, you know, I had some leeway where I could get some help.

Professionalism as Nonjudgmental

Marissa, a recent immigrant to the United States, described her confusion and embarrassment when she first came see Pete. She was overwhelmed by the problems she faced: a high-risk pregnancy, her young daughter's severe asthma, recent separation from an abusive husband, and being fired from her job. What brought her to NELS was the denial of health benefits because of her immigration status:

And then I was going through a lot. I was going through a lot I didn't know. At times I cried. I would talk and [Pete] would talk and I would cry and I would stop talking. I didn't know what to do. I didn't know what to say, I didn't know how to go about explaining. I felt ashamed that I was like, you know. But he made me feel that it wasn't my fault, he explained certain things to me. And gradually I started talking to him about it.

Marissa's difficulty sharing her story with Pete and the NELS social worker was exacerbated by the shame associated with discussing such problems with strangers from outside of her community. When I asked if there was anything that Pete did to make her feel more comfortable, Marissa responded:

He said stuff. He calmed me down. He talked to me quietly in a reassuring voice. That was it. He told me that everything I said to him is going to be confidential, that he would not judge me, that he's not here to do that, and he's just here to help me.

Marla, a client who worked with Joanne, spoke of her first encounter with the lawyer at NELS who Joanne replaced after his death. She underscored that he did not try to judge her or assess her guilt or innocence, but rather was interested in helping as best he could:

He was very soft-spoken . . . He very—he definitely understand, you know, and it wasn't never, it was never a like "Well [pause] I got another client" [in a bored voice]. You know how you get clients, they're guilty or not guilty, it was never thought I was guilty or never thought—Not saying that I wasn't. He was there to help me. To get my child back.

Marissa and Marla were not alone in noting how important it was that their respective lawyers did not judge them. In describing how Martin made her feel more comfortable, Florence told me that he did not look down on her:

Well, I think this is going to sound stupid, but I didn't know I was poor until I got to be an adult. I mean, I didn't feel like I was lacking anything. We didn't have anything, but I didn't feel like I was lacking anything. When, sometimes when you don't have anything, people put you in a position of feeling like you're begging, so to speak. He didn't do that.

He made me feel really, really comfortable. He was very sympathetic. He understood my plight, and I just felt like he was, you know, he was going to help me and that he would do the best that he could.

Florence's quote reveals another aspect of the lawyer-client encounter that clients highlighted as important: the lawyer's willingness to provide the best service that they can. Many clients came to NELS with trepidation. Several said that they came despite their expectation of being treated poorly.[2] As people who are poor, they often receive inferior services and are expected to make do with meager resources. These generally stigmatized, less than desirable benefits are hard-won and clients are made to feel beholden and second-class in the process of accessing them. While clients often had few expectations from NELS, they had no other recourse. Clients are surprised when the lawyers put their best professional efforts to work on their behalf.

Florence and Marissa felt comfortable with their respective lawyers, at least in part, because of the professional role each assumed. Martin and Pete made clear in word and attitude that it was their job to serve as lawyers. A lawyer's professional demeanor reassures clients because it emphasizes the lawyer's role as legal adviser and advocate rather than as a judge.

Ben also saw his job this way. He makes an effort to remember that his clients' lives are complicated and to reserve judgment even if he believes they have made bad decisions or have repeated their mistakes:

[Our job] is to represent as much people as we can, doing the best job that we can. . . . The relationship with the clients . . . I don't say it's uniformly great . . . [but] we're not saying no to a lot of people, and the cases that I'm handling basically they're happy endings and people are satisfied. But I . . . don't feel real confident that we sort of change their lives sufficiently to know if they won't be back again. . . . We've saved a lot of houses and then have the clients go out and take out a mortgage and they're back six years later and you notice, oh my God, like right after I got them out of trouble they walked into this other thing. And, you know, you can't be too judgmental.

Family advocacy is a practice area where it seems particularly difficult to be neutral or to withhold judgment about clients' choices. As noted earlier, lawyers in NELS's family advocacy unit represent clients who have been accused of child abuse and neglect. Most have had their children taken from them. Lawyers in this unit and in others acknowledged that this was one of the most difficult areas of practice. As Joanne pointed out, it is hard for lawyers not to put themselves in their clients' place and imagine how they would act.

> I think it's widely accepted throughout [NELS] that this is the hardest unit with the hardest clients . . . who have the most to lose. You know, you lose your house, you go to a shelter—you get back on your feet eventually. You lose your kid, what do you do? You know? Half of us here would commit suicide if we lost our kids. That's just, you know, we would never be able to recover from a loss like that. I don't have kids. I want kids. I love kids. I don't know what my feelings about this work are going to be once I have kids . . . it would be very challenging to go home and look at your baby after a day of talking about abused babies [pause]. It really, really is a roller coaster so I live for the good days. And try to remind myself on the bad days that it's not my fault and that . . . clients have, for good or bad, gotten themselves to the place that they are. Even if they've had bad luck or obstacles—unfair obstacles—thrown in their way.

Although Joanne finds her clients' circumstances difficult, like other lawyers, she tries to meet clients where they are. This allows her to avoid judging them and, perhaps more important, to absolve herself of responsibility for their predicament and for the outcomes of their cases. As a lawyer, she resolves to do the best she can in the given circumstances with each particular client and his or her strengths and limitations, but she recognized the limits of her capabilities. Suzanne, also a lawyer in the family advocacy unit, shared this view.

> I kind of went into this knowing that I wasn't anyone's savior. I mean, I can always tell myself this in the abstract although then I still get upset and have bad days. But I can go in saying . . . I'm not their savior . . . that's really arrogant of me to think that. . . . At best, I'm their lawyer, and, you know, at best I'm going to try to like stand up for them and get them the services that they're owed by the law and make sure that their rights aren't trampled. . . . A lot of people had messed up lives before I came and their lives are still going to be messed up when I leave. And they're poor. And my clients I don't think are ever going to be anything other than poor. Like I don't think they have the ability to lift themselves out of the situation that they're in.

Joanne and Suzanne provided examples of how lawyers use their understanding of the professional role as a way to cope with the intense intimacy of their involvement with clients as well as their frustration with their limited ability to change clients' life circumstances. It allows them to set boundaries that are beneficial for them and for their clients. Boundaries release lawyers from taking their clients' behaviors personally and from many of the judgments that certain behaviors or attitudes might incur. Lawyers have little control over clients' life circumstances, which can make strategic legal planning difficult. This is compounded when clients themselves behave erratically due to mental or emotional difficulties which are often the result of or exacerbated by stress. As noted earlier, many lawyers care deeply about their clients and can become frustrated when the course of a legal procedure is thrown off track by a client's failure to appear at a hearing or a relapse of addiction. Recognizing their mutual limits and the unpredictability of legal action allows lawyers and clients to work together without taking out their frustrations on each other.[3]

Attending to Clients

Lawyers try to signal their concern for clients not only through their professional mien but also in gestures of attentiveness and care. Attending means to be present, concentrate, and listen. Marcia slows down so that her clients understand that they have her "undivided attention." She believes that this can help her cases. If clients feel at ease, they are more likely to "focus." Worried clients are understandably distracted, and this can hamper lawyers' ability to work on their cases. "Sometimes the situation is so desperate that they're worrying about the fact that they don't have a token to get home. And if I can clue in to where they are and say, 'You know! [snaps fingers] I have an extra token, how about—?' And then we can focus."

Like Marcia, other lawyers considered ways to enhance their rapport with clients, thinking about how to make clients comfortable and signal interest, while minimizing social and professional distance. Lawyers in this study variously noted using client surnames, standing up when a client entered the room, shaking a client's hand, and offering a legal pad for clients to take notes. Such gestures comprise what Gerald López refers to as "practical moments" that "often arise in the course of activities that many others treat either as trivial or mechanical to good lawyering."[4] Lawyers and clients alike use the practical moments to shape the lawyer-client relationship. Despite their apparent unimportance, lawyers' use of practical moments to show clients respect and attentiveness can make a difference in client perception of the legal services process. In light of clients' previous experiences with government agencies, these practical moments assume personal and political import. While I have discussed in great detail how individual encounters can have social justice ramifications (see chapter 3), this chapter focuses on the significance of clients' perception of lawyers' treatment of them as a meaningful part of progressive lawyering.

For most clients, sharing their experiences with a lawyer who listens was important beyond any legal or strategic advantage gained. Dara described her evolving relationship with Marjorie. It began with Dara's suspicion that Marjorie did not (in fact, could not) understand her plight. Dara believed that anyone who has not experienced difficulty cannot truly understand those who suffer, and she perceived Marjorie as "professional but distant." This changed over time, and Dara said of Marjorie "that she kind of, at some point, understood—because she really, really, really worked hard on my case, she did. She really did work hard on my case. She really worked hard on it." It was Marjorie's apparent dedication to Dara's case that led Dara to believe that Marjorie had some sense of the difficulty of her situation.

Clients were often surprised at the dedication lawyers showed to their cases. They viewed such dedication to cases as analogous to dedication to them as clients and as human beings, an indication that lawyers "got it" and that they cared. Lawyers bore out Dara's assessment, often stating that their recognition of clients' dire needs led them to expend enormous efforts. Marjorie's actions, more than her manner or her words, are what proved to Dara that she would not let her down or misperceive her as others had. This is a crucial component of what Peter Margulies has termed "engaged empathy," advocating that lawyers move beyond passive expression of superficial or instrumental empathy, which can have the effect of taming clients and depoliticizing their claims.[5] Margulies chiefly focuses on the way that lawyers and clients share across difference and open themselves up to one another (as I will discuss below). Clients like Dara indicate an even more engaged kind of empathy that involves *doing*, showing *in deed* that they understand and are open to their clients' needs. As Lilly summed up what was special about what she called her lawyer Liz's "lawyerism": "It's the fact that she's empathetic. She listens. She's caring. And she's productive."

Many clients were not accustomed to displays of empathy in word or deed, and clients worried that their lawyers might revoke their goodwill. Both Lorna and her lawyer Steve described their relationship as one characterized by trust, real affection, and respect. Nevertheless, when asked whether there was anything that she felt uncomfortable discussing with Steve, Lorna expressed fleeting concern that he might misjudge her even though they had been working together for some years and each spoke of the other fondly. Ultimately, it was her trust in Steve and her estimation of the strength of their relationship that led her to speak with him candidly.

> You know the hardest thing was to be honest with him about the sale of the house and whether that would affect my benefits. To ask him questions, but not sound like I needed to hide money or that I was trying to do something illegal because that's not what I'm trying to do. But I am trying to protect my interests and prevent a situation that I'm not going to be able to afford.
>
> So how did you figure out then how to talk to him about that?
>
> I just decided that he was open enough and honest enough and very caring with me that he would see me as who I was and that my fears [that he would see me as somebody trying to mess with the system] weren't really rational.

Clients' fears stemmed from their prior encounters and embarrassment, perceptions of their own worthiness, perceptions of lawyers' empathy and interest, and clients' dependency upon their lawyers and fear of being judged. These different (but related) fears combined in ways that affect lawyer-client relationships.

Nancy's experiences illustrate how these factors interact. It was very difficult for Nancy to expose her troubles to Marjorie, but she recognized that to get the help she needed in bankruptcy proceedings, she had to provide her lawyer with information she found difficult to share.

> I felt like I was scared to tell her everything [thoughtful]. . . . Why are you behind on your mortgage? Uhhh [gagging noise, as if her words are getting stuck] . . . it was hard to talk about why you behind in your bills if you spent the money! And it went towards this or it went towards that and I had to pay the electric Peter, Peter to pay Paul . . .
>
> So you felt you had to explain to her why?

> She was asking me and she has to know why. Why are you coming here for my help if you can't answer my questions? You have to be honest with your lawyer if you want them to help you. And I didn't have nothing to hide but I just felt bad having to tell her that I'm behind on my mortgage and I'm not with my husband, and I don't have—I'm not proud of everything I say [sighs].

What eventually put Nancy at ease was her sense that Marjorie both understood and believed her. Nancy credited her own honesty (and Marjorie's ability to discern it) as the reason for Marjorie's understanding. In other words, Nancy, like many other clients, made a point of championing her own worthiness and honesty as responsible for engendering her lawyer's goodwill and trust, counterposing this against hypothetical others who try to get things "over" on their lawyers or on the system.

> Not saying she's been in my situation before, but I think she understands and I think she sees and feels honesty with me. Sometime you feel a person . . . I think she feels a vibe, a vibration of honesty in what I'm saying to her. I think she feels that. Because if I was dishonest, I think she would feel that, too. She's been around I'm sure a lot of clients that didn't tell the truth but they want them to defend her. [Shouts] "I didn't really do it!" [laughs] But, no, I really am sincere when I come to her.

Summarizing her thoughts on the interaction, Nancy imagined what it would have been like to work with a different lawyer, one who either judged her or ignored her.

> Had they got me a guy, a 80-year old guy with a beard, I'm not saying it would have been any different if he was a nice person. . . . I didn't see her come across to me as [in a disgusted voice], "Oh you're a ghetto being and you're this person that I got to help" and blaming everything on me that I brought to her attention. . . . She didn't really come across to me like I had to feel guilty and bad about my thoughts to come and ask her for help. . . . As I said, she was just so eager and willing to help me! And I was just glad that she was willing to help me. 'Cause sometimes you can go to people and they say [in mock boredom] "Next in line . . . well never mind, I really have to go now" and see the disinterest in the lawyer. . . . She never seemed that way to me. . . . 'Cause she was hanging right in there with me. . . . I felt, you know, connected [laughs].

Clients perceived lawyers' hard work on their behalf as an expression of caring and in some cases as a testimony to their own credibility. Clients like Nancy work hard to transmit "vibes of honesty." Some, like Dara, help their lawyers gain a better understanding of the obstacles they face. Still others, like Lorna, decide to trust their lawyer even when doing so is difficult in light of past experiences that include betrayals, callousness, and dehumanizing treatment. From this vantage point, the formation of relationships between lawyers and clients is mutual and goes beyond lawyers' attempts to make clients feel at ease. Lawyers and clients are involved in an ongoing process of gauging their working relationships, which contain both professional and personal elements.

The Professional-Client Relationship as Friendship

Several clients in this study, in describing their relationship with their lawyers, said that they thought about their lawyer as a friend. Clients realized that they were unequally beholden to and dependent on their lawyers and acknowledged that, in the course of representation, they must often reveal intimate information, unreciprocated, to lawyers. They therefore did not use the term "friend" to indicate a fully reciprocal relationship but rather to indicate a dimension of care. Maryann acknowledged that while her relationship with Pete was for her unique and special, Pete likely has other clients who feel that they, too, have a special connection with him.

> He's just like a friend, you know, I think that I felt like I've known, he's a family friend for years or something. And he has this type of thing with him where, I guess it's the aura, I guess, he makes you feel like he's totally just your friend [laughs]. You know? And he probably just totally somebody else's friend, too.

Latonya also understood that although her relationship with Joanne is like a friendship in some ways, she and Joanne are not "friends" in the common sense of the word:

> I would say, like I talk to Joanne. I talk to her. . . . like a friend, like! You know? That's how I talk to her. I say, "Jo, well this—" you see I call her Jo, I don't say Joanne. . . . I talks to her . . . and I look at her like a friend. I mean, I know that she's not my friend but like, I trust her. I trust her. I really do.

This was echoed by Ruth, also a client of Joanne's:

> I mean, she generally acted like she cared. You know, some of them don't. A lot of them just had a attitude like [in bored voice], "Okay well, you know, I have to do this for you, that's all." But she, it was more like a personal thing like we was almost friends, like? I could tell her anything, as hard as it was. 'Cause so much stuff had happened and she just made me feel like she was going to actually try to do anything she could. I guess that's what made the difference. All of them aren't like that, I mean, I'm sure. I wasn't expecting her to be like that [laughs].

Latonya, Ruth, and Maryann viewed their lawyers "like a friend" because they found in them something different than what they expected from a lawyer. Latonya and Ruth, although they explicitly compared their respective relationships with Joanne to friendship, at the same time acknowledged that it is not a friendship. Familiarity (for Maryann), trust (for Latonya), and caring and commitment (for Ruth) marked the relationship as one *like* (although not the same as) friendship. It is telling that clients struggled to find a word to express the idea of a professional relationship that is characterized by elements of warmth and respect. As Ruth pointed out, this is not something that clients have come to expect, particularly when services are offered free of charge. Clients expected such services to be given grudgingly or with disinterest, if at all, and expressions of empathy and caring were viewed as anomalous or outside of the professional helping relationship.

Martin viewed friendship and professionalism as mutually exclusive. When I asked him to describe his rapport with clients, he specifically noted that he did not want to be regarded as a friend.

> I view myself as playing a professional role in their life. And I try to keep the relationship on a professional basis. Now that doesn't mean it's not cordial, but I don't want them to regard me as their friend, I want them to regard me as their lawyer. So, for example, I would never call a client by his or her first name, even though they will frequently call me by my first name.

Martin's commitment to such a formal professional role was uncharacteristic of the lawyers in this sample, although it may also in part be attributed to his general demeanor, which was relatively formal. However, it demonstrated a respect for clients and sensitivity to their needs that was shared by other lawyers. Clients come to Martin for his professional services. He makes a point of treating them with dignity and providing services at the highest level of professionalism. Martin felt that too informal a manner was at odds with respect for clients and their needs; he emphasized the professional aspect of his relationship with clients at least in part by acting *other than* as a friend. NELS reinforces this organizationally. Justin invited Pete and his partner to dinner after the successful resolution of Justin's case. Pete initially declined the invitation, telling Justin that it broke NELS's rules against receiving gifts from clients. Pete noted that NELS's rules were murky, but that he preferred to err on the side of caution because he did not want clients to feel beholden or to consider his professional representation as a favor rather than an entitlement. When Justin informed him that to decline the invitation would be considered an insult, Pete changed his mind. Lawyers struggle with what is the most respectful and appropriate stance in a relationship with any given client.

Pete was more representative of the lawyers. Despite his own ambivalence about boundaries, he was gratified to hear that the clients I interviewed characterized their relationships with him as "friendly." He understood friendship in this context much as Maryann (his own client), Joanne, and LaTonya did.

> I think it's more warmth, is what the friendship thing is. There's a mutual warmth and I think a crossing of barriers and joining of empathy and a sense of connection between the client that this means something to the lawyer beyond that that's my case— that he's really there for me because he cares about me or she's really there for me because she cares about me. And I think that's what we ought to be doing.

Empathy and openness can also counter clients' negative experiences with public agency employees, who clients report as suspicious and rude. Some lawyers foster their relationships with clients by sharing of themselves. For clients like Lorna, their lawyers' openness signals receptivity as a fellow human being:

> He's also been very open about who he is personally, you know, his children. He's shared some of that so he has made me feel like he's not just a lawyer but he's a human being and that has helped a lot. Most lawyers,

they don't have enough time to get personal. He found time to get personal. Which is a good thing. It reassures people that you're human.

As discussed in chapter 3, when government agencies dehumanize clients and dismiss their claims, they teach clients that their grievances are illegitimate. In such a climate, lawyers' treatment of poor clients with courteousness and respect has political import as it counters such messages.

Limitations to Lawyer-Client Relationships

Despite the centrality of the lawyer-client relationship, lawyers and clients alike acknowledged a number of limits, both personal and institutional. Lawyers with heavy caseloads cannot develop the level of engagement described here with all clients. Lawyers also admitted to having affinities for some clients or "types" of clients and dislike of others, such as one lawyer who was uncomfortable with clients with mental illness. Several lawyers discussed clients' anger as interfering with their relationship. Vicki, the most recent law school graduate in the study, was still learning how to respond to hostile clients.

> The very first time it happened to me I was so upset and like took it so personally and thought . . . "Am I going to have to deal with this all the time?" And then I talked to other people about it and they said, "You don't have to take that. . . . You have to understand where they're coming from, you have to be polite. But you certainly don't have to take . . . someone yelling at you." And so more recently I had a client who . . . was really upset with me and I said, "You know what? I can't talk to you, you can't talk to me like this and I can't explain anything to you if you're yelling at me." And hung up. And it just felt so much better [sounding relieved] 'cause I didn't feel guilty about it and I didn't feel bad about myself.

Suzanne, on the other hand, had a different way of coping with distraught and angry clients.

> Especially in the beginning, they're like really upset. Like their children have just been taken, they feel like they've been lied to by the [child welfare] worker. They feel that everyone's lying about their situation. They're just furious. And sometimes I think they yell at me 'cause I'm the only

one who'll like let them yell at me. Like I don't usually yell back, and, you know, if they need to work off their frustrations somewhere I'd rather they yelled at me than . . . their worker and that'll go on their file. . . . "Mother has problem with anger management, mother has called worker son of a bitch. . . . " There's times when I just feel like really crappy and then you just sort of go home and try not to take it home with you. . . . I know it has an effect on me. Like, I don't work on their case as much as I should. Although I have to admit the ones that are really . . . on me, even if they're mean, I'll still work them.

Despite differences in approaches, client hostility may dampen lawyers' efforts.[6]

While lawyer and client personalities certainly played a role in relationships (and in part explain the difference in Vicki's and Suzanne's approaches to clients), differences also arose from the nature of their different kinds of legal work. For example, Vicki's work involved limited contact (often entirely over the telephone) with clients concerning employment issues. Suzanne's work, in contrast, entailed long-term relationships with clients involved in the child welfare system, many of whom struggled with mental health problems or mental retardation. When I asked Suzanne what she learned from her clients, she told me that working with Erica, a particularly volatile client with what lawyers describe as "mental health issues," has taught her the importance of "hanging in there and not getting—not taking things too personally." By understanding the frustration and anguish that her clients experience, she distances herself from what might otherwise feel like abusive behavior. She can thus "hang in there" for and with them. Such distancing helps clients to trust their lawyers, especially in the dependency unit in which clients are involved in a system that is characterized by suspicion and a high level of surveillance. Ruth, a client of Joanne's (also in the dependency unit), explained that when a lawyer stands by her client in spite of the tensions between them, the client can stay with the legal process rather than give up or act in a way that might jeopardize her case.

I didn't have to like put on no façade. Like for those social workers, I had to pretend. Well I was angry anyway—screw them. But I'm saying, I didn't have to pretend like everything was all right when it wasn't with Joanne. You know, if I was angry, she didn't care. You know, she would try to come out and talk to me if I walked out or whatever, and I couldn't do that with nobody else. I had to correct myself, you know, talk to them. 'Cause I know when I be angry it tears off of my eye,[7] it hurts so much [laughs].

Resource Constraints

While lawyers attempted to fashion a client-centered practice grounded in respect for clients, they universally lamented interrelated funding, personnel, and time constraints that impede their efforts. Paul Tremblay has argued that resource limitations and the practice of triage they necessitate do not end with intake.[8] When resources are limited, lawyers must ration their time and efforts, even in the face of greater client need. As noted in chapter 2, triage criteria (and whether or not lawyers should engage in it) are highly contentious. Like other legal services programs, NELS has too few lawyers and support staff. Lawyers have large caseloads. Some expand their work hours, allowing the job to encroach upon their personal lives. Denise, who complained about the difficulty of reaching Martin, told me that he gave her his home phone number. Martin, a self-described workaholic with a heavy caseload, admitted that it was difficult for clients to reach him and therefore he routinely returns phone calls from his home at night and on weekends. Many lawyers believe that they spend insufficient time with clients and on clients' cases despite working long hours. Despite the overwhelming caseloads, like Steve, most lawyers are reluctant to turn away clients.

> If I'm too swamped, I just stop taking cases. And that's a decision that I make. Now I am known not to do that. And I take on too many cases. And when I get way swamped, then I stop. But I have too many cases, I know that. And when I get overloaded is when it gets just too crazy. When I lose things. . . . Or, you know, there are . . . signs. For example when a client calls and I don't know who they are. Or when I wake up in the middle of the night and think, oh my God, I didn't file the appeal and then of course I go find the file and, yeah, I filed the appeal two months ago but I have no recollection of it. Then I know that I have got too much going on. Or, I mean, look at this! [pointing to piles of paper on his desk and all over his office]. . . . But right now, I'm totally overloaded, I got too much on my plate . . . But I just can't say no to my clients.

At least in hindsight, clients seemed to appreciate that they were one case of many and that the lawyers were overwhelmed. Denise described the frustration of not being able to reach Martin.

> And I felt as though, every time I called since we had to start going to court, they say, "Well, Mr. Reynolds is in court." And sometimes he wouldn't return my calls 'cause he was so busy, and he might have forgotten, you know. See, I'm realizing that now, but you know at that time I didn't want to hear nothing about "He at a meeting" [laughs]. You know, look, I want him to report to me, to take care of me, and that was it. But that was being selfish. That was really being selfish. But I was really, I'm tell—I mean—I know a lot of people is need for service and stuff like that but I felt as though my time was limited. I didn't have but so much time.

Clients of under-resourced bureaucracies are socialized to anticipate and accept the limitations of bureaucracies, so client satisfaction may be as much a matter of low expectations as of good service.[9] The power of this socialization is evidenced by Denise's consideration for Martin's time, while herself dealing with the extreme pressures and constraints of her and her teenage daughter's homelessness. Many of the lawyers were more sensitive to what clients might (or should) be dissatisfied with than were clients themselves. While lawyers deplored the lengthy waiting time or the sparseness of the waiting room (particularly at the branch office) which they thought clients experienced as poor treatment, most clients did not share that perception even when asked about this explicitly. Limited resources experienced by lawyers and clients exacerbate the difficulty of delivering services. The limitations serve to lower clients' expectations of the manner and quality of the services they receive. Where clients and lawyers were least likely to compromise their expectations for service is in providing time to listen to clients.

Progressive lawyering literature views the technique of empathetic understanding or listening in an attentive, nonjudgmental way as an important tool for communicating with clients.[10] It makes clients more apt to speak honestly and at length, increasing the likelihood that lawyers will better understand client goals and concerns and will obtain information important to their cases. Despite time constraints, most lawyers tried hard to allow clients to tell their stories fully. The lawyers viewed this as necessary to understand what the client was trying to accomplish. Martin said that he found it useful to let the client talk first. . . . Sometimes it's frustrating because we're all pressed for time, and they throw in extraneous stuff, or they don't put it in appropriate order in terms of chronology, but, um, at least you get a sense of what the client wants. You know, altogether too often when I was a very, very young attorney I would assume that that's what the client wanted—and it wasn't really the client's concern at all. They had something very different on their agenda. So I think you have to listen to that stuff to figure out what your client wants in terms of problem-solving. And then go back and ask lots of questions and lots of details, too, based upon what the client's concern is. And that process even in simple cases usually takes a half hour. And I've found that people appreciate it if you don't rush them.

Like Martin, other lawyers and clients viewed empathic listening as an essential component of fostering a better lawyer-client relationship. It respects a client's need to give her own narrative of events—however chronologically disjointed or "nonlegal." Lawyers regretted the necessity to "focus" or "redirect" a client; they took pains to legitimate the clients' need to talk and to explain why the legal process required certain information or a particular focus. Lawyers and clients recognized the importance of empathy and mutual respect in maintaining a satisfactory relationship. However, the intensity of such a relationship can also be a strain.

The Problem with Caring

The stress that the lawyers experienced is not only the result of limited resources, but resources limited in the face of what has been called "brutal need."[11] Lawyers know that individuals turned away by NELS, even with a referral, may not receive assistance. Elena, a former NELS attorney working at another legal services program in Northeast City, characterized the frustration of allocating scarce resources to people in need:

It's just very draining, this day-to-day. And you'll have to say no to the clients, and sometimes I think, at least in family law, I mean we only represent probably 5 percent of the people who request assistance. It's just, we just can't—the number of attorneys we have, so we're just continuously telling people: "Well, no, I'm sorry you're going to lose your children, but I can't do anything for you." Or, our consumer housing unit, there aren't that many of them, so: "I'm sorry you're going to lose your house today, but—." And you're on the front line all the time doing stuff like that. It's really overwhelming.

Many NELS clients have few other people to turn to. Clients of the elderly law unit often live alone or with sick spouses or are homebound. Clients in the family advocacy units find it difficult to trust others in light of their experiences with child welfare agencies, especially since many of these cases are initiated through anonymous tips that many suspect come from neighbors or former friends. In other units, too, clients may not want to turn to others if they are embarrassed about their situation. NELS lawyers understand this isolation, and it complicates the problem of saying no. Awareness of clients' predicaments is even more poignant when a client's case is not going well.

Bearing Bad News

Lawyers found it hard to give clients bad news.[12] It is particularly hard when they themselves are critical of the legal institutions and outcomes. Marjorie tried to explain to me what it feels like to realize during an initial interview that she probably will not be able to help the client:

> I'll just ask why they fell behind and what their income is and what their family situation is, just to kind of get a sense of what the situation is. . . . Some people, if they don't have any income there's no chance they're going to save their house and I tell them that [sarcastically] "Some people are just too poor to live-," which are the worst cases to deal with. . . . I just hate it, it's the worst. It's like one of the only things that I hate about this job . . . telling people that they're too poor to own a house. That's only costing them $150 a month!
>
> That must be so hard.
>
> It's awful. It is awful. It'll make me cry right now.

Several lawyers remarked on their emotional frustration; Marjorie was one of four who, unprompted, mentioned crying with clients or about client predicaments.

Some NELS units turn potential clients away more often than others. This is partly a result of resource constraints and partly a result of the paucity of legal remedies available. Martin noted the public housing unit turns down the majority of potential clients because they are unable to help them.

I would say that anywhere from 50-75 percent of the people who contact us, the most that we can do is give them some advice and we won't be able to do anything else to help them. So for the paralegals and actually the attorneys [who] take their turn in intake too, it's sometimes a discouraging thing because you find there's lots and lots of people that we just can't help . . .

Internally it was a little bit difficult for me, because I don't particularly like to tell people bad news. I don't think anybody does. Um, and I don't like to tell people that there's nothing that we can do for them. So that I think it was difficult for me to *do*, more than to conceptualize how to deal with it. But over time, I found that people really do appreciate your being honest about what you're doing and they understand why you're doing it, and may not be totally happy about it but they're also going to accept it.

Ironically, it is the clients' understanding that ultimately helps Martin cope with the necessity of delivering the discouraging message. Again, clients' understanding and acceptance should not be confused with passivity. Rather, it confirms what clients expect from a system that is unfair, unhelpful, and uncaring, a point of view largely shared by the lawyers at NELS. For Vicki, this shared understanding can make it even more difficult to inform clients of the legal status of their claims.

Some people just say okay 'cause they've heard it before or they just expect the system to be that way. Some people get really upset and they think that there is something I should be able to do for them. And then some don't get upset at me, they get upset at the way things are and, you know, I can only agree and say, "Yeah, it's really unfair. And it's a law out there and most states have this law and if you really feel this strongly about it you should write to your legislators because they're the ones who are going to change it. But right now that's the way it is." [W]hen I first came here and I was talking to people they told me how they handled this conversation 'cause we all have our own way of dealing with it, and it, it's difficult every time. Right before I'm about to launch into it I sort of have to take a deep breath and say, "Okay [sighing]. You've just told me like this whole horrible set of events that happened to you on the job and now I have to tell you that there's nothing that I can do."

Even in ongoing relationships, lawyers understand that the information or "instructions" they convey will likely contribute to their client's stress.

Lawyers want to assist clients and thus dislike it when their professional role demands that they convey distressing information. Marjorie commented on this:

> I understand that my clients have a lot of stress and I hate to be the source of more stress. Like I'd hate to write them another letter that they don't want to open. Even though I need to write a letter that says, like, "Make your payment or else your bankruptcy's going to be dismissed and you're going to lose your house." You know, I'm conscious of that when I'm writing letters, probably less so when I'm talking to clients, actually, but when I'm writing letters I always want it to sound like—I don't want to create more stress. Like I see my job as trying to alleviate one point of stress. So I never want them to get a letter from me, if they're behind on their payments, that they go: "Oh I don't want to open that because she's going to be yelling at me for not making my payments."

The lawyers are not dealing with abstractions but individuals. They see the clients, they hear them, and they are distressed when they must turn someone away or when a case goes badly or a client experiences setbacks in another area of her life.

Coping Mechanisms

There are several difficulties in figuring out when personal involvement is more likely to be helpful or harmful. Kathleen Sullivan has outlined a number of them in her discussion of the relationship between clinical law professors and students that illuminate similarly hierarchical relationships in a legal setting.[13] While Sullivan's discussion of intimacy focuses largely on self-disclosure, it raises questions of the proper balance between separation and connectedness. One problem is the inverse relationship between the perception of professionalism and intimacy that includes self-disclosure.[14] Another difficulty is assessing when expressions of intimacy and connectedness are appropriate and when they may instead be a burden, self-serving, or otherwise inappropriate.[15] Most of the lawyers in this study, however, seem most concerned about the emotional toll of their connections with clients.

A relatively new field in legal scholarship, therapeutic jurisprudence, notes the importance of understanding emotional aspects of lawyer-client relationships. Lawyers face difficulties when they open themselves to the suffering of clients. Mills calls the practice of opening oneself to the emotional aspects of lawyering, particularly client engagement, "affective lawyering." While the vicarious trauma to lawyers is incommensurate with the trauma that clients experience, lawyers must develop coping mechanisms to stay healthy.[16]

Steve credited his temperament for giving him the ability to compartmentalize his work. Although he sympathizes with his clients, and develops ongoing relationships with some of them, Steve sets boundaries that enable him to continue working at NELS.

> I don't think that it's that I'm not sympathetic and empathetic and angry and sad, but it doesn't sort of make me go home and pull my hair out and take out all the money from my bank account and give it to all of my clients. I mean, it just doesn't overwhelm me. Which is fortuitous. I don't think it's anything that I get credit for. It just doesn't—maybe I should be banged up a bit because it doesn't and maybe it should more. But it doesn't make me—I mean, there's some people in our office that go home and do more good works. Much more than I do. I mean, there's some people in the office that they spend, they spend their vacations building houses in Mexico. It's like, "Oh my God, how can you do that?!" I don't do that! You know, I don't do that. I mean, for example, just silly things. We went to Jamaica once for vacation. I won't go back to Jamaica. There's too many poor people in Jamaica. I don't want to go on vacation and see poor people. I don't need it. Which is totally selfish. You know, I have—No. No, no thanks. That's not what I want to be confronted with when I get away from it all. And you got to have a bit of a sense of humor about what we do. If you take it home with you every day and it overwhelms you every day, you're done.

Steve distinguished between empathy and a complete identification with clients. Empathy is important because it allows lawyers to care about their clients and to understand them. As we have seen, clients perceive empathy as a defining aspect of their relationship with their lawyer. This does not mean that the lawyer need abandon his or her own lifestyle, nor should empathy occasion despair that may ultimately be debilitating. No client wants or expects her lawyer to renounce his position and salary, nor do they want the lawyer to dissolve in a pool of emotion. They want competent assistance, after all. Indeed, none of the five clients who spoke of wanting to be a lawyer at some point in their lives expressed an interest in doing so out of altruism, but rather saw a legal career as a means to improve their lives through better incomes and more prestige.[17] Lawyers' ability to empathize without losing their separate identity is a coping mechanism that allows them to continue in a difficult line of work, assisting clients who experience trauma while avoiding the dangers of burnout and compassion fatigue.

The lawyers in this study characterized NELS as a collegial workplace that provided strong support, both professionally and emotionally. Liz told me that when she felt her "humanity slipping away," she would turn to the head of her unit whom she admired as a role model and who was willing to listen to her. Marjorie told me that the family advocacy unit was close-knit and that the attorneys shared a black humor that helps them cope.

> They have this really unique way of laughing at their clients. You know, like kind of as a survival skill . . . that develops as a way to cope with these tragedies that you're dealing with or difficulties that you're dealing with every day. To an outsider it might sound almost gross, but they've got that going on down there. And it gets them through. And they're completely, they only get away with it because they are completely compassionate about their clients and they love their clients and go to the ends of the earth for them, but it's an interesting, they poke fun at their clients.

Not only are lawyers able to laugh together, but they are able to turn to colleagues when they need to cry. They also rely on each other to learn techniques to cope with difficult clients. Marcia and Steve, who are perceived by other lawyers in their respective offices as being able to communicate well with people experiencing mental illness, both told me that other lawyers or staff members at NELS call on them for help with clients. Many of the less experienced lawyers also spoke of getting advice or support from more experienced colleagues, illustrated by the example of Vicki's learning how to cope with hostile clients, described earlier.

Perhaps the most interesting paradox in affective lawyering, however, is that its greatest source of difficulty, that is, working with and being open to clients, also appears to provide the closest thing to a cure. The same work with clients that so troubles lawyers provides a sense of connectedness to the people they set out to serve, inspirational models of human resilience, and an impetus to continue "Sisyphean work" (as Jeff put it in a paper he wrote in law school). Joanne's contact with clients reminds her why she chose to be a lawyer and allows her to see how her work and the law affect people.

I think that it's easy to lose sight of what you're doing and why you're doing it. I mean, the law that I learned about in law school is nothing at all like the law that I'm practicing every day and there are so very few people who connect to the law that I learned about in law school. It's like a very insular group. And these are the everyday people and this is how law affects the everyday people, or clients at [NELS].

Vicki explained that one reason she went to law school after working with kindergartners in a federally sponsored teaching program was to influence policy in order to make a bigger impact. With time, Vicki has come to realize that small, tangible results are meaningful, and she translates this understanding into her goals for future law practice.

I didn't feel like I was having enough impact with the 30 students I had in my classroom every year. But then, having seen the policy of it, like, I don't, I know that—I could measure the impact I had on each kid. I could tell you how far they came from the beginning to the end of the year. I could tell you these kids couldn't read and now they can read. And I think having stepped away from that for three years and looked at the bigger picture to see the broader impact you can have? That I think I might like the smaller impact. And I'd like to deal with the 30 kids every year or the 30 clients every few months, or whatever the case may be.

Steve expressed similar sentiments, and relishes the satisfaction he gets when he is able to help secure material assistance for a client.

And every day we—I get victories. And I don't think I'm unique. Which is great. You know—I mean, it's like I had one yesterday where, and it was a hassle, but finally my client got what she needed, and it was like, "Yes!" That's another one, we can close that one. And it was great, I mean it was great to call the client and say, "Yes, the food stamps are on and yes, you're getting the cash!" 'Cause it had been such a struggle. So there's a lot of positive reinforcement.

Affective lawyering carries risks and benefits, and lawyers must suffer the former if they are to experience the latter. For most NELS lawyers, the benefits outweigh the risks.

Being affected by clients also provides lawyers with the incentives they need to continue to practice law in systems that feel unresponsive and stingy. Allen used quotation marks to describe his clients as the ones "helped" because he believes he gains more from the representation than his client:

> Sometimes helping people "in the smallest sense" is important. It's important personally to me because it keeps me going, it's important to the individuals "affected" or "helped," and it's important to the organization to have the credibility that comes with helping people in individual problems. . . . If at the end of the day—there are some clichés that never used to be clichés—if you prevented a family from being forced to move into a homeless shelter, you've done something with that day, you've accomplished something. Sometimes, the biggest benefit of that goes to you. Well, at least it's a tie, I suppose. You may have been at a low energy point and all of a sudden, the job, you remember why you're doing it. And it gives you as much as, almost as much as, it gives to the families.

When I asked Marcia if her clients affected her, she said that her understanding of her clients' dire circumstances gives her the necessary energy to work hard for them.

> I hope and feel that most of my clients really affect me. And they affect me both negatively and positively. . . . I think I'd start being burnt out if they didn't affect me. I think if I became hardened to what they're experiencing . . . and my job wouldn't mean much to me, . . . I wouldn't have the energy to do it well. I mean, not all the time, but there are times I get up at 4:00. If I've got a hearing, you know, first thing in the morning and . . . to find that energy to do that at [mid-50s], you know, I think it's because I do, I want to get them that money . . . because their life is so hard because it is so hard to be so poor. I mean, it's not really anything more dramatic than that. I mean, it's just really hard to be that poor. You know, year in and year out. And this $579 . . . is a big, big help.

Marcia not only drew strength from her clients' needs, but was inspired and touched by stories of their bravery, resourcefulness, and caring for others in the face of them. Many lawyers told me that they marveled at their clients' resilience. I talked with Ben about his client, Elinor, who suffered from lupus. Elinor came to Ben for help with bankruptcy proceedings. During the course of their relationship, he also assisted her in obtaining help against an abusive husband who attempted to place her in a mental hospital against her will under false pretenses and later threatened her life and home by smoking crack near her oxygen tank. Ben visited Elinor in the hospital at one point while she was being treated for complications of lupus, and although he had not seen her since closing her case, told me he thought of her and was sorry that he did not have the time to keep up the relationship. Discussing Elinor's hopeful outlook despite her devastating troubles, Ben said that while work with clients was at times depressing, it was more often inspirational.

> And that sometimes translates from my end into—some days walking down the street in front of the office and seeing all the trash and the crazy people wandering around and I think I'm like walking through hell or something. And then some days I'm seeing all this strength that is, um, kind of—the tremendous survival ability that many of the clients sort of present. And um, um, and you know I would say in terms of it translating to me most of the time I'm feeling very positive about the clients and what we're doing. But there certainly are days when I'm feeling overwhelmed. Like many of the clients do.

Tempering Abstract Notions of Progressive Lawyering With Compassion For Clients

Face-to-face encounters bring out the tensions in progressive practice. Lawyers in situated practice with actual clients must carry out their values and visions of ideal practice in a context of limited resources and imperfect and unsatisfying legal remedies. Lawyers are conscious of this and strive to meet clients' needs and their own professional goals to the best of their abilities within these constraints.[18] While other forms of cause lawyering allow for the elevation of a cause over clients, the lawyers in this study viewed their clients as their primary causes. NELS does engage in policy as well as bread-and-butter legal services work, but the lawyers in this study were a group that self-selected in responding to my call for lawyers who were interested in reflecting on their relationship with clients. From interviews with these lawyers and their clients, it is clear that they pursue the kind of "lawyerism" that opens them up to their clients in a way that went beyond the instrumental and allowed for a dialogue.

Pete's concern over an interaction with one of his clients illustrates how such dialogic encounters have the potential to transform lawyers' ideals.

I have a client who came in last week who is going through a ton of different things. She's got a tremendous amount of anxiety and depression and we've been worried that she might also be suicidal. But she came in so wound up. . . . It was this little tiny thing that means nothing. I said . . . "You've explained this, I'm going to take care of it from here. Take this off your mind. You don't need to worry about this problem, you've got enough things to try and deal with, don't worry about this one. This is taken care of. She was completely relieved, you can tell the stress just [indicates washing away].

When I asked Pete what troubled him about this, he responded:

The part where it's problematic from an empowerment perspective is you really shouldn't be saying, "Give it to me, I'll handle it, I'll call you when it's fixed," which I basically said in that case. But I think it was appropriate for that case.

Pete's consternation is, in part, shaped by his professional training. Law school education teaches explicitly and implicitly that being affected by clients is not considered lawyerly.[19] The law school socialization that teaches students to "focus on the issue at hand, strip away what is not in question, not open to questions, or not obtainable in this forum"[20] discourages lawyers from opening up to client experiences and examining the implications of the legal process and outcomes for clients and their lives. In ignoring the way that lawyers can be affected by clients, lawyers are left without a vocabulary to explore this possibility.

Pete's unease is compounded because his judgment as to what constitutes an ideal notion of progressive lawyering is informed by limited conceptions of autonomy (discussed in chapter 4). It is also likely that Pete acted not according to ideals of progressive lawyering that privilege autonomy, but rather, according to other values that he fails to identify, like compassion. He is clearly affected, in the sense of being open to his client's distress and trauma, by his assessment of her vulnerability. As a result, he tempered his ideals of progressive lawyering in response to his client's needs. If progressive lawyering literature paid greater heed not only to the emotional aspects of practice, but to situated practice more generally, then Pete might have a greater vocabulary to articulate the different factors that informed his decision.

Clients cited in this chapter feel most comfortable with lawyers who respond to them with openness and empathy and show in word and in deed that they will work for clients to the best of their ability. Working with competent lawyers who care counteracts clients' dehumanizing and stigmatizing experiences with government agencies and services and validates clients grievances as legitimate. Clients understand the difference between competence and caring, and are perhaps more sophisticated than lawyers in demanding both and refusing to consider them mutually exclusive.

Drawing on early social change workers, Jane Addams emphasized the effect of interactions between intended recipients and would-be benefactors. For Addams, it was not the client who needed changing (although she might need material assistance) so much as the professional helper, and it was the mutual encounter and learning that formed the basis of social change. Would-be beneficiaries had a better understanding of contextual realities than the professional. Professionals learn from their encounters with clients:

> [T]he contact with the larger experience, not only increases her sense of social obligation but at the same time recasts her social ideals. She is chagrined to discover that in the actual task of reducing her social scruples to action, her humble beneficiaries are far in advance of her, not in charity or singleness of purpose, but in self-sacrificing action. . . . She has socialized her virtues not only through a social aim but by a social process.[21]

In this view, it is the lawyers who interact with clients on an ongoing basis who are most likely to be transformed. This may lead to more effective lawyering, as such lawyers will have a better understanding of issues that impact their clients and their clients' cases. It may also lead to greater client satisfaction, as indicated by the importance that clients attach to listening, caring, engaging, and acting on their behalf. Perhaps more important, lawyer-client openness is most likely to produce change: change in the practice of law to suit the individual needs and desires of particular clients involved in particular cases with particular legal institutions and change in the balance of values and ideals that inform legal practice. It is also more likely to produce change in the clients' and lawyers' understanding of their claims and grievances and in our understanding of the way poor people are impacted by policies and practices.

7

Progressive Lawyering and the Ethic of Risk

Critiquing the Critical Mind-Set

Theorists of progressive lawyering, critical and otherwise, tell lawyers how to act. They set out guidelines that assume client goals and desires and attempt to mold client behavior. Underlying such advice is the presumption that observers of public interest lawyering know better than lawyers and clients engaged in practice about everything from the nature of the client-professional relationship to the goals they should pursue and their chances of achieving them. Drawing on Paul Ricoeur's hermeneutic of suspicion, Paul Schiff Berman has pointed to some of the dangers of the almost exclusively critical focus of sociolegal and critical scholarship about progressive lawyering.[1] Berman acknowledges the value of postmodernist-inspired deconstruction that seeks to unmask the delusions of false consciousness of legal actors. Critiques that are "relentlessly suspicious," however, exact a price.

Decontextualized critical scholarship fails to recognize and give credence to the stories that lawyers and clients tell about the work they do together in ways that reproduce hierarchies. They are elitist, discounting the knowledge and experiences of those engaged in practice. They further privilege outsider perspectives but do not subject such perspectives to similar scrutiny. This has the effect of making fewer voices and perspectives available. It also distances those who practice or "do" from those who observe and critique. Such distancing creates a counterproductive, potentially dangerous, division between the processes of doing and reflecting, leaving both activities impoverished. Relentless suspicion is also discouraging. With no hope and no reason to try to make the world a better place (even with a contingent understanding of what "better" might be), relentlessly suspicious critique can lead to disengagement and paralysis.

Progressive lawyering critiques have added a burden of abstract goals that confuse rather than clarify because they do not incorporate how actual lawyers and clients work together or their aspirations. Lawyers and clients judge themselves (and each other) when actions and behaviors do not meet idealized expectations of progressive lawyering. Further, the burden is not balanced by a complementary understanding of the trade-offs or reflections that illuminate lawyers' and clients' work together. This is a missed opportunity to produce a dialogue about the pitfalls and promises of progressive lawyering that is rich in nuance, complexity, and perspectives.

Exploring the perspectives of lawyers and clients enhances our understanding of practices. This in turn will lead us to better understand and revise what it means for lawyers and clients to work together for social justice, including what social justice might look like (and for whom). Investigating practices on the ground allows us to debate the goals of public interest law practice not merely in an abstract discussion of their merits, but also by how they were determined, including who played a role in formulating them, how they play out in real life, and how amenable they are to revision when necessary. Re-examining the practice of working with clients may lead to changes in goals—for instance, from the empowerment of individuals to cope with the welfare system independently to the empowerment of individuals to hold the welfare system accountable through the law. The distinction I have just outlined is not *merely* a matter of focus. It is shared by many theorists who call for contextualizing philosophy and ideals in ways that make a difference for very real people because it is both more efficient and morally sound.[2]

John Gilliom's study of welfare beneficiaries in Appalachia reveals another danger of disengaged skepticism, which is the failure to recognize everyday practices as acts of resistance. "Skeptical readers of recent works of everyday resistance have noted the frequent absence of something that we might normally expect or hope to see in political struggles."[3] Gilliom suggests that we do not find them because we are not looking properly, not because they are not there. This is due, at least in part, to the valorization of protest in traditional political arenas and broad-scale demonstrations.[4] It is also (not unconnectedly) a result of the failure to understand the daily realities of the least powerful. The actions and insights of Gilliom's study participants, poor women who are dependent upon the state to support themselves and their families, refute such skepticism. Their attempts to thwart state surveillance show that everyday resistance can be both powerful and principled.[5]

The practices of lawyers and clients, when measured against amorphous goals, have been similarly understudied and undervalued. Viewed from afar, their efforts look largely piecemeal. To outsiders, lawyers and clients might appear so mired in responding to crises that they cannot and do not reflect upon the work that they do. Listening to what lawyers and clients say about what they do refutes the notion that their work is nothing more than a haphazard muddling through. Lawyers and clients in this study articulate a coherent ethic that informs their actions. They engage in principled acts of resistance when, where, and how they can. They articulate a critique of the systems in which they work and a theory of justice. These may be influenced and constrained in ways that they are unaware of that can be illuminated by critical scholarship. As Berman points out, however, revealing the sources of delusion (as if lawyers and clients are unaware of what constrains them) or offering alternative explanations are not the *only* stories that might be told. Nor are they inherently better or worse than any other stories, including the stories that lawyers and clients formulate for themselves.

Focusing our analysis on lawyers' and clients' practices and perceptions more comprehensively helps ascertain whether they reveal a more systematic and integrated ethic that guides their work toward social justice, and if so, what that ethic is. In this study, I have discussed lawyers' and clients' attitudes toward social change, autonomy, collaboration, and lawyer-client relationships. Lawyers' and clients' approaches to these themes reveal striking similarities and consistencies that are also shared by many social change proponents who are themselves, or who work closely with, intended beneficiaries. The most striking, perhaps, is their principled ethical grounding.

The Feminist Ethic of Risk

Lawyers and clients in this study practice what Sharon Welch has described as the "feminist ethic of risk":

> The ethic of risk is characterized by three elements, each of which is essential to maintain resistance in the face of overwhelming odds: a *redefinition of responsible action, grounding in community,* and *strategic risk-taking* [italics added]. Responsible action does not mean the certain achievement of desired ends but the creation of a matrix in which further actions are possible, the creation of the conditions of possibility for desired changes.[6]

Working for social change is a daunting prospect, particularly in a political climate that is hostile to the types of changes envisioned. I have explained how and why lawyers and clients continue to work for desired social change in the face of apparently insurmountable challenges, deep-seated frustration, and limited resources. Although it is based on a small sample of legal services lawyers and some of their clients, this study sheds light on other client-professional relationships where similar concerns exist.

Progressive lawyering theorists do not generally grapple with the "how and why" of practice but create ideal types for lawyers to follow. It is easy to forget that these are not Platonic ideals but ideal types in the Weberian sense. Weber's ideal types were meant to be heuristic devices that did not necessarily exist in practice but were useful in enhancing our ability to understand social phenomena.[7] This is in contrast to the Platonic ideal, which has an independent existence and is to be striven for with the understanding that perfect practice would lead to the closest achievement of this idea.[8] Grounded social science research recasts ideal types as I believe they were intended, that is: to serve as guides, to red-flag the potential pitfalls and benefits of different practices, and more generally to exhort a more reflective practice.[9]

It is telling that lawyers who participated in this research asked me what I found, as if my research would disclose something to them that they do not already know. This is despite the fact that I viewed them as experts whose knowledge would help inform others, not necessarily themselves. Social science research helps lawyers and clients to articulate the practice understandings that they often use subconsciously, much in the way that Schon describes the practitioner who has not yet tried or been asked (or has the time) to be reflective about how she acts. Intensive interviews are valuable in helping lawyers and clients see what they already know. Focused conversation provides a platform for them to analyze and articulate often intuitive understandings. It also acknowledges lawyer and client practices as something more comprehensive, integrated, and ethically informed than many critics realize. Practicing law in this way is not just muddling through as best they can, but it is the art of navigating in a way to make one's own work rewarding and strategically viable. Beyond this, the ethic of risk that emerged from conversations with lawyers and clients provides a normative framework that explains "how" and "why" lawyers and clients make the choices that they do far better than abstract social justice goals or tangible resource constraints alone. The ethic of risk holds a healthier respect for the abilities and practices of lawyers and clients, recognizing the decisions they make as ethical in that their values guide their practice. In this chapter, I use the ethic of risk as defined by Welch as a comprehensive framework.[10]

Responsible Action

The pragmatists of the late nineteenth century believed that although we may not be able to know the truth, even if we saw it, this should not preclude us from acting responsibly.[11] Living with limited epistemological ability does not preclude us from action that is informed by moral or normative judgments. Acknowledging the limited state of our knowledge, it is incumbent upon each individual to act based on accumulated knowledge and experiences. Further, responsible individuals, according to the pragmatists, must actively seek to question the state of their knowledge and revise it as new experiences and intellectual understandings accumulate.

Living as if imagined ideals existed might be sufficient for the complacent who refrain from acting in the world, but those who test their ideals and ideas in real situations cannot ignore the occasions when their experiences provide them with contradictory input. This does not necessarily mean giving up ideals, although it is possible they too will be revised. It does, however, require acknowledging the gap between the desirable and the possible. Lawyers and clients concerned with social justice often learn from their experiences that their ideal visions are not realizable in the foreseeable future. To continue to act in the world without giving up these visions, they must acknowledge this discrepancy.

Responsible actions are those that acknowledge the boundaries of power while continuing to imagine something different.[12] One possible danger of focusing on abstract ideals is that it can lead to paralysis. If public interest lawyering risks further marginalization of oppressed people, the only sure way to avoid this danger is by eschewing such work.[13] This, however, would not be the responsible course to take, since it would also eliminate the possibility of positive change. The commitment to a vision of social justice is what sustains many lawyers in their pursuit of social change despite the limited scope of potential achievements. This is coupled with a desire to help individuals, particularly those with whom they have developed relationships. Rather than a mere ratcheting down of expectations, lawyers and clients make positive, informed decisions as to what actions are possible, and what actions have potential to help with the least potential to harm. Responsible action involves evaluating potential harm and acknowledging that strategies might need to be changed if they are to benefit clients. Clients themselves come to define responsible action based on what they know of the legal system. This is not to be confused with accepting the system. Most clients view responsible action as one that acknowledges the faults of the system and takes steps to maximize their chance of success based on their understanding of how best to navigate or manipulate the legal system. This process generally relies on assistance from lawyers. Clients in this study take action and exhort others to act within a faulty and unjust system, often facing fundamental risks to themselves and their families.

Grounded in Community

This study emphasizes the personal relationship as one of the more important facets of legal services lawyering (and arguably all lawyering) and as such it deserves further study. As this study also makes clear, although professional ethics grounded in community can be rewarding for both clients and professionals, it can also be difficult. Delineating "community" is not a clear-cut process, nor are communities themselves homogeneous. Lawyers and clients have conflicting interests, priorities, and understandings of similar situations. Work that is grounded in community is the most likely to challenge our understanding of the world, and to change us. Despite the religious metaphor and perspective, Jane Addams's eloquent description of the difficulty of working *with* clients can be easily applied in all present-day helping relationships:

> "[T]o walk humbly with God" . . . may mean to walk for many dreary miles beside the lowliest of his creatures, not even in peace of mind, that the companionship of the humble is popularly supposed to give, but rather with the pangs and misgivings to which the poor human understanding is subjected whenever it attempts to comprehend the meaning of life.[14]

Addams is critical of those social change workers who invoke religion to make themselves feel worthy. For her, the religious and social imperative is radical because it challenges what we think we know, and it acknowledges that engagement with others is the only way to correct our misunderstandings.

The social reformers who avoid the charitable relationship with any of their fellow men take a certain outside attitude toward this movement. They may analyze it and formulate it: they may be most valuable and necessary, but they are not essentially within it. The mass of men seldom move together without an emotional incentive, and the doctrinaire, in his effort to keep his mind free from the emotional quality, inevitably stands aside. He avoids the perplexity, and at the same time loses the vitality.[15]

For Addams, complacency is a sign that something is amiss; it means that we are not truly open to the lives and perceptions of others. This not only results in a misperception of reality, but is also more likely to lead to a loss in "vitality" or the motivation to continue.

In any professional helping context, responsible action must be grounded in community in order to reflect reality and sustain action. Lawyers base their strategic decisions with an awareness of and respect for (and a sense of responsibility toward) the clients they wish to serve, which is best summarized by Enisa, a former NELS lawyer:

The best people are the people who understand, be they doctors or lawyers or whatever, that they are taking responsibility for other people's lives, and that is a huge responsibility. Anyone who ever takes for granted that other people are putting their trust in them and counting on them to come through, whoever takes that responsibility lightly, I don't think should be doing it.

Clients, for their part, provide lawyers with feedback for the work they do, and victories for these clients give lawyers the motivation they need to continue despite what may feel like meager gains.

Lawyers and clients help each other safeguard their ability to imagine a different system. Responsible action is also characterized by the lawyers' and clients' recognition of their mutual responsibility for each other. This is evident in their acknowledgment of each others' humanity and respect for each others' decisions and understanding of one another's situations, abilities, and limitations.

Redefining responsible action grounded in community to include this component of responsibility for, and responsiveness to, others helps to broaden our understanding of legal services work and to recognize a field of action that goes largely unacknowledged. When I discuss my research with legal services lawyers and law students, most are surprised to hear that lawyers and clients viewed the interpersonal exchanges as a valuable part of representation. This runs counter to most understandings of professional legal representation held by both lawyers and clients. Lawyers who participated in this study were surprised[16] that I found their self-deprecating comments about doing "social work" worthy of analytic attention. None had ever considered these well-worn remarks seriously, and were surprised at the resonance and power they held when articulated as an ethic of concern that focuses on the centrality of the personal working relationship. Legal education often looks to avoid emotion and interpersonal skills that risk clouding "the facts" or strictly rational legal analysis.[17] It also cultivates emotional and contextual detachment in a way that obscures power relations on the societal and the individual levels.[18] Arthur explained the traits he most admired in the late Supreme Court Justice Brennan as "his warmth" and that "he valued every person as an individual." Arthur, who teaches at a law school, looks to role models like Brennan to help fight so-called professional detachment:

> As people advance professionally they too often become devoid of what it means to be a human being and the value of human . . . interaction and contact and what's important in life. And unfortunately, I see law students already developing a distance from all of that. And I think that's so dangerous. And so people who can keep those values in context, and teach us how to keep those values in context, are the most important mentors. . . . They can be a teacher . . . I like to think that they can be a loved one, they can be our peers.

For lawyers in this study, they can also be clients.

Strategic Risk-Taking

Strategic risk-taking involves challenging authority when it is possible to do so and with full knowledge of the risks involved and awareness of who will bear the burden of failure.[19] This, too, is grounded in the personal relationship and the desire for social justice, despite the limited possibilities in any given time or situation. Welch emphasizes that the ethic of risk is one that simultaneously acknowledges limitations and seeks to act within them to maximize potential for future change. One way lawyers and clients do this is to assist each other in confirming the unfairness of current arrangements and using the law and legal challenges to imagine a different future to offer to others. The law can be deployed for symbolic uses that can affect change in the social, if not legal, world. For example, McCann's study of the pay equity movement shows that even if there are no viable legal remedies in many instances of unequal pay, when employees and employers *believe* that there are, the outcomes are often the same as if there were effective legal recourse.[20] A sense of unfairness can fuel clients' (and lawyers') beliefs that it is the system that must be changed, rather than those who are oppressed by it. This helps both continue to see the *ethical* locus of responsibility for change with those in power, even if this is not the *practical* locus of responsibility. Moral righteousness is a valuable source of strength and energy for both clients and lawyers, particularly in the face of opposing views and resource limitations that sap that energy.

Any action involves a risk, and as its name implies, the ethic of risk recognizes the ethical value of taking risks for change. Those who are willing to put their foot into the muddy waters in order to effect change are the only ones who stand any chance of success, and it is therefore an ethical imperative to continue to try. The ethic of risk accepts this challenge and exhorts us to be aware of the process so as to be able to revise our actions and update our assessment of what is possible by remaining grounded in the social, political, and cultural contexts and the lives of intended beneficiaries. This is very similar to the approach of the pragmatists who insisted that we must act on our existing state of knowledge and experiences and make ethical decisions despite the fact that we know our knowledge and experiences to be imperfect. What distinguishes this ethical process from haphazard actions is that it is reflective. If we cease to open ourselves to the experiences of others, to the possibility of our own fallibility, and to the dynamic nature of social life, then we are not practicing responsible action and an ethic of risk, but just bumbling along with no direction. When we remain open to these, we are engaged in an ethical and informed practice of risk-taking.

Implications

This study has several implications for all proponents of social change. Underlying all other implications is that this research shows the importance of taking reflective practice seriously. Given the academic valorization of theory over practice,[21] it is not surprising that insufficient attention has been paid to lawyers' and clients' knowledge. It is also not surprising that it is through feminist analysis that the ethic of risk is best recognized and characterized, as feminists have historically insisted on the connection of theory to direct action and the personal to the political.[22] If theory is to make a difference, it must connect the profound with the prosaic. Taking clients and lawyers seriously means honoring their willingness to get their hands dirty. This is not a call for the hollow praise of good intentions. It is a call for researchers and theorists to provide grounded understandings that can help lawyers and clients work for social justice and that acknowledges the complexity of the work that they do together. This means taking seriously the voices of lawyers and clients in progressive lawyering scholarship: from the setting of future research agendas, to providing perspectives, interpreting results, and considering the value and implications of progressive lawyering theories. Empirical research grounded in the perspectives of lawyers and clients can bridge the gap between theorists and practitioners to pave the way for theory that contributes to practice in a number of ways.

A grounded theory of progressive lawyering helps lawyers and clients reflect about choices in order to mitigate the potential for continuing oppression. This means that assumptions, goals, and strategies must be revised based on accumulated knowledge and experiences. Lawyers and clients must work together and share information on individual cases. On a more systemic level, lawyers and legal services organizations can help by acting as a node or repository for client knowledge when clients are dispersed or may be unaware of others who share similar problems. Clients can help lawyers by sharing the information and experiences they have with others, including how and where to access services. Perhaps more important, clients and lawyers can work together to articulate and spread their concerns and discontent with the current state of affairs in order to better understand which issues are systemic and how they might be critiqued and changed.

Reflection reminds us that though many client-professional decisions may be necessarily strategic, there is an ethic that guides the strategies. This ethic needs to be acknowledged and nurtured in law schools, in practice settings, and in the professional literature. Making the ethic explicit respects professionals and clients engaged in social change by understanding their actions as an expression of an ethical stance. Awareness of the different factors that lawyers and clients weigh in making decisions can help both groups make informed choices. Such is the case with lawyers who are so worried about client autonomy that they fail to give full attention to the equally important value of compassion. If these are both acknowledged, then it is easier to locate and understand the dilemmas of practice grounded in community. While these are by definition irresolvable, lawyers and clients can at least debate the relative merits of choices explicitly to make decisions that are enriched by input from a variety of stakeholders.

Explicit choices can elicit greater support from peers and others, something that we have seen is necessary to sustain commitment in the face of work that can be stressful and draining. Visions of idealized practice fail to acknowledge the risks involved in "doing." They are not "messy" enough to be representative of, or resonant with, practitioners and their experiences. One unintended consequence of this is that it implicitly blames the lawyers and clients for failed strategies. Focusing on the possibly inherent disempowerment in highly unequal professional-client relationships deflects blame from the more systemic causes of limited options.

It is important to continue to explore what practices might disempower clients or work against social justice goals. It is also important to question the extent to which such critiques can themselves be used and turned against legal services lawyers and clients. For example, we should question why lawyers and clients are told that clients need to be "autonomous," and what we mean by autonomy. As this study shows, atomistic definitions of client autonomy do not serve clients well, nor do they sit well with many lawyers. More careful investigation shows that such a definition of autonomy is compatible with the prevailing U.S. discourse that valorizes the individual and stigmatizes as dependency most forms of social assistance, particularly for the poor. Lawyer-client relationships belie these myths because they are rooted in more comprehensive, and thus more complex, understandings of the contexts in which clients and lawyers live and work. When these relationships are not congruent with the prevailing wisdom and ideals, it results in tension. It is easy to hold lawyers and clients culpable for these tensions and to assume that if they would only act *properly*, then clients would be autonomous. Such an understanding of the all-powerful individual is consistent with widespread cultural beliefs in the all-responsible individual.

A more critical analysis questions the validity of this ideal and its underlying assumptions. When concepts like autonomy or empowerment are narrowly viewed in the legal services context, it appears that reluctant legal services clients need to be coaxed to become autonomous, collaborative clients. A comprehensive vision would recognize that every one of us is dependent in some way or another at one time or another, and that this does not necessarily diminish our capacity to make decisions or to collaborate when (and how) this is warranted. Such an understanding situates the choices of legal services clients alongside those made by paying clients. This is important for understanding clients and for deconstructing lawyers' angst over "capitulating" by not hounding clients to conform to some ideal mold. It also shifts the locus of blame from the individual to society, which is primarily responsible for most clients' social, political, and economic subordination.

To come full circle: Lawyers and clients must remind themselves that their working relationship takes place in a context and that their responsible action is delineated as much by the possibilities created by outside systems as they are by their own choices. Simultaneously, lawyers and clients need to walk a line that holds lawyers (and other professionals) responsible by calling them to act reflectively and holding them to an ethic of risk. This is an ethical framework for action that holds the promise of creating change, even in politically conservative times.

APPENDIX A

Supplemental Methods

Protection of Confidentiality and Ethical Issues

Lawyers interested in participating were asked to contact me directly via e-mail or telephone to set up an interview. All interviews took place in their respective offices and were tape-recorded: I transcribed all interviews and removed identifying information from the transcripts. Names of participants were changed and same-gender pseudonyms assigned. I eliminated or altered possible identifying references in the transcripts, such as names of cities, law schools, or specific positions held within NELS, although I retained the identity of the division. Any e-mail correspondence with lawyers was deleted electronically. All informed consent forms (appendix C) were retained and stored in a locked file cabinet.

I requested permission to contact the attorneys for clarifications or questions, should these arise during the study. Identifying information necessary to match initial and follow-up interviews was stored in a locked file cabinet until completion of data analysis. The interviews were then given a matching code, and any identifying information was destroyed.

Lawyers who identified potential study participants asked a client's permission to provide me with contact information (see appendix D). I made contact with clients by their mode of choice, which in most cases was by telephone. While most clients agreed to participate, several referrals did not result in interviews, as described in chapter 2. In one case, the referring lawyer warned me via e-mail that his conversation with his client regarding study participation had been strange, that she said she would "do anything for him," and he was not sure she had agreed to participate independent of her gratitude to and dependence upon him. He also noted that the client had some "mental health issues." Because the lawyer was concerned that the client would be distressed if I failed to call, I did contact the client and thanked her for her interest, but did not conduct an interview with her.

If a client agreed to participate in the project after discussing it with me, interviews were set up at the client's location of choice. Most interviews took place in clients' homes, with the exception of five conducted at the NELS offices and one telephone interview. I employed the same confidentiality procedures with client interviews as those outlined above (client consent forms are attached as appendix E). However, special attention was paid to the more vulnerable status of the clients seeking legal services. Because the research question concerned the lawyer-client relationship and the legal process, clients were only asked to elaborate on substantive issues to the extent that they were relevant. Although the attorneys considered for this study provide legal services only for civil matters, I specifically requested at the outset that clients refrain from discussing any behavior that could be considered illegal or incriminating. In cases where clients asked my advice on legal questions, I reiterated that I was not their lawyer, and suggested that they contact their lawyer with such questions. Participating clients received $20 for their time.

Data Collection

Lofland and Lofland describe intensive interviewing as a "guided conversation" which "seeks to *discover* the informant's *experience* of a particular topic or situation."[1] This is the best method to obtain the in-depth perceptions of lawyers and clients about the work they do together. My interviews lasted from one to two and a half hours and used an interview guide with open-ended questions and topic areas to be explored. The open-ended format allowed for exploration of topics that the participants brought up, in the order that they wished to follow.

I used separate interview guides for clients (appendix F) and lawyers (appendix G).[2] Interviews were designed to elicit rich descriptions of the relationship between the lawyer and the client. Interviews also explored issues that had been flagged in the literature; for example, conflict or tension between lawyers and clients regarding goals or strategies (see appendix F, second page). Some questions about client satisfaction were based loosely on survey questions from a telephone study that William Felstiner conducted (questionnaires received from Felstiner via e-mail, June 2000).

Unscripted interviewing is a collaborative process. Although there are areas or topics the interviewer seeks to explore, semi-structured interviews allow respondents to guide the conversation. I did not employ the entirely unstructured interview approach that "attempts to understand the complex behavior of members of society without imposing any a priori categorization that may limit the field of inquiry."³ I did direct the conversation to the subject of lawyer-client relationships, and specific topic areas came from my prior understanding of and curiosity about the field and specific issues. However, I allowed clients to tell me as much or as little they liked about legal problems, their lives, and their thoughts as they came up in the conversation—however apparently tangential.

Interviews generally started with "small talk" before the client signed the consent form, often about the weather or children. Many clients asked questions. Participants often asked what I did; what degree I was going for (and what *is* a dissertation?); when would I become a lawyer; or why did I leave the practice of law? Questions were also personal: Did I have any children, how old were they (and how old was I), who was taking care of them? I answered such questions. Instrumentally, I felt that to do so would facilitate rapport with clients. Morally, I felt that since I was asking intrusive questions about difficult topics (albeit for a purpose),⁴ it was only fair to answer the ones they asked me. Perhaps most compelling, I felt that my interviews were conversational, open and trusting, and the flow of conversation and reciprocity of interest made me feel as though it was "natural" to answer questions. Answers were brief, however, so as not to focus the conversation upon myself and to minimize the social desirability bias that any answer might elicit.

Although it was entirely clear that as the interviewer I shaped the conversation, my approach was to try to elicit the clients' understandings. I explained the interview to participants as an opportunity for me to learn from them as experts or knowledge holders about the topic at hand.⁵ I often used phrases such as "you went through this, so I'd like to know what you thought"; or "what would you tell a friend or a relative in the same situation?" I also asked respondents if my interpretation of their words or my understanding of an emerging theme made sense to them.

Participants led the discussion, covering most of the questions and topic areas in the interview guide. Whenever possible, I asked participants to provide examples, often using phrases such as "can you walk me through that?" The specificity allowed better understanding of what they were explaining, and steered participants away from vague generalizations.⁶ I requested clarification of what participants meant if they assumed that I knew something, particularly when lawyers who knew I had practiced law assumed that we shared an understanding of the legal situations or processes.

Many participants offered to show me legal documents, correspondence, or records about events relevant to the cases to provide background information or to clarify a point. Although I perused some of these documents in the interviews, I stressed to the participants that I was interested in their impressions and that it was not necessary to show me documents to back them up.[7]

I revised the interview guide as unanticipated issues emerged during data collection. For example, as the concept of "transformation" emerged about halfway through the study, I began to probe lawyers about how clients influenced them or changed the way they thought of their goals or their practices. Early on, many clients talked about stress, so I devised questions to probe that concept as well. In later interviews, as saturation was reached, I tested emerging interpretations of the data for resonance with study participants. More informal member-checking took place when a number of lawyers and the NELS director asked to read my research as it progressed. In response to this request, I shared drafts of an article based on preliminary analysis of the data.[8] Three of the lawyers who read the draft provided feedback that corroborated my understanding of their (and their colleagues) experiences and confirmed that my analysis added insight to *their* understanding.

Lawyers were requested not to provide background information about the clients whom they referred so that I would not to come to the interview with the referring lawyer's perception in place. Only in follow-up interviews with lawyers did I ask them to reflect on the clients they referred and to explain how "typical" (or not) they considered them to be. I also asked the lawyers to explain why they referred each client, and how their cases were going if they were still open. Outside of these questions, each follow-up interview was tailored to reflect the previous interview with the lawyer and interviews with the clients who were referred. Data from interviews with participating lawyers were supplemented with data from interviews with three lawyers who had formerly worked at NELS and two current NELS employees that were collected as part of another study.

Data Analysis

My transcriptions were verbatim, with the exception of one from an interview with a very tangential discussion. All grammatical errors were retained, although accents and dialects were not indicated (e.g., the word "going" was written even if the respondent pronounced it "goin'"). I made notations when participants laughed or made other noises or gestures, such as sighs or pounding the table.

After transcribing the interviews and prior to the follow-up interview with the lawyer, I read all the interviews from that set, that is, the initial interview with the lawyer and all three client interviews. I coded each interview as I read it, often adding codes with subsequent readings as my analysis progressed. Using an open-coding technique, I coded interviews as wholes (to indicate gender, type of legal problem, and whether the participant was a lawyer or client).[9] I also coded interviews on a line-by-line basis. Initially, I did all coding by hand on hard copies of the transcripts. At about the midpoint of data collection, I employed the N4 version of the qualitative data analysis software NUD·IST. As others have pointed out,[10] software is a tool. It does not replace the researcher's task of interpreting the data, although it can make it easier and more comprehensive. I used software to better manage the large quantity of data[11] and to ensure a systematic approach to the coding of each interview.[12]

In coding, I examined the interviews for sensitizing concepts suggested by the relevant literature and my pilot interviews.[13] For example, to appreciate power dynamics, I looked for instances of conflicting interests, resistance, and conflicting opinions between lawyers and clients.[14] I also looked for differences and convergences of expectations and anticipated outcomes, particularly between clients and lawyers.[15] In reviewing different legal strategies and practice structures, I searched for discussions of trade-offs. Sensitizing concepts[16] that occurred to me prior to data collection were updated throughout analysis using the constant comparative method.[17] As the interviews were analyzed and more specific categories emerged, prior interviews were revisited to look for confirming and disconfirming statements.

Open-coding yielded 66 codes (see appendix H for a list of codes used). An explanatory memo accompanied most codes. Some were as brief as one line, but others were several pages long. Memos contained an explanation of the code, and if applicable, noted relevant material such as literature or a quote from an interview that typified the code. As codes became more complicated, I sometimes split them. For example, a code labeled "social work" indicated a lawyer's observations that his or her work was like social work, something that came up in nearly all interviews. The first few participants explained this as work that was largely characterized by coordinating their efforts with social services. As more lawyers explained their use of the term, it became clear that other lawyers used it differently, to indicate when they used relationship skills or showed empathy to clients in a way that they imagined a therapist might. After these two different meanings emerged, I split the code "social worker" into subcategories. In many cases, portions of the interviews were coded using overlapping codes.

When two codes included nearly identical data, I merged them. More frequently, however, as analysis proceeded I noted that I often coded portions of the interview with the same group of codes. For example, discussions of competency often accompanied discussions of autonomy. As I reviewed codes that recurred together, I tried to understand how they might be related and formed major themes, or what Miles and Huberman call "bins" which contained related codes.[18] I also referred to the "progressive lawyering" literature to enhance my emerging understanding. All of the major themes changed at various points, as did their contents, which shifted in different combinations through several iterations of the analysis and changed as new codes emerged. Perhaps the most important component in the emergence of major themes was the writing process itself.[19] In writing to produce reports for presentations, my understanding of the data changed each time, which in turn led me to revise and write more. The resulting four themes that emerged from these groups are the four empirical chapters in the body of this book: Collaboration, Client Autonomy, Transformation, and Notions of Social Change.

APPENDIX B

Corey S. Shdaimah
210 Williamsburg Road
Ardmore, PA 19003
cshdaima@brynmawr.edu
610-642-2358

Public Interest Lawyering, Professionalism, Power, and the Pursuit of Social Justice

Summary Project Description

Critical literature has questioned public interest lawyering as an appropriate tool for the pursuit of social justice. While critical scholarship has been important in raising awareness of lawyers and academics concerning issues of power and empowerment within the public interest lawyering context, it has not always been grounded sufficiently.

Although much of the literature relies on the first-hand experiences of a small number of practitioners, it has failed to account satisfactorily for the daily expectations, practices, and experiences of many public interest lawyers. It also does not address sufficiently the self-reflection in which many of these lawyers engage or the adaptations they make so that their practice of public interest law is more compatible with other ideals or goals they embrace. Furthermore, virtually no studies have been made with legal services clients.

My research seeks to address these gaps. Research that is empirically grounded in the experiences of lawyers and clients will allow us to better understand and assess the credibility of critical scholarship. It will also help to direct this scholarship in ways that are useful to practicing lawyers and their clients as well as to legal scholars.

I would like to interview 8–10 public interest lawyers who practice in nonprofit organizations dedicated to the provision of direct legal services, either exclusively or in combination with other legal tools. Lawyers who are interested in participating will be asked to contact me to set up an interview, which will take approximately 90 minutes and will be tape-recorded. Interviews will be transcribed, disguising any names or identifying characteristics of people or of organizations, and then the tapes will be destroyed. Lawyers will be asked to agree to a second interview at a later date. I expect these follow-up interviews to be shorter.

Each participating lawyer will be asked to refer three consenting clients to be interviewed. If a client thinks they may be interested in participating, you will ask them to indicate their consent by signing a contact form that I will give you, which requests a telephone number and the best time of day to call. Client interviews will be governed by the same confidentiality procedures indicated above, and participating clients who agree to be interviewed will receive a $20 stipend.

As I am chiefly interested in the lawyer-client relationship and the legal process, the clients will only be asked to elaborate on substantive issues concerning their representation to the extent that they are relevant. I will specifically request at the outset that clients refrain from discussing any behavior that could be considered illegal or incriminating. I will reiterate this during the interview, if necessary.

Interviews can take place at the public interest law organization or at another location designated by the participating lawyer or client. This will depend on the organization and the participant, with an eye toward minimizing any inconvenience or disruption. All methods and procedures, including informed consent forms for lawyers and clients, have been submitted for prior approval to Bryn Mawr College's Institutional Review Board.

Lawyer Informed Consent Form

The Practice of Public Interest Law:
Power, Professionalism, and Social Justice

The purpose of this study: This research is a study of public interest lawyers and their clients. I am interested in talking to you about your practices and experiences as a lawyer pursuing legal solutions to individual and social problems. I am particularly interested in how you view the work that you do and your relationships with your clients.

The researcher: I, Corey Shdaimah, am conducting this research in partial fulfillment of my Ph.D. requirements at the Graduate School of Social Work and Social Research, Bryn Mawr College. The Institutional Review Board of Bryn Mawr College has approved the proposed research project.

Participation: If you choose to participate, I will conduct an interview with you at the location of your choice, which will take approximately 90 minutes. During the interview, I will ask you questions about your experiences practicing public interest law. The interview will be recorded on cassette tape, which I will later transcribe. I will also conduct a shorter follow-up interview. In addition to your participation, you will also be asked to refer three clients who agree to be interviewed by me, and who will receive $20 for their time and effort. Your participation is voluntary, and you may refuse to participate or discontinue the interview at any time.

By signing this consent form, you also indicate that you agree to inform your study client that whether he or she participates in the study or not will in no way affect your organization's provision of legal services to them in the future.

Confidentiality: Anything that you say during the interview will be held confidential. I will transcribe our interview within five days. I will then destroy the tapes and store the transcripts in a locked cabinet and will not share them with anyone else. In any transcripts as well as in any publications that may result from this study, your name and any identifying information will be deleted or disguised. Your name and your contact information matched up with the pseudonym will be held in a locked file until the follow-up interview. Once I conduct the follow-up interview, your contact information will be destroyed. I will complete the follow-up interview upon completion of interviews with the clients which you refer and as soon as possible. These interviews will have priority over any interviews with new clients.

Risks: Although I believe it to be unlikely, in the event of a civil liability claim involving the behavior recorded in the interview, if the tapes (before destruction) or transcribed interviews are subpoenaed, I will produce them. As noted, I will take all precautions possible to eliminate any identifying information as outlined above in order to minimize this risk.

Benefits: There are no direct benefits to you from this study. It is my hope that this research will contribute to a better understanding of the practice of public interest law and issues of importance to practicing lawyers and their clients.

Rights: You have the right to refuse or discontinue participation in this interview at any time or to refuse to answer any question that we ask. Your confidentiality will also be protected as outlined in this consent form.

By signing this consent form, you are indicating that you have read and understood the above information and that you have been given the opportunity to discuss any questions about the study and your participation with the interviewer. If you have any further questions or concerns, please contact Corey Shdaimah at 610-642-2358 or the Director of my Dissertation Committee, Jim Baumohl, at 610-520- 2621.

_____	_____	_____
Participant Name	Participant Signature	Date
_____	_____	_____
Researcher Name	Researcher Signature	Date

Referral Consent Form

The Practice of Public Interest Law:
Power, Professionalism, and Social Justice

You have been asked to participate in a study of public interest lawyers and clients being conducted by Corey Shdaimah, a doctoral student at Bryn Mawr College. If you agree to participate, the researcher will meet with you to talk with you about your experiences as a client receiving legal services. Your refusal or agreement to participate in this study will in no way affect your receipt of services.

If you think you are willing to participate, Corey Shdaimah will contact you in order to answer any questions about the research and to set up an interview at a time and place of your convenience. You will receive a $20 stipend at the end of the interview.

If you have any questions or concerns, you may contact the researcher, Corey Shdaimah, at 610-642-2358.

Please sign below if you agree to be contacted, and indicate the best way contact you:

_____ _____ _____
Name of Participant Referred   Signature   Date

Please contact me at telephone # _____

Alternative telephone # _____

The best time of day to contact me is _____

_____ _____ _____
Name of Referring Lawyer   Signature   Date

Client Informed Consent Form

The Practice of Public Interest Law:
Power, Professionalism, and Social Justice

The purpose of this study: This research is a study of public interest law-yers and their clients. I am interested in talking to you about your expe-rience as a client receiving legal services. I am particularly interested in what you thought about the services that you got, and how you felt about your interaction with your lawyer. Your lawyer _____ recommended you for the study.

The researcher: I, Corey Shdaimah, am conducting this research in partial fulfillment of my doctoral requirements at the Graduate School of Social Work and Social Research, Bryn Mawr College. The Institutional Review Board of Bryn Mawr College has approved the proposed research project.

Participation: If you choose to participate, I will conduct an interview with you at the location of your choice, which will take approximately one hour. During the interview, I will ask you questions about your experi-ences with your lawyer and legal services. I will also be talking to your lawyer about how you work together, but I will not share any information that you tell me in this interview with your lawyer or anybody else in a way that would identify you. The interview will be recorded on cassette tape, which I will transcribe. If you agree, I may contact you for further information or a shorter follow-up interview.

Your participation is voluntary, and you may refuse to participate or discontinue the interview at any time. Your refusal or participation will not affect the legal services that you receive in any way.

Confidentiality: I will transcribe the tapes within five days of our in-terview. I will then destroy the tapes and store the transcripts in a locked cabinet and will not share them with anyone else. In any of the transcripts as well as in any publications that may result from this study, your name and any identifying information will be deleted or disguised.

Risks: I do not foresee any risks associated with your participation in this study. I am a researcher and not your lawyer, so although our conversation is confidential it is not covered by attorney-client privilege. That means that I cannot refuse to provide tapes (before they are destroyed) or transcripts of our interview if they are subpoenaed. Therefore, please do not share with me any information about yourself that may be illegal or incriminating.

Benefits: There are no direct benefits to you from this study. I hope this research will contribute to a better understanding of issues of importance to clients who receive legal services and their lawyers. You will receive $20 for your time and effort in participating in this study.

Rights: You have the right to refuse or discontinue participation in this interview at any time or to refuse to answer any question that I ask. Your confidentiality will also be protected as outlined in this consent form.

By signing this consent form, you are indicating that you have read and understood the above information and that you have been given the opportunity to discuss any questions about the study and your participation with the interviewer. If you have any further questions or concerns, please contact Corey Shdaimah at 610-642-2358 or the Director of my Dissertation Committee, Jim Baumohl, at 610-520-2621.

Participant Name	Participant Signature	Date

Researcher Name	Researcher Signature	Date

Client Interview Guide

The Practice of Public Interest Law:
Power, Professionalism, and Social Justice

I will thank the client for agreeing to meet with me. I will briefly introduce myself, the research project, and the interview format and ask if he or she has any questions.

Together, we will review the consent form. I will place particular emphasis on the fact that I do not need to know detailed information about the legal problems that prompted the client to seek legal assistance, except if they want me to know about it. Furthermore, I will reiterate that the client should not inform me of any behavior that may be illegal or make them vulnerable in any way. I will explain that I am not protected by the same kind of confidentiality that they have with their lawyer. If necessary, I will remind the client of this during the interview.

If the client agrees to participate and indicates this by signing the consent form, I will begin the interview. At the outset, I will inform the client that I am interested in his or her "personal take" on his or her experience with the lawyer and the legal process.

Interview:

I. BACKGROUND

Personal information
How did you hear about <u>organization</u>?
What made you decide to seek legal assistance from <u>organization</u>?
How did you first contact them (phone/walk-in)?
How did you explain your legal problem to the person who took your call/the intake worker?
Have you ever used a lawyer before? (Describe.)
Have you ever sought legal assistance before from <u>organization</u>?

II. ENCOUNTER WITH THE ORGANIZATION

What did you hope that <u>organization</u> could do for you?

Can you walk me through your first encounter at <u>organization</u>? (Prompt—telephone, intake.)

Did you see a lawyer during your first visit?

III. RAPPORT WITH THE LAWYER

How would you describe your meeting with <u>lawyer</u>?

How did you explain your problem to <u>lawyer</u>?

Do you think <u>lawyer</u> acted professionally/unprofessionally? In what way?

How easy was it to talk about your problem?

How well did you feel that the lawyer understood what you were telling him/her?

Is there anything that you felt that you wanted to tell the lawyer but couldn't/didn't? (If yes, explore.)

IV. COMMUNICATION ABOUT THE LEGAL PROCESS

How did <u>lawyer</u> explain your legal situation?

Did you ask <u>lawyer</u> any questions about that?

What choices did <u>lawyer</u> give you to make about taking care of your legal problem?

How did you decide what to do?

How did <u>lawyer</u> help you decide?

How well did <u>lawyer</u> understand your problem?

Did you understand what <u>your lawyer</u> told you about handling your legal problem?

What is your next step with your legal problem?

V. CONFLICT

Did you want to do something that your lawyer told you wouldn't be a good idea? (Probe.)

Did you want your lawyer to do something that you knew he/she would not do? (Probe.)

How did you resolve that?

How do you feel about the way that worked out?

Did you discuss that incident with anybody?

VI. INVOLVEMENT IN THE LEGAL PROCESS

Where are you at now with your legal problem?

Are you satisfied with that?

How have your ideas about the law changed since you have had this legal problem? (Explain.)

How have your ideas about the law changed since you started working with lawyer? (Explain.)

VII. ASSESSMENT

Would you feel comfortable coming back to organization again for help?

Would you feel comfortable working with lawyer again?

What do you think you would tell a friend or relative with a similar legal problem to do?

Is there anything that lawyer did or said that made you feel comfortable?

Is there anything that lawyer did or said that made you feel uncomfortable?

Is there anything that you think could be done differently at organization to help make it easier for clients like yourself?

Is there anything else about your experience with lawyer or organization that you want to tell me/ that you think I should know?

CONCLUDING QUESTIONS AND PARTICIPANT ASSESSMENT OF INTERVIEW

I will thank the participant for agreeing to meet. I will ask how he/ she found the interview, and if he/she has any suggestions or comments regarding the interview format or anything that he/she would like to talk about or expand on that we have not covered.

If the client has a legal problem that requires ongoing legal services with the organization, I will ask permission to contact him or her again for a follow-up interview as the case progresses.

Lawyer Interview Guide

The Practice of Public Interest Law:
Power, Professionalism, and Social Justice

I will thank the lawyer for agreeing to meet with me. I will briefly intro-duce myself, the research project, and the interview format and ask if he or she has any questions. Together, we will review the consent form. If the lawyer agrees to participate and indicates this by signing the consent form, I will begin the interview.

At the outset, I will emphasize that I am interested in the participant's point of view—his or her "personal take" on things.

Interview:

I. BACKGROUND

Personal information
How long have you been practicing law?
How did you decide to go into law?
How did you decide to go into public interest law?
What does the term social justice mean to you?
Do you have a specific vision of social justice?

II. INDIVIDUAL WITHIN ORGANIZATION

How long have you been at <u>organization</u>?
What made you decide to work here/in this field?
Can you describe what you do at <u>organization</u>.
How do you decide what kind of cases or issues to work on? (Probe for priority-setting criteria—organizational or personal.)

III. RELATIONSHIP WITH CONSTITUENTS

Who are your clients/intended beneficiaries?

How do you come into contact with them?

How do you figure out which clients you can provide with legal services?

How do you see your relationship to them?

Do you or does your organization have ties with a particular community? If so, what kinds of things do you do with/for them? How would you describe your relationship with that community?

IV. RAPPORT WITH CLIENTS

Can you walk me through a typical first meeting with a client?

How do you find out the information that you need to know?

How would you describe your rapport with most clients?

Do you have any personal guidelines for interacting with clients?

Can you think of a situation in which you had trouble communicating with a client? How did you handle that?

Is there anything that you would like to change about the way you interact with most clients now?

Has your approach to clients or your work changed over time? How? Why do you think that is?

V. COMMUNICATION ABOUT THE LEGAL PROCESS

How do you explain the client's legal situation?

How do you present clients with information about possible options or strategies?

How do you handle a situation where a client asks your opinion in choosing between various options? (Ask to describe an example.)

How do you handle a situation where a client asks you to decide for him or her? (Ask to describe an example.)

VI. CONFLICT

Do you ever find that you have misunderstandings with clients about the legal process or about what you can do for him or her?

Do you ever have different opinions with a client about what course of action to pursue?

Can you describe one or two incidents when that happened?

How did you resolve that?

Were you satisfied with the resolution?

Did you discuss that incident with anybody?

VII. CRITIQUE

Are you familiar with some of the criticisms that say that certain legal tools work against empowering people for social change? (If not, provide brief explanation.)

What do you think of that idea?

Has this, or similar thoughts that you yourself have had, influenced your practice?

Has it influenced the way that you approach your clients?

VIII. SATISFACTION AND INTERVIEW CONCLUSION

Is there anything you would like to talk about or expand on that we have not covered?

Do you like your work?

What about your work do you find satisfying? Unsatisfactory?

To conclude, I would like to ask whether you have you had any mentors in your life or career who have influenced your work?

(If the previous question doesn't "speak" to the respondent) Do you have a guiding value in your work?

CONCLUDING QUESTIONS AND
PARTICIPANT ASSESSMENT OF INTERVIEW

I will thank the participant for agreeing to meet. I will ask how he/she found the interview, and if he/she has any suggestions or comments regarding the interview format.

I will explain that I will be contacting him or her again for a follow-up interview some time in the next few months.

I will thank the participant for agreeing to refer three clients, and provide the participant with a referral consent form. I will then suggest that I call some time in the next two weeks to check and see whether the participant has any clients who have agreed for me to contact them.

List of Codes

Hierarchical Codes

1. Participant
   1.1. Lawyer
   1.2. Client
2. Group
   11 interview groupings of lawyers and clients who work together, indicating also whether they were in the main or branch office.
3. Gender
   3.1 Female
   3.2 Male
4. Lawyer-Client Relationship
   4.1 Retainer Model
   4.2 Friendship Model

Free Codes

1. Respect/dignity
2. Motivation
3. Law as a tool
4. Political engagement/advocacy: Are clients engaged in anything that could be construed as political in the sense of seeing grievances as not merely their own private bad luck?
5. Social work: What lawyers and I see as their "social work" role. Also instances where social workers are involved
6. Resource constraints
7. Triage/screening: Including also screening at the front desk or during intake, maybe this needs to be in a separate, administrative node with separate branches.
8. Lawyer/client communication

9. Background information
10. Main/branch dynamics
11. Work environment
12. Specialization
13. Attorney autonomy: vis-à-vis NELS and vis-à-vis clients
14. Social change/social justice
15. Direct service
16. Outreach/community education
17. Representing the client to others
18. Stress/calming clients: This node includes stress on attorneys and stress on clients.
19. Listening to clients
20. Complexity
21. Redirecting
22. Satisfaction/dissatisfaction: Here also clients and attorneys. For attorneys, job satisfaction; for clients, (dis)satisfaction with lawyers.
23. Lawyer as being there for the client: also cases of clients coming back to NELS or a particular lawyer for services after having used them in the past.
24. Client autonomy/decision-making
25. Multiple problems
26. Values/mentors
27. Stereotypes of lawyers
28. Judging clients
29. Access
30. Clients "doing my part"/documentation
31. Interactions with the system
32. Learning/imparting knowledge: This can be about learning from the system or the lawyer but also about clients helping other clients.
33. Feeling/making clients comfortable: This includes references to trust.
34. First impressions/expectations
35. Support networks
36. Transformative
37. Unit info: people, job description, specialty-related issues
38. What is the lawyer's role: What is the function of the lawyer, the scope of what he or she does for clients? This also includes the preferred model for lawyering.
39. Bearer of bad tidings

40. Referrals: This can refer to lawyers referring to other professionals or other lawyers, or to clients referring or being referred by friends/family/acquaintances.
41. Paralegals
42. Empathy/concern
44. Alienation of legal process from clients' lives.
45. Who are my clients/constituents: These are all questions directed at lawyers, but may also be used with clients who describe their group belonging.
46. Lawyer/community relationships
47. Collaboration
48. Personal/professional guidelines
49. Empowerment
50. Professional ethics
51. Practice/theory
52. Duration
53. Health problems
54. Client's understanding of the legal system
55. Trust
56. Justice/thoughts about the law or the legal system
57. Thoughts about free legal aid
58. "Uppity" clients: Comes from Steve's complimentary description of a client as a fighter.
59. Arbitrary/capricious
60. Resourcefulness/persistence
61. Boundaries
62. Client goals
63. Coping mechanisms
64. Self-reflection
65. The importance of a (good) lawyer
66. Abdication of responsibility/rules from higher up
67. Lawyers and social change: This should be a subcategory of social change, perhaps replacing the social change category for lawyers.
68. Justice and the legal system

Notes

PREFACE

1. Lorde gave her 1979 speech, entitled "The Master's Tools Will Never Dismantle the Master's House," at a New York University Conference. It was published in *Sister Outsider, Essays and Speeches*.

2. Northeast City and all names, places, and organizations referred to in this book are pseudonyms in order to protect the confidentiality of the participants in the study upon which this book is based.

3. This is based on Sharon Welch's *A Feminist Ethic of Risk*, which I discuss in greater detail in chapter 7. The ethic of risk acknowledges that actions carried out in the real world are unpredictable and potentially harmful. Ethical actors respond to this; they do not become paralyzed by the potential of harming others, but rather reflect thoughtfully and in dialogue with others about the actions they have taken in the past and will take in the future.

CHAPTER 1

1. See Feldman, "Political Lessons"; also see, criticizing Feldman, Houseman, "Political Lessons—A Commentary."

2. People from around the state and around the country contact NELS for their experience and expertise.

3. The unit that serves elderly clients is an exception to this income limitation. Because it receives funding from the local federally funded aging services organization, it does not have an income ceiling, but rather serves all clients who come with a qualifying substantive issue. However, most clients who enlist this assistance cannot afford a private attorney and thus are similar to NELS's other clients in financial status, although there are some more financially secure, lower middle-class clients.

4. For resasons of confidentiality, the brief description of Northeast City does not cite any specific data or refer to any particular sources. The demographic information provided in this paragraph is available from a number of national and local sources.

5. Cahn and Cahn, "The War on Poverty"; and Reich, "The New Property."

6. See Davis, *Brutal Need;* and Hilbink, "Constructing Cause Lawyering."

7. See Davis, *Brutal Need;* and Katz, *Poor People's Lawyers,* for detailed histories of two legal services programs. Davis focuses on New York and Katz on Chicago.

8. On bar support, see Hilbink, "Constructing Cause Lawyering"; and Houseman and Peete, *Securing Equal Justice for All.* For criticism by the bar association, one of the more famous attacks was levied by Spiro Agnew (1972). Hilbink's history also provides a detailed account of vying for the support of the organized bar in the creation of the Legal Services program within the Office of Economic Opportunity.

9. Jim Baumohl has suggested that the aging of legal services lawyers may also contribute to their *perceptions* of neighborhood problems such as drugs and crime rather than indicators of change (see "The 'Dope Fiend's Paradise'"). As lawyers aged, they may have become aware of their own vulnerabilities and become attuned to things that they had ignored earlier. This stems not only from concern for self; as they became involved in relationships with partners and children, they might also have taken on a sense of responsibility that made them more aware of risks and less likely to take chances.

10. See Trubek, "The Worst of Times."

11. On the career opportunities and trajectories of legal services lawyers, see Thomson, "Negotiating Cause Lawyering"; and Jones, "Exploring the Sources"; on the lack of access to legal services the Legal Services Corporation, *Documenting the Justice Gap.*

12. In *Pathologies of Power,* Paul Farmer argues that the everyday deprivation and oppression that shapes the lives of people who are disadvantaged are some of the most pervasive yet unrecognized forms of violence.

13. López, *Rebellious Lawyering.*

14. Felstiner, Abel, and Sarat, "The Emergence and Transformation of Disputes."

15. Soss, "Lessons of Welfare."

CHAPTER 2

1. Sarat and Felstiner, *Divorce Lawyers and Their Clients.*

2. Gerald López characterizes much of the literature as resorting to facile, polarized caricatures of public interest lawyers and clients rather than developing complex but more accurate depictions (see *Rebellious Lawyering*). For one oft-cited study of legal services clients, see Sarat, "The Law Is All Over."

3. Shdaimah, Stahl, and Schram, "When You Can See the Sky."

4. In his situated study of case management of severe mental illness, *Meds, Money and Manners,* Jerry Floersch provides an excellent discussion of the need for studies better grounded in practice. Schon, in *The Reflective Practitioner,* criticizes the gap between theory and practice in professions generally, and

Lipsky, *Street Level Bureaucracy*, discusses how what he refers to as "street level bureaucrats" mediate between policies and practice realities and how policies, in large part, are implemented with full knowledge that they provide insufficient resources to accomplish goals.

5. See Tremblay, "Critical Legal Ethics."

6. López, "An Aversion to Clients," speaks to lack of attention to clients in the critical legal services literature.

7. Becker, Geere, Hughes, and Strauss, *Boys in White*; Edelman, *Political Language*; and Goode, "The Theoretical Limits."

8. See Auerbach, *Unequal Justice*, on the legal profession.

9. Auerbach, ibid., provides historical evidence for this in the professional context and, more recently, Guinier, Fine, and Balin, *Becoming Gentlemen*, in the law school context.

10. On law, see White, "Subordination, Rhetorical Skills, and Sunday Shoes." On social work, see Rose, "Reflections."

11. See Sarat and Felstiner, *Divorce Lawyers and Their Clients.*

12. See Rhode, "Policing the Professional Monopoly."

13. On professional codes, see Gustafson, "Professions" and Wilensky, "The Professionalization"; on altruism, see Merton and Gieryn, "Institutionalized Altruism."

14. Kronman, *The Lost Lawyer.*

15. Brint, *In an Age of Experts.*

16. Edelman, *Political Language.*

17. On rebellious lawyering, see López, *Rebellious Lawyering*; on client-centered lawyering, see Ellman, "Client-Centeredness Multiplied"; on collaborative lawyering, see White, "Collaborative Lawyering"; on critical lawyering, see Trubek, "Critical Lawyering"; and on facilitative lawyering, see Marsico, "Working for Social Change." "Cause lawyering" is a term coined by Austin Sarat and Stuart Scheingold, to encompass all forms of lawyering in service of a "cause" and thus it is broader than the progressive lawyering that is the subject of this study, encompassing, for example, right-wing cause lawyers and pro bono practitioners. (See *Something to Believe In* for a history of this conceptual catagory). As an example of the disconnect between some of the social science research on legal services lawyering and legal services practice, it is telling that none of the lawyers in this study were familiar with the term "cause lawyering," a term that I myself employ elsewhere.

18. Polikoff, "Am I My Client?" 443.

19. Freire, *Pedagogy of the Oppressed.*

20. For examples of each of these, see López, *Rebellious Lawyering*; White, "Facing South"; Polikoff, "Am I My Client?"; Ellman, "Client-Centeredness Multiplied"; and Trubek, "The Worst of Times."

21. Ibid., and Southworth, "Business Planning for the Destitute." Southworth

also admonishes such critics for failing to acknowledge the broad range of non-adversarial services that legal services actually provide.

22. White, "Facing South," 825.

23. Determining who constitutes a community, particularly where issues are contested, is also problematic. Michael Diamond, "Law, the Problems of Poverty," and "Community Lawyering," has grappled with questions of identifying "community" as well as determining which course or tactic to pursue in the case of conflicting interests within a community served by a public interest lawyer or organization. In his guidelines for making such difficult choices, the public interest attorney is not asked to renounce his or her ethical or moral commitments or do the impossible task of choosing only uncontested neighborhood issues. Instead, he or she is encouraged to choose a "defensible community interest" that is in line with his or her own guiding values (while not losing sight of community politics and the importance of trust).

24. Trubek, "Critical Lawyering," 56.

25. On the view of law as a vehicle for social change, see Ewick, Kagan, and Sarat, "Introduction: Legacies of Legal Realism"; on neutrality, see Bumiller, *The Civil Rights Society*.

26. Berger and Luckmann, who developed the concept of social constructionism in *The Social Construction of Reality*, did not take the extreme position that there is no objective reality, although they did indicate that the search for it may be fruitless, and that we cannot be sure that we know it when we see it. Their view is that despite certain constraints (societal, structural, and physical), there is, to varying degrees, room for people to apprehend, interpret, and modify their own reality and that of others. This type of scholarship has been applied to the creation and implementation of policy; see, for example, Gusfield, *The Culture of Public Problems*, as well as to interactions between individuals (e.g., Sarat and Felstiner, *Divorce Lawyers and Their Clients*). On law and society scholarship, see Silbey and Sarat, "Critical Traditions in Law," 165-174.

27. Shdaimah, "Dilemmas of Progressive Lawyering."

28. See Schon, *The Reflective Practitioner*, and more recently, Flyvbjerg, *Making Social Science Matter*.

29. Garth and Sarat, "Justice and Power in Law."

30. Foucault, *The History of Sexuality: An Introduction*, 93.

31. See, for example, the exchange between Jonathan Simon, "Between Power and Knowledge"; and Winter, "Cursing the Darkness," in the context of lawyering for social justice.

32. For this more optimistic take on power, see Cruikshank, *The Will to Empower*; and Winter, "Cursing the Darkness."

33. Simon, "Between Power and Knowledge."

34. Abu-Lughod, "The Romance of Resistance."

35. See, for example, the work of Sarat and Felstiner, *Divorce Lawyers and*

Their Clients, on divorce lawyers and clients; and Chambon, Irving, and Epstein, *Reading Foucault*, on power in the social work context. More generally, see Cruikshank, *The Will to Empower*; and Schram, *After Welfare*.

36. On nontraditional legal communication as a means of resistance, see Wanitzek, "The Power of Language." On "law talk" generally, see Probert, "Law Talk."

37. Polikoff, "Am I My Client?" and White, "Subordination, Rhetorical Skills, and Sunday Shoes."

38. Hughes, *The Sociological Eye*.

39. Sarat and Felstiner, *Divorce Lawyers and Their Clients*.

40. Gordon, *Pitied but Not Entitled*. See also Flyvbjerg, *Making Social Science Matter*; and Lemert, *Social Things*, on the importance of localized studies of power.

41. Gilliom, *Overseers of the Poor*.

42. Glaser and Strauss, *The Discovery of Grounded Theory*.

43. On the dangers of this and strategies to mitigate, see Melia, "Producing 'Plausible Stories.'"

44. Sarat, "The Law Is All Over." Shdaimah, "Not What They Expected."

45. In contrast to the experiences of Danet, Hoffman, and Kermish, "Obstacles to the Study," who experienced tremendous difficulty with lawyer cooperation, the NELS director and the lawyers and clients in this study were enthusiastic and encouraging, eager to participate in the study. The NELS director was very accommodating, providing me with data as the study progressed and offering access to conference rooms and feedback on the research.

46. Reported, for example, in Sarat and Felstiner, *Divorce Lawyers and Their Clients*. Details regarding these safeguards were explained in separate personal communications with Austin Sarat, 2000, and William Felstiner, 2000.

47. See appendix A.

48. This is likely due to a combination of factors. Women are overrepresented among the poor in general and the elderly poor in particular. This is reflected in NELS's general client population and in the unit that serves the elderly (six clients in my sample were drawn from this population, two men and four women). Further, one-third of the clients interviewed were represented by NELS's family advocacy unit (representing parents accused of abuse or neglect) or the public benefits unit. The vast majority of people involved in these systems are women, as they overwhelmingly act as the advocate parent even if they are not officially one-parent households, as many are. As client stories unfold, we see that many of their legal problems in other units are also related to their activities as caregivers, a category in which women are again overrepresented.

49. Shdaimah, "Not What They Expected."

50. I discuss this in greater detail in Shdaimah, "Dilemmas of Progressive Lawyering."

51. Such as those outlined in Trubeck, "The Worst of Times," or Houseman, "Political Lessons."

CHAPTER 3

1. See Hunt and Baumohl, "Now Invited to Testify," on the similar experiences of former beneficiaries of the Social Security Administration's drug addiction and alcoholism program.

2. Thomson, "Negotiating Cause Lawyering"; and Jones, "Exploring the Sources."

3. See, for example, Feldman, "Political Lessons," and Kennedy, "Legal Education."

4. See Auerbach, *Unequal Justice*, on a historic view of these practices; and Guinier, Fine, and Balin, *Becoming Gentlemen*, on law school socialization more recently.

5. Tremblay, "Theoretics of Practice," 949-50.

6. Mills, *The Power Elite*.

7. See, for example, Piven and Cloward, *Regulating the Poor*; and Stone, *The Disabled State*.

8. Hunt and Baumohl, "Now Invited to Testify."

9. See, for example, Rosenberg, *The Hollow Hope*.

10. See, Davis, *Brutal Need*, for a detailed account of such discussions that took place in the 1960s and early 1970s.

11. Tremblay, "Theoretics of Practice," provides a moral defense of legal services work along these lines.

12. See Bell, "Serving Two Masters," on desegregation cases and the way in which the lawyers who mounted *Brown v. Board of Education* were at odds with many of the families whose interests lawyers purported to represent.

13. McMunigal, "Of Causes and Clients," provides a thorough discussion of this using the example of Sarah Weddington's representation of Norma McCorvey in *Roe v. Wade*.

14. Feldman, "Political Lessons."

15. Karl Marx is often cited on the intersection of agency and structure: "Men make their own history, but they do not make it just as they please; the do not make it under circumstances chosen by themselves but under circumstances directly found, given and transmitted from the past"(*The Eighteenth Brumaire*, 595). C. Wright Mills refines this further in his examination of the intersection between history and biography (Mills, *Sociological Imagination*). People are limited by their circumstances; some circumstances are more limiting to some people than others.

16. Soss, "Lessons of Welfare."

17. Lesnick, "The Wellsprings of Legal Responses."

18. Lesnick distinguishes a radical perspective (described on pages 435-437) from a liberal perspective, which accepts the basic premises of the legal status quo and acknowledges the rules and roles it dictates (433-435). He asks lawyers

to resist polarizing choices between liberal and radical distinctions in order to find a way to practice law that acknowledges constraints without succumbing to paralyzing pessimism. Lawyers can:

> Infuse the day-to-day choices of "liberal" practice with the insights suggested by a radical perspective. Such an effort tries to steer clear of two polar hazards: to avoid adopting—falling prey to, some would say—the "nothing can change until everything changes" consciousness of a pure radical view, and to avoid succumbing (more than momentarily, at least) to the strong pull that the practice of law has toward regarding "radical" insights as just too counter-productive to hold on to. (p. 435)

Lesnick's definition is based on an understanding of the liberal perspective as what Kaufman has described as hollow liberalism. Hollow liberalism has been exploited by conservative politicians and thinkers and is different from the classic liberal perspective, which is "the belief that the ultimate aim of public policy is the protection and promotion of each person's equal opportunity to develop his potentialities as fully as possible" (p. 430); and a conviction of the necessity of "political democracy . . . to the realization of a good society" (*The Radical Liberal*, p. 431).

19. Schram, *After Welfare*.
20. Schram, *Praxis for the Poor*, 51.
21. Gil, *Confronting Injustice and Oppression*, 101.

CHAPTER 4

1. López, *Rebellious Lawyering*.
2. Mandatory autonomy and optional autonomy are the terms that Carl Schneider (*The Practice of Autonomy*) uses to refer to these brands of autonomy in the doctor-patient relationship. On what Schneider terms mandatory autonomy in the lawyer-client relationship, see Simon, "Lawyer Advice and Client Autonomy."
3. Minow, "Lawyering at the Margins."
4. See also Mather, "Ethics Symposium"; Minow, "Lawyering at the Margins"; and Simon, "Lawyer Advice and Client Autonomy."
5. Law school professor Carl Schneider (*The Practice of Autonomy*) explored autonomy in the context of doctor-patient relationships.
6. Ibid., 18.
7. Ibid., 22.
8. Soss, "Lessons of Welfare."
9. Schneider, *The Practice of Autonomy*, 23.
10. Fraser and Gordon, "A Genealogy of 'Dependency,'" explain how dependency has been made to appear pathological. Any behavior that evidences or

encourages people to rely on others (juxtaposed against self-reliance) is not only undesirable but downright dangerous. One classic example of this is the rhetoric around and language of the Personal Responsibility and Work Opportunity Reconciliation Act of 1996.

11. Ellman, "Symposium: Clinical Education," 777.

12. NELS does not receive any federal funding. Thus, individuals and the program as a whole are less constrained in their choice of representation tactics than many other legal services programs. It is likely that this institutional constraint did not come up in my study to the extent that it would in a study of federally funded organizations.

13. See also Polikoff, "Am I My Client?" for a general discussion of the double-edge sword of representing clients as a lawyer.

14. For a related discussion in the context of relationships between academic researchers and community-based political advocates, see also Shdaimah and Stahl, "Reflections on Doing Phronetic Social Science."

15. Sinden, "Why Won't Mom Cooperate?" 390.

16. The term "triage" is derived from battlefield medicine and it is broadly used in the legal services literature. Paul Tremblay defines it as "a practice of distinguishing among several clients in determining which should receive what level of service, acknowledging that each cannot receive an unlimited delivery of service" ("Toward a Community-Based Ethic," 1104). While some disagree with triage practices, it is widely accepted as necessary by many in the legal services community and among scholars of legal services. "Poverty lawyers will inevitably encounter more potential poor persons than they have the resources, time, and money to serve. That scarcity is a fact of life for all public interest practice and will remain so for the realistic future" (Tremblay, "Acting 'A Very Moral Type of God,'" 2475). For a different view, see Dunlap, "I Don't Want to Play God."

17. Minow, "Lawyering at the Margin."

18. The most famous example of this is in White, "Subordination, Rhetorical Skills, and Sunday Shoes."

19. American Bar Association, Model Rules of Professional Conduct.

20. "Back pay" refers to retroactive Social Security benefit payments. See Hunt and Baumohl, "Now Invited to Testify," for a discussion of "dangerous cash" as it relates to payment of retroactive benefits to beneficiaries of the Social Security drug addiction and alcoholism program.

21. Simon, "The Dark Secret of Progressive Lawyering," 1099.

22. Mackenzie and Stoljar, "Introduction: Autonomy Refigured."

CHAPTER 5

1. López, *Rebellious Lawyering*.

2. Southworth, "Taking the Lawyer."

3. Shdaimah, "Not What They Expected."

4. Piomelli, "Appreciating Collaborative Lawyering."

5. Ibid., 439.

6. *Pro se* is the legal term for self-representation in legal matters.

7. AFDC was the program commonly referred to in the United States as "welfare" prior to 1996. SSDI provides benefits to the disabled calibrated in some part to their histories of wage earning. SSDI beneficiaries do not get "welfare," and are not generally stigmatized as are their AFDC counterparts.

8. Felstiner, Abel, and Sarat, "The Emergence and Tranformation of Disputes."

9. For a wonderful discussion on this regarding her research with welfare beneficiaries, see Hays, *Flat Broke with Children.*

10. Hunt and Baumohl, "Now Invited to Testify."

11. McCann, *Rights at Work*; Concha, "Cause Lawyering for Indigenous Cases"; and Meili, "Cause Lawyering for Collective Justice."

12. Hasenfeld, "Organizational Form." The term *moral entrepreneurship* was coined by Becker, *Outsiders.*

13. Hasenfeld, "Organizational Forms."

14. See, for example, Shamir and Hacker, "Colonialism, Culture, and the Law."

15. See further discussion in chapter 6.

16. See also Michael Diamond on choosing among competing community interests—mentioned in chapter 2, footnote 18.

17. See McCoyd and Shdaimah, "Revisiting the Benefits Debate," and the literature reviewed there.

18. Green, *Cultural Awareness*, 145.

19. Literature on the social construction of social problems has highlighted how what C. Wright Mills, *Sociological Imagination*, has called "private troubles" can be transformed into "public issues."

20. McCann, *Rights at Work*, 11.

21. Engel and Munger, *Rights of Inclusion.*

CHAPTER 6

1. This attorney, who was not a participant in the study, noted that the same breakdown of advice provided and clients accepted would also apply to the unit that represents parents in child welfare proceedings. Twelve of the 30 clients in this study were served by these two units.

2. Shdaimah, "Not What They Expected."

3. In *The Lost Lawyer*, Kronman extols the virtue of lawyers' simultaneous professional commitment to sympathy and detachment. Lawyers in this study do not necessarily combine adherence to these seemingly conflicting values as a professional virtue, but rather as a response to practice concerns. That this

adaptive response is adopted or that it is widely shared may in part be due to the professional norms to which they, as lawyers, are socialized and the acceptability of striking such a dual commitment within the profession at large.

4. López, *Rebellious Lawyering*, 62.

5. Margulies, "Legal Education," specifically discusses the clinical law school setting, but his insights and suggestions about the importance of the client-professional encounter at both the personal and political levels are corroborated by my data.

6. In "We Don't Care About What Happened," Hosticka reports that the legal services lawyers he interviewed actually expended greater efforts on behalf of clients that they perceived negatively as persistent (599). Suzanne's qualification here indicates that, like the lawyers in Hosticka's study, even when clients are hostile, if they persist, she will continue to expend an effort in the case. Her quote does indicate, however, that the quality of service or her investment in the case might be compromised.

7. I understood Ruth to mean here that it makes her so angry that it is painful, making it hard to control her temper and her expression.

8. Tremblay, "Toward a Community-Based Ethic."

9. Lipsky argues that street-level bureaucracies, which are frequently under-resourced, are forced to ration services. It is in the interest of such bureaucracies to institute policies and practices that deter clients from applying and/or lower the expectations of clients regarding service. See *Street Level Bureaucracy*.

10. Binder and Price, *Legal Interviewing and Counseling*, are oft-cited proponents of this approach. See Margulies, "Legal Education," and the literature cited therein for a review of the critiques of Binder and Price's understanding of empathy.

11. *Goldberg v. Kelly*, 1970. Davis, *Brutal Need*, uses this term in the title of her history of legal services from 1960 to 1973.

12. This is not unique to legal services lawyers. Margulies notes that "most lawyers shy away from giving clients bad news, for a range of reasons including money, power, and ideology" ("Lawyers' Independence," 954). Lawyers in this study seemed most averse to communicating bad news due to their empathy for clients, as discussed in this section.

13. Sullivan, "Self-Disclosure, Separation, and Students."

14. Ibid., 115-116, 128.

15. Ibid., 132.

16. Mills, "Affective Lawyering." See also Afek, "'Touchy-Feely' Is OK." Affective lawyering is a form of therapeutic jurisprudence, which is a relatively new field (see Stolle, Wexler, and Winick, *Practicing Therapeutic Jurisprudence*). It is subject to some of the same criticism that William Simon raises in "'Homo Psychologicus,'" to the extent that it may depoliticize clients and lawyers and

focus on their inner lives to the detriment of recognizing societal and systemic concerns. However, for the same reason that I argue here (and Margulies, "Legal Education," argues) regarding the political importance of empathy, this is not necessarily the case.

17. For a detailed discussion of this, based on data from this study, see Shdaimah, "Not What They Expected."

18. See also McCann and Silverstein, "Rethinking the Law's Allurement."

19. Lesnick, "Infinity in a Grain of Sand," 1181, citing López at note 31.

20. Ibid., 1172.

21. Addams, *Democracy and Social Ethics*, 69.

CHAPTER 7

1. Berman, "Approaches to the Cultural Study of Law," 98, 118.

2. See Habermas, *Between Facts and Norms*; Toulmin, *Return to Reason*; and Welch, *A Feminist Ethic of Risk*.

3. Gilliom, *Overseers of the Poor*, 109.

4. Warren, Indigenous Movements; see also Belenky, Bond, and Weinstock, *A Tradition that Has No Name*.

5. Gilliom, *Overseers of the Poor*.

6. See Welch, *A Feminist Ethic of Risk*, 46.

7. See Elwell, "The Sociology of Max Weber," 90.

8. See Plato, *The Republic*.

9. Schon, *The Reflective Practitioner*.

10. Welch, *A Feminist Ethic of Risk*.

11. Menand, *The Metaphysical Club*.

12. See Welch, *A Feminist Ethic of Risk*.

13. See Illich, "To Hell with Good Intentions."

14. Addams, "The Subtle Problem of Charity," 75.

15. Ibid., 74.

16. Six lawyers (all of whom were included in this study except the director of NELS) asked to read my work in progress. I received unsolicited comments from three of them.

17. See Guinier, Fine, and Balin, *Becoming Gentlemen*; and Sturm, "Gender and the Higher Education Classroom."

18. Williams, *The Alchemy of Race and Rights*.

19. See Welch, *A Feminist Ethic of Risk*.

20. McCann, *Rights at Work*.

21. See Flyvberg, *Making Social Science Matter*; and Schon, *The Reflective Practitioner*.

22. See Nussbaum, "Professor of Parody."

APPENDIXES

1. Lofland and Lofland, *Analyzing Social Settings,* 18.
2. See Seidman, *Interviewing as Qualitative Research.*
3. See Fontana and Frey, "The Interview."
4. See Seidman, *Interviewing as Qualitative Research.*
5. See Fontana and Frey, "The Interview," 77, citing Wax, 1960.
6. See Weiss, *Learning from Strangers.*
7. Particularly with clients, this was often to emphasize work they had done and how organized they were, which I discuss in greater detail in chapter 5.
8. Shdaimah, "Dilemmas of Progressive Lawyering."
9. See Padgett, *Qualitative Methods.*
10. See Weitzman, "Software and Qualitative Research."
11. See Kelle and Lauries, "Computer Use in Qualitative Research."
12. See Lee and Fielding, "User Experiences of Qualitative Data."
13. Beeman, "Maximizing Credibility and Accountability."
14. See Foucault, *The History of Sexuality;* and Abu-Lughod, "The Romance of Resistance."
15. See White, "Subordination, Rhetorical Skills, and Sunday Shoes"; and López, "An Aversion to Clients."
16. Beeman, "Maximizing Credibility."
17. See Strauss and Corbin, *Basics of Qualitative Research.*
18. Miles and Huberman, *Qualitative Data Analysis.*
19. Richardson, "Writing."

References

Abu-Lughod, Leila. "The Romance of Resistance: Tracing Transformation of Power through Bedouin Women." *American Ethnologist* 17, no. 1 (1990): 41–55.

Addams, Jane. *Democracy and Social Ethics*. Chicago: University of Illinois Press, 1911/2002.

———. "The Subtle Problem of Charity." In *The Jane Addams Reader*, edited by Jean B. Elshtain, 62-75. New York: Basic Books, 2002.

Afek, Dina. "'Touchy-Feely' Is OK: Teaching Emotional Competence in Law School." Paper presented at the annual meeting for the Law and Society Association, Pittsburgh, PA, June 07, 2003.

American Bar Association. "Model Rules of Professional Conduct," available online at http://www.abanet.org/cpr/mrpc/mrpc_toc.html.

Auerbach, Jerold S. *Unequal Justice: Lawyers and Social Change in Modern America*. New York: Oxford University Press, 1974.

Baumohl, Jim. "The 'Dope Fiend's Paradise' Revisited: Notes from Research in Progress on Drug Law Enforcement in San Francisco." *The Drinking and Drug Practices Surveyor* 24 (1992): 3-16.

Becker, Howard S. *Outsiders: Studies in the Sociology of Deviance*. New York: The Free Press, 1963.

Becker, Howard, Blanche Geere, Everett C. Hughes, and Anselm Strauss. *Boys in White: Student Culture in Medical School*. Chicago: University of Chicago Press, 1961.

Beeman, Sandra K. "Maximizing Credibility and Accountability in Qualitative Analysis: A Social Work Research Case Example." *Journal of Sociology and Social Welfare* 22, no. 4 (1995): 99-114.

Belenky, Mary, Lynne A. Bond, and Jacqueline S. Weinstock. *A Tradition that Has No Name: Nurturing the Development of People, Families, and Communities*. New York: Basic Books (Harper Collins), 1997, p. 13.

Bell, Derrick A., Jr. "Serving Two Masters: Integration Ideals and Client Interest in School Desegregation Legislation." *Yale Law Journal* 85 (1976): 470-516.

Berger, Peter L., and Thomas Luckmann. *The Social Construction of Reality: A Treatise in the Sociology of Knowledge*. New York: Doubleday, 1966.

Berman, Paul Schiff. "Approaches to the Cultural Study of Law: Telling a Less Suspicious Story: Notes toward a Non-Skeptical Approach to Legal/Cultural Analysis." *Yale Journal of Law and the Humanities* 12 (2001): 95-139.

Binder, David A., and Susan C. Price. *Legal Interviewing and Counseling: A Client-Centered Approach*. St. Paul, MI: West Publishing, 1977.

Brint, Steven. *In an Age of Experts: The Changing Role of Professionals in Politics and Public Life*. Princeton: Princeton University Press, 1994.

Bumiller, Kristen. *The Civil Rights Society: The Social Construction of Victims*. Baltimore: Johns Hopkins University Press, 1988.

Cahn, Edgar S., and Jean Cahn. "The War on Poverty: A Civilian Perspective." *Yale Law Journal* 73 (1964): 1317-1352.

Chambon, Adrienne S., Allan Irving, and Laura Epstein. *Reading Foucault for Social Work*. New York: Columbia University Press, 1999.

Concha, Hugo. "Cause Lawyering for Indigenous Cases in Mexico: The Use of Legal Strategies for Political Participation in Mexico." Paper Present at the Cause Lawyering Conference, Cachan, France, October 2003

Cruikshank, Barbara. *The Will to Empower: Democratic Citizens and Other Subjects*. Ithaca: Cornell University Press, 1999.

Danet, Brenda, Kenneth B. Hoffman, and Nicole Kermish. "Obstacles to the Study of Lawyer-Client Interaction: The Biography of a Failure." *Law and Society Review* 14 (1980): 905-922.

Davis, Martha. *Brutal Need: Lawyers and the Welfare Rights Movement, 1960-1973*. New Haven: Yale University Press, 1993.

Diamond, Michael. "Law, the Problems of Poverty, and the 'Myth of Rights.'" *Brigham Young University Law Review* 1980 (1980): 785-795.

———. "Community Lawyering: Revisiting the Old Neighborhood." *Columbia Human Rights Law Review* 32 (2000): 67-131.

Dunlap, Justin A. "I Don't Want to Play God—-A Response to Professor Tremblay." *Fordham Law Review* 67 (1999): 2601-2616.

Edelman, Murray. *Political Language: Words that Succeed and Policies that Fail*. New York: Academic Press, 1977.

Ellman, Stephen. "Symposium: Clinical Education: Lawyers and Clients." *UCLA Law Review* 34 (1987): 717-778.

———. "Client-Centeredness Multiplied: Individual Autonomy and Collective Mobilization in Public Interest Lawyers' Representation of Groups." *Virginia Law Review* 78 (1992): 1103-73.

Elwell, Frank. "The Sociology of Max Weber." http://www.faculty.rsu.edu/~felwell/ Theorists/Weber/Whome.htm (accessed November 15, 2004).

Engel, David M., and Frank W. Munger. *Rights of Inclusion: Law and Identity in the Life Stories of Americans with Disabilities*. Chicago: University of Chicago Press, 2003.

Ewick, Patricia, Robert Kagan, and Austin Sarat. "Introduction: Legacies of Legal Realism: Social Science, Social Policy and the Law." In *Social Science, Social*

Policy and the Law, edited by Patricia Ewick, Robert Kagan, and Austin Sarat, 1-38. New York: Russell Sage Foundation, 1999.

Farmer, Paul. *Pathologies of Power: Health, Human Rights, and the New War on the Poor*. Berkeley: University of California Press, 2005.

Feldman, Marc. "Political Lessons: Legal Services for the Poor." *Georgetown Law Journal* 83 (1995): 1529-1608.

Felstiner, William L. F., Richard L. Abel, and Austin Sarat. "The Emergence and Transformation of Disputes: Naming, Blaming, Claiming . . . ." *Law & Society Review* 15 (1980-81): 631-654.

Floersch, Jerry. *Meds, Money, and Manners: The Case Management of Severe Mental Illness*. New York: Columbia University Press, 2002.

Flyvbjerg, Bent. *Making Social Science Matter: Why Social Inquiry Fails and How It Can Succeed Again*. Cambridge: Cambridge University Press, 2001.

Fontana, Andrea, and James H. Frey. "The Interview: From Structured Questions to Negotiated Text." In *Collecting and Interpreting Qualitative Materials*, edited by Norman K. Denzin and Yvonna S. Lincoln. Thousand Oaks: Sage Publications, 2003.

Foucault, Michel. *The History of Sexuality: An Introduction*. Vintage Books Edition ed., vol. 1. New York: Vintage Books, 1990/1978.

Fraser, Nancy, and Linda Gordon. "A Genealogy of 'Dependency': Tracing a Keyword of the U.S. Welfare State." In *Justice Interruptus: Critical Reflections on the "Postsocialist" Condition*, by Nancy Fraser, 121-150. New York and London: Routledge, 1997.

Freire, Paolo. *Pedagogy of the Oppressed*, Revised 20th-Anniversary ed. New York: Continuum, 1970/1990.

Garth, Bryant G., and Austin Sarat. "Justice and Power in Law and Society Research: On the Contested Careers of Core Concepts." In *Justice and Power in Sociolegal Studies*, edited by Bryant G. Garth and Austin Sarat. Chicago: Northwestern University Press, 1998.

Gil, David G. *Confronting Injustice and Oppression: Concepts and Strategies for Social Workers*. New York: Columbia University Press, 1998.

Gilliom, John. *Overseers of the Poor: Surveillance, Resistance, and the Limits of Privacy*. Chicago: University of Chicago Press, 2001.

Glaser, Barney, and Anselm Strauss. *The Discovery of Grounded Theory: Strategies of Qualitative Research*. Chicago: Aldine, 1967.

Goode, William J. "The Theoretical Limits of Professionalization." In *The Semi-Professions and Their Organization*, edited by Amitai Etzioni. New York: Free Press, 1969.

Gordon, Linda. *Pitied but Not Entitled: Single Mothers and the History of Welfare, 1890-1935*. New York: Free Press, 1994.

Green, James W. *Cultural Awareness in the Human Services: A Multi-Ethnic Approach*, Third ed. Needham Heights, MA: Allyn & Bacon, 1999.

Gruinier, Lani, Michelle Fine, and Jane Balin. *Becoming Gentlemen: Women, Law School, and Institutional Change.* Boston: Beacon Press, 1997.

Gusfield, Joseph R. *The Culture of Public Problems: Drinking-Driving and the Symbolic Order.* Chicago: University of Chicago Press, 1981.

Gustafson, Joseph M. "Professions as 'Callings.'" *Social Service Review* 56 (1982): 502-515.

Habermas, Jurgen. *Between Facts and Norms: Contributions to a Discourse Theory of Law and Democracy.* Translated by William Rehg. Cambridge: MIT Press, 1998.

Hasenfeld, Yeheskel. "Organizational Forms as Moral Practice: The Case of Welfare Departments." *Social Service Review* 74 (2000): 329-351.

Hays, Sharon. *Flat Broke with Children: Women in the Age of Welfare Reform.* New York: Oxford University Press, 2003.

Hilbink, Thomas, M. "Constructing Cause Lawyering: Professionalism, Politics, and Social Change in 1960s America." Ph.D. diss., New York University, 2006.

Hosticka, Carl J. "We Don't Care About What Happened, We Only Care About What Is Going to Happen: Lawyer-Client Negotiations." *Social Problems* 26 (1979): 599.

Houseman, Alan W. "Political Lessons: Legal Services for the Poor—A Commentary." *Georgetown Law Journal* 83 (1995).

Houseman, Alan W., and Linda E. Peete. *Securing Equal Justice for All: A Brief History of Civil Legal Assistance in the United States.* Washington, DC: Center for Law and Social Policy, 2007. http://clasp.org/publications/legal_aid_history_2007.pdf (accessed September 12, 2007).

Hughes, Everett C. *The Sociological Eye: Selected Papers.* Chicago: Aldine-Atherton, 1971.

Hunt, Sharon R., and Jim Baumohl. "Now Invited to Testify: Former Beneficiaries Praise the SSI Drug Addiction and Alcoholism Program." *Contemporary Drug Problems* 30 (Spring-Summer 2003): 455-499.

Illich, Ivan. "To Hell with Good Intentions." In *Combining Service and Learning*, edited by J. C. Kendall, vol. 1, 314-320. Raleigh: National Society for Internships and Experiential Education, 1968/1990.

Jones, Lynn C. "Exploring the Sources of Cause and Career Correspondence Among Cause Lawyers." In *The Worlds Cause Lawyers Make: Structure and Agency in Legal Practice,* edited by Austin Sarat and Stuart Scheingold. Stanford: Stanford University Press, 2005.

Katz, Jack. *Poor People's Lawyers in Transition.* New Brunswick, NJ: Rutgers University Press, 1982.

Kaufman, Arnold S. *The Radical Liberal: The New Politics: Theory and Practice.* New York: Simon & Schuster, 1968.

Kelle, Udo, and Heather Lauries. "Computer Use in Qualitative Research and Issues of Validity." In *Computer-Aided Qualitative Data Analysis Theory,*

Methods and Practice, edited by Udo Kelle. Thousand Oaks: Sage Publications, 1995.

Kennedy, Duncan. "Legal Education and the Reproduction of Hierarchy." *Journal of Legal Education* 32 (1982): 591-615.

Kronman, Anthony T. *The Lost Lawyer: Failing Ideals of the Legal Profession.* Cambridge: The Belknap Press of Harvard University Press, 1993.

Lee, Raymond M., and Nigel G. Fielding. "User Experiences of Qualitative Data Analysis Software." In *Computer-Aided Qualitative Data Analysis Theory, Methods and Practice,* edited by Udo Kelle. Thousand Oaks: Sage Publications, 1995.

Legal Services Corporation. *Documenting the Justice Gap in America: The Current Unmet Civil Legal Needs of Low-Income America.* Washington, DC: Legal Services Corporation, 2005. http://www.lsc.gov/JusticeGap.pdf (accessed August 10, 2007).

Lemert, Charles. *Social Things: An Introduction to the Sociological Life.* Lanham: Rowman and Littlefield Publishers, 2002.

Lesnick, Howard. "Infinity in a Grain of Sand: The World of Law and Lawyering as Portrayed in the Clinical Teaching Implicit in the Law School Curriculum." *UCLA Law Review* 37 (1989-1990): 1157-1197.

———. "The Wellsprings of Legal Responses to Inequality: A Perspective on Perspective." *Duke Law Journal* 1991(2): 413-454.

Lipsky, Michael. *Street Level Bureaucracy: Dilemmas of the Individual in Public Service.* New York: Russell Sage Foundation, 1980.

Lofland, John, and Lyn H. Lofland. *Analyzing Social Settings: A Guide to Qualitative Observation and Analysis.* Third ed. Belmont: Wadsworth, 1995.

López, Gerold P. *Rebellious Lawyering: One Chicano's Vision of Progressive Law Practice.* Boulder: Westview Press, 1992.

———. "An Aversion to Clients: Loving Humanity and Hating Human Beings." *Harvard Civil Rights-Civil Liberties Law Review* 31 (1996): 315-323.

Lorde, Audre. "The Master's Tools Will Never Dismantle the Master's House." In *Sister Outsider, Essays and Speeches.* Trumansburg: Crossing Press, 1984.

Mackenzie, Catriona, and Natalie Stoljar. "Introduction: Autonomy Refigured." In *Relational Autonomy: Feminist Perspective on Autonomy, Agency and the Social Self,* edited by Catriona Mackenzie and Natalie Stoljar, 3-31. New York: Oxford University Press, 2000.

Margulies, Peter. "Legal Education: Reframing Empathy in Clinical Legal Education." *Clinical Law Review* 5 (Spring 1999): 605-637.

———. "Lawyers' Independence and Collective Illegality in Government and Corporate Misconduct, Terrorism, and Organized Crime." *Rutgers Law Review* 58 (2005-06): 939-982.

Marsico, Richard. "Working for Social Change and Preserving Client Autonomy: Is There a Role for 'Facilitative' Lawyering." *Clinical Law Review* 1 (1995): 639-663.

Marx, Karl. "The Eighteenth Brumaire of Louis Bonaparte." In *The Marx-Engels Reader,* edited by R. C. Tucker. Second ed., 594-607. New York: W. W. Norton, 1852/1978.

Mather, Lynn. "Ethics Symposium: What Do Clients Want? Fundamental: What Do Clients Want? What Do Lawyers Do?" *Emory Law Journal* 52 (2003): 1065-1087.

McCann, Michael. *Rights at Work: Pay Equity Reform and the Politics of Legal Mobilization.* Chicago: University of Chicago Press, 1994.

McCann, Michael, and Helena Silverstein. "Rethinking the Law's Allurement: A Relational Analysis of Social Movement Lawyers in the United States." In *Lawyering: Political Commitments and Professional Responsibilities,* edited by Austin Sarat and Stuart Scheingold, 261-292. New York: Oxford University Press, 1998.

McCoyd, Judith L. M., and Corey S. Shdaimah. "Revisiting the Benefits Debate: Does Qualitative Social Work Research Produce Salubrious Effects? *Social Work* 52, no. 4 (2007): 340-349.

McMunigal, Kevin C. "Of Causes and Clients: Two Tales of *Roe v. Wade.* Hastings *Law Journal* 47 (1996): 779-819.

Melia, Kath M. "Producing 'Plausible Stories': Interviewing Student Nurses." In *Context and Method in Qualitative Research*, edited by Gale Miller and Robert Dingwall. Thousand Oaks: Sage Publications, 1997.

Meili, Stephen. "Cause Lawyering for Collective Justice: A Case Study of the Amparo Colectivo in Argentina." In *The Worlds Cause Lawyers Make: Structure and Agency in Legal Practice*, edited by Austin Sarat and Stuart Scheingold. Stanford: Stanford University Press, 2005.

Menand, Louis. *The Metaphysical Club: A Story of Ideas in America.* New York: Farrar, Straus and Giroux, 2002.

Merton, Robert K., with Thomas F. Gieryn. "Institutionalized Altruism: The Case of the Professions." In *Social Research and the Practicing Professions*, edited by Robert K. Merton. Cambridge: ABT Books, 1982.

Miles, Matthew B., and A. Michael Huberman. *Qualitative Data Analysis: An Expanded Sourcebook,* Second ed. Thousand Oaks: Sage Publications, 1994.

Mills, C. Wright. *The Power Elite.* New York: Oxford University Press, 1956.

———. *Sociological Imagination, 40th Anniversary Edition.* New York: Oxford University Press, 1999.

Mills, Linda G. "Affective Lawyering: The Emotional Dimensions of the Lawyer-Client Relation." In *Practicing Therapeutic Jurisprudence: Law as a Helping Profession,* edited by Dennis P. Stolle, David B. Wexler, and Bruce J. Winick, 419-446. Durham: Carolina Academic Press, 2000.

Minow, Martha. "Lawyering at the Margins: Lawyering for Human Dignity." *American University Journal of Gender Social Policy and Law* 11 (2003): 143-170.

Nussbaum, Martha C. "Professor of Parody." *The New Republic.* http://www.tnr. com/archive/0299/nussbaum022299.html (accessed February 1999).

Padgett, Deborah K. *Qualitative Methods in Social Work Research: Challenges and Rewards.* Thousand Oaks: Sage Publications, 1998.

Piomelli, Ascanio. "Appreciating Collaborative Lawyering." *Clinical Law Review* 6 (2000): 427-515.

Piven, Frances F., and Richard A. Cloward. *Regulating the Poor: The Functions of Public Welfare.* New York: Pantheon Books, 1971.

Plato. *The Republic.* Translated by Desmond Lee. Second revised ed. London: Penguin Books, 1987.

Polikoff, Nancy D. "Am I My Client? The Role Confusion of a Lawyer Activist." *Harvard Civil Rights-Civil Liberties Law Review* 31 (1996): 443-471.

Probert, Walter. "Law Talk and Words Consciousness." *General Semantics Bulletin* 41-43 (1974-76): 49-55.

Reich, Charles A. "The New Property." *Yale Law Journal* 73 (1964): 733-787.

Rhode, Deborah. "Policing the Professional Monopoly: A Constitutional and Empirical Analysis of Unauthorized Practice and Prohibitions." *Stanford Law Review* 34 (1981): 64-99.

Richardson, Laurel. "Writing: A Method of Inquiry." In *Collecting and Interpreting Qualitative Materials,* edited by Norman K. Denzin and Yvonna S. Lincoln. Thousand Oaks: Sage Publications, 2003.

Rose, Stephen M. "Reflections on an Empowerment-Based Practice." *Social Work* 45, no. 5 (2000): 403-405.

Rosenberg, Gerald N. *The Hollow Hope: Can Courts Bring About Social Change?* Chicago: University of Chicago Press, 1991.

Sarat, Austin. "'The Law Is All Over': Power, Resistance, and the Legal Consciousness of the Welfare Poor." *Yale Journal of Law and the Humanities* 2 (1990): 343-379.

Sarat, Austin, and William L. F. Felstiner. *Divorce Lawyers and Their Clients: Power and Meaning in the Legal Process.* New York: Oxford University Press, 1995.

Sarat, Austin, and Stuart Scheingold. *Something to Believe In: Politics, Professionalism, and Cause Lawyering.* Stanford: Stanford University Press, 2004.

Scheingold, Stuart. "The Struggle to Politicize Legal Practice: A Case Study of Left-Activist Lawyering in Seattle." In *Cause Lawyering: Political Commitments and Professional Responsibilities*, edited by Austin Sarat and Stuart Scheingold. New York: Oxford University Press, 1998.

Schneider, Carl E. *The Practice of Autonomy: Patients, Doctors, and Medical Decisions.* New York: Oxford University Press, 1998.

Schon, Donald A. *The Reflective Practitioner: How Professionals Think in Action.* New York: Basic Books, 1983.

Schram, Sanford F. *After Welfare: The Culture of Postindustrial Social Policy.* New York: New York University Press, 2000.

———. *Praxis for the Poor: Piven and Cloward and the Future of Social Sciences in Social Welfare.* New York: New York University Press, 2002.

———. *Welfare Discipline: Discourse, Governance and Globalization.* Philadelphia: Temple University Press, 2006.

Seidman, Irving. *Interviewing as Qualitative Research: A Guide for Researchers in Education and the Social Sciences.* New York: Teacher's College Press, 1998.

Shamir, Ronen, and Dafna Hacker. "Colonialism, Culture, and the Law: Colonialism's Civilizing Mission: The Case of the Indian Hemp Drug Commission. *Law & Social Inquiry* 26 (2001): 435-461.

Shdaimah, Corey S. "Dilemmas of Progressive Lawyering: Empowerment and Hierarchy." In *The Worlds Cause Lawyers Made: Structure and Agency in Legal Practice,* edited by Austin Sarat and Stuart Scheingold. Stanford: Stanford University Press, 2005.

———. "Not What They Expected: Legal Services Lawyers in the Eyes of Legal Services Clients." In *The Cultural Lives of Cause Lawyers,* edited by Austin Sarat and Stuart Scheingold. Cambridge: Cambridge University Press, 2008.

Shdaimah, Corey, and Roland Stahl. "Reflections of Doing Phronetic Research: A Case Study." In *Debating Flyvbjerg: Making Political Science Matter,* edited by Brian Caterino and Sanford F. Schram. New York: NYU Press, 2006.

Shdaimah, Corey, Roland Stahl, and Sanford F. Schram. "When You Can See the Sky Through the Roof: Policy Analysis from the Bottom Up." In *Political Ethnography,* edited by Edward Shatz. Chicago: University of Chicago Press, Under Review.

Silbey, Susan S., and Austin Sarat. "Critical Traditions in Law and Society Research. *Law & Society Review* 21, no. 1 (1987): 165-174.

Simon, Jonathan. "Between Power and Knowledge: Habermas, Foucault, and the Future of Legal Studies." *Law & Society Review* 28, no. 4 (1994): 947-961.

Simon, William H. "Homo Psychologicus: Notes on a New Legal Formalism." *Stanford Law Review* 32, no. 3 (1980): 487-559.

———. "Lawyer Advice and Client Autonomy: Mrs. Jones's Case." *Maryland Law Review* 50 (1991): 213-226.

———. "The Dark Secret of Progressive Lawyering: A Comment on Poverty Law Scholarship in the Post-Modern, Post-Reagan Era." *University of Miami Law Review* 48 (1994): 1099–1114.

Sinden, Amy. "'Why Won't Mom Cooperate?': A Critique of Informality in Child Welfare Proceedings." *Yale Journal of Law & Feminism* 11 (1999): 339-396.

Soss, Joe. "Lessons of Welfare: Policy Administration, Political Learning and Political Action." *American Political Science Review* 93 (1999): 363-380.

Southworth, Ann. "Taking the Lawyer Out of Progressive Lawyering." *Stanford Law Review* 46 (1993): 213-234.

———. "Business Planning for the Destitute: Lawyers as Facilitators in Civil Rights and Poverty Practice." *Wisconsin Law Review* 1996 (1996): 1121-1169.

Stolle, Dennis P., David B. Wexler, and Bruce J. Winick, eds. *Practicing Therapeutic Jurisprudence: Law as a Helping Profession.* Durham: Carolina Academic Press, 2000.

Stone, Deborah A. *The Disabled State.* Philadelphia: Temple University Press, 1984.

Strauss, Anselm, and Juliet Corbin. *Basics of Qualitative Research: Grounded Theory Procedures and Techniques.* Newbury Park: Sage Publications, 1990.

Sturm, Susan. "Gender and the Higher Education Classroom: Maximizing the Learning Environment." *Duke Journal of Gender Law & Policy* 4 (1997): 119-147.

Sullivan, Kathleen A. "Self-Disclosure, Separation, and Students: Intimacy in the Clinical Relationship." *Indiana Law Review* 27 (1993): 115-155.

Thomson, Douglas. "Negotiating Cause Lawyering Potential in the Early Years of Corporate Practice." In *The Worlds Cause Lawyers Make: Structure and Agency in Legal Practice,* edited by Austin Sarat and Stuart Scheingold. Stanford: Stanford University Press, 2005.

Toulmin, Stephen. *Return to Reason.* Cambridge: Harvard University Press, 2001.

Tremblay, Paul R. "Toward a Community-Based Ethic of Practice." *UCLA Law Review* 37 (1989-1990): 1101-1156.

———. "Theoretics of Practice: The Integration of Progressive Thought and Action: Rebellious Lawyering, Regnant Lawyering, and Street-Level Bureaucracy." *Hastings Law Journal* 43 (1992): 947-966.

———. "Acting 'a Very Moral Type of God': Triage among Poor Clients." *Fordham Law Review* 67 (1999): 2475-2252.

———. "Critical Legal Ethics: Review of Lawyers' Ethics and the Pursuit of Justice: A Critical Reader." Edited by Susan D. Carle, paper 185. Boston College Law School: Boston College Law School Faculty Papers, 2007.

Trubek, Louise G. "Critical Lawyering: Toward a New Public Interest Practice." *1 Public Interest Law Journal* 49 (1991): 49–56.

———. "The Worst of Times. And the Best of Times: Lawyering for Poor Clients Today." *Fordham Urban Law Journal* 22 (1995): 1123-1140.

Wanitzek, Ulrike. "The Power of Language in the Discourse of Women's Rights: Some Examples from Tanzania." *Africa Today* 49, no. 1 (2002): 3-19.

Warren, Kay B. "Indigenous Movements as a Challenge to the Unified Social Movement Paradigm for Guatemala." In *Culture of Politics, Politics of Culture, Re-Visioning Latin American Social Movements,* edited by Sonia E. Alvarez, Evelina Dagnino, and Arturo Escobar, 165-195. Boulder: Westview Press.

Weiss, Robert S. *Learning from Strangers: The Art and Method of Qualitative Interview Studies.* New York: Free Press, 1994.

Weitzman, Eben A. "Software and Qualitative Research." In *Collecting and Interpreting Qualitative Materials,* edited by Norman K. Denzin and Yvonna S. Lincoln. Thousand Oaks: Sage Publications, 2003.

Welch. Sharon D. *A Feminist Ethic of Risk.* Revised Edition. Minneapolis: Fortress Press, 2000.

White, Lucie. "Subordination, Rhetorical Skills, and Sunday Shoes: Notes on the Hearing of Mrs. G." *Buffalo Law Review* 38 (1990): 1-58.

———. "Collaborative Lawyering in the Field? On Mapping the Paths from Rhetoric to Practice." *Clinical Law Review* 1 (1994): 157-172.

———. "Facing South: Lawyering for Poor Communities in the Twenty-First Century." *Fordham Urban Law Journal* 25 (1998): 813-829.

Wilensky, Harold L. "The Professionalization of Everyone." *The American Journal of Sociology* 70, no. 2 (1964): 137-158.

Williams, Patricia J. *The Alchemy of Race and Rights: Diary of a Law Professor.* Cambridge: Harvard University Press, 1991.

Winter, Steven L. "Cursing the Darkness." *University of Miami Law Review* 48 (1994): 1115-1132.

Index

Clients (*continued*): representation, xi,
50, 56, 79–81, 100, 114–15, 117,
120, 134, 158, 168; resilience, xi,
61, 118, 158; responsible action,
165, 167–68, 169; self-advocacy, 69,
89, 100, 105, 107–9, 111, 118–19,
128; socialization, 72, 150; stress, x,
85–86, 134–36, 140, 153–54, 160;
trust, 142, 144, 145, 148; voices, 12,
13–14, 18, 19, 22, 26, 59, 63, 67–69,
70–71, 76, 92, 96–98, 99, 116, 131,
164, 165, 172–73
"Co-eminent problem solvers," 14, 99
Collaborative lawyering, xiii, 14, 21,
99, 100–102, 128; client participation, 100, 102–3, 109–16, 140, 172;
client perception of, 109–11, 114–
16, 118, 164; lawyer as resource, 78,
88, 114–15; lawyer's perception of,
102–3, 116–17, 155, 157–59, 164;
obtaining resources, 100, 102, 149–
50, 151, 152, 159; "sequentially,"
14, 107; teamwork, 107–9, 109–11,
113, 114–15, 140
Communication, 27, 82, 85, 104–5,
109–11, 114–15, 131, 132–34, 136–
40, 140–44, 145–47, 148, 150–51,
159–60, 169, 172; communicating
bad news, 151, 152–54
Community group, representation, 52,
125–26
Community outreach, 2, 5, 52, 54,
123–24, 125
Consumer law, 43, 52, 110, 115, 128,
134, 151; student loan frauds,
123–24

Decision making, 22, 63, 67, 69–70,
71–73, 75–76, 78, 81, 85, 89–91,
93–95, 107–9, 117–18, 119, 122,
131, 166–67, 167–68, 172–73
Discrimination, 54, 56–57

Education, 52, 54, 100, 102, 104, 109,
115
Elderly clients, ix-x, 2, 5, 5n3, 152
Empathy, 15, 141–42, 147–48, 151,
155–56, 161; empathetic listening,
150–51; "engaged empathy," 141
Empowerment, 19, 23, 27, 54, 59, 67,
70, 75, 83, 93, 95, 96, 103, 116, 118,
160, 164, 173; disempowerment,
xii, 6, 29–30, 173
Ethic of risk, xiii, 16, 165, 166–67,
170–71, 174; chapter 7

Facilitative lawyering, 21
False consciousness, 71–72, 163
Family advocacy, 2, 46, 111–13, 133,
138

Government agencies, 47–48, 51,
55–56, 61, 78, 82–84, 117–18, 133,
144–47, 161

Hermeneutic of suspicion, 163

Immigrants, 2, 10, 33, 107, 114,
136–37
Impact practice, 5, 11, 51–53, 55,
58–59, 132
Incremental Change, 58, 64, 65, 66,
157
Individual representation, 11, 52,
54–55, 58, 131, 132–33, 156–57;
complementing systemic work, 60,
61, 172; vs. systemic change, 54–55,
58–59, 64
Interpretivist framework, 17

Law: limitations of, 51, 54–55; sym-
bolic uses of, 127–28, 171
Law and society research, 24–26
Law school, 77, 157, 160, 170, 172
Lawyer-client relationships, 18, 25,

About the Author

COREY SHDAIMAH is an assistant professor at the School of Social Work, University of Maryland, Baltimore.